HARLEM MOON
BROADWAY

4/06 B~T 16.00

UNCLE TOM
OR
NEW NEGRO?

African Americans Reflect on
BOOKER T. WASHINGTON
and
UP FROM SLAVERY
One Hundred Years Later

Edited by Rebecca Carroll

HARLEM MOON
Broadway Books
New York

Published by Harlem Moon, an imprint of Broadway Books,
a division of Random House, Inc.

UP FROM SLAVERY was originally published in 1902 by Doubleday.

PRINTED IN THE UNITED STATES OF AMERICA

HARLEM MOON, BROADWAY BOOKS, and the HARLEM MOON logo, depicting a moon
and a woman, are trademarks of Random House, Inc. The figure in the Harlem
Moon logo is inspired by a graphic design by Aaron Douglas (1899–1979).

Visit our website at www.harlemmoon.com

First Edition

Book design by Michael Collica

Library of Congress Cataloging-in-Publication Data

Uncle Tom or new Negro : African Americans reflect on Booker T. Washington
        and Up from slavery 100 years later / edited by Rebecca Carroll.
      p.   cm.
    Includes index.
      1. Washington, Booker T., 1856–1915.   2. Washington, Booker T.,
    1856–1915. Up from slavery.   3. African Americans—Biography.
    4. Educators—United States—Biography.   I. Carroll, Rebecca.
    II. Washington, Booker T., 1856–1915. Up from slavery.

    E185.97.W4U53 2006
    370'.92—dc22
                                                              2005050161

ISBN 0-7679-1955-6

10   9   8   7   6   5   4   3   2   1

For Chris, because there's very little that isn't

CONTENTS

for *Uncle Tom or New Negro?*

———————

UP FROM SLAVERY

Complete text with a new Editor's Note follows page 164.

ACKNOWLEDGMENTS

This book would not be possible without the ongoing support and encouragement of my editor, Janet Hill, who continues to find my ideas interesting and makes them even more so with her careful guidance and dedicated insights. Much thanks to Meredith Bernstein, my agent of more than ten years who would do her enthusiastic best to sell a book on my behalf about polar bears and gas stations if that's what I felt most passionate about. Love and appreciation to my parents, whose creative and artistic influence is omnipresent in all of my work—in my life and everything I do. And finally, endless thanks to my husband, Chris Bonastia, who never fails to read whatever I write with anything other than a championing spirit and an engaged mind.

UNCLE TOM
OR
NEW NEGRO?

INTRODUCTION

When I finally read *Up from Slavery* in its entirety as an adult, it was the second or third time the book had been assigned or recommended to me. I had started reading it the other times but had never felt gripped or engaged by Washington's writing. His story was justly remarkable, but not extraordinary; many former slaves had gone on to become great educators and activists and writers. Harriet Tubman, Frederick Douglass, Ida B. Wells, Sojourner Truth—all had been slaves, all had made outstanding examples of their freedom, and all, it seemed, were better and more compelling writers than Booker T. Washington. That I felt behooved to judge the quality of writing more than the actual content is indicative of my generation's relative insulation from the anguish and reality of slavery.

What I did not appreciate then but understand now after rereading *Up from Slavery* again as an adult is that what makes Washington and this book extraordinary is in fact how ordinary it is, how evenhanded, poised, and frank a personal account he crafted for publication in 1901, a time when learning how to read and write was still a life-threatening endeavor for black people. Furthermore, the style and tone of Washington's writing, while perhaps not poetically striking, do succeed in mirroring its message in near-precise measure. Humility, consistent hard work, attentive behavior, and great faith in humanity can well set the foundation for a strong sense of self and the achievement of individual sovereignty. "Every persecuted individual and race should get much consolation out of the great human law, which is universal and eternal, that merit, no matter under what skin found, is, in the long run, recognized and rewarded. This I have said here, not to call attention to myself as an individual, but to the race to which I am proud to belong."

But possibly even most important, Booker T. Washington's *Up from Slavery* is a human legacy in narrative form. For someone who did not grow up with parents passing down or referencing stories of African American history and folklore, and maybe also for those at that awkward point of generational disconnect where everything "back then" seems so irrelevant and annoying, *Up from Slavery* is a poignant primer not because it has been called by jacket flap copywriters "one of the greatest American autobiographies ever written," but because it is the very embodiment of legacy, something that has been handed down from the past from an ancestor. "Years ago," writes Washington within the first thirty pages of *Up from Slavery*, "I resolved that because I had no ancestry myself I would leave a record of which my children would be proud, and which might encourage them to still higher effort."

Much has been made in today's vernacular, and indeed discussed in this book's narrative interviews, of the notion that

Washington was an "Uncle Tom," a term and stereotype that find their origin in the docile and dutiful Uncle Tom character of the classic novel *Uncle Tom's Cabin* by Harriet Beecher Stowe, in which Uncle Tom is a fairly intelligent man, if without formal education. It is a curious notion, as the Uncle Tom stereotype has become primarily qualified by a passive nature, if also by an eagerness to please white people. Booker T. Washington was certainly many things, but he was not passive. One cannot serve as founder of an institution (at twenty-five years of age), raise hundreds of thousands of dollars for that institution, serve as adviser to United States presidents and congressmen (in the postslavery Reconstruction era), or preach the value and necessity of human progress and self-reliance whilst being passive in nature.

But over the years *passive* became *house nigger* became *spineless* and finally became *sellout*. In some ways it seems there is a kind of involuntary reflex among African Americans, particularly in the twentieth and twenty-first centuries, to brand one of our own—usually one of our famed own—as an unforgivable sellout. From Clarence Thomas to Colin Powell and Henry Louis Gates, black people (most often men) who negotiate with white people are frequently labeled "sellouts" no matter what they are selling. Men who, for better or worse, as leading black British scholar Stuart Hall was once quoted as saying of Gates in a 2002 article for the *Guardian*, follow the "strand of black politics" represented by Booker T. Washington. Whereby, Stuart continues, "you advance your cause by making yourself acceptable to white society, not by political struggle but economic self-advancement: going into big business, not grassroots politics."

I wish there were some way to make *Up from Slavery* sexy for those young people reading it for the first time, a way to make it as prevalent to twenty-first-century youth as are fashion and hip-hop and cell phones. In its own time this book might well have been the latest Jay-Z record; no living black American was more famous than Booker T. Washington in the early 1900s. He was a celebrity of the first order; random people approached him on the train and in the streets to make the honor of his acquaintance. His eloquence as a public speaker and his established role as the leading spokesperson for black America placed him in high demand on the lecture circuit, and he was constantly traveling to meet that demand.

Booker T. Washington was the first black American to have his face on a United States postage stamp—in 1940, nearly fifteen years before *Brown v. Board of Education* and the beginning of the civil rights movement. And even as history has been much kinder to Washington's contemporary and much-hyped adversary W. E. B. Du Bois, Washington was by far the better known of the two. Washington never boasted of this fact amid his travels, never played it as a card to win more favor.

But apart from the man himself, a large part of reading (or rereading) and understanding Washington's *Up from Slavery* is simply about learning legacy, an integral and not always clear concept for black people in America to understand, and a legacy with origins unimaginable to many, perhaps even less clear. In a letter dated January 27, 1901, found in the Booker T. Washington papers, white abolitionist and activist Emily Howland wrote this to Washington about his then newly published autobiography: "The book will last, not only for its

own merits . . . but because your career began in the most interesting and complicated periods of our nation's history,
when it was casting out slavery, and that you are one of the
most important factors in the working out [of] the problem
of reconstruction."

So perhaps the book will continue to last, but it is up to
those in this and coming generations to decide just how and
in what vein.

To that end, naturally, not all aspects of *Up from Slavery* are
agreeable. For example, it is hard for any generation to swal-
low the notion that "notwithstanding the cruel wrongs inflicted upon us, the black man got nearly as much out of
slavery as the white man did." Or that, after word had filtered
through of the Emancipation Proclamation, among southern
slaves, Washington himself included, "there was great rejoicing, and thanksgiving, and wild scenes of ecstasy. But there
was no feeling of bitterness." Really?

If not as an Uncle Tom, Washington's reputation as an accommodationist is not altogether far-fetched, he said things
that white people wanted to hear, sometimes at the risk of
sounding like a traitor to his race. Famously, during his Atlanta Exposition address, published in *Up from Slavery*,
Washington says:

As we have proved our loyalty to you in the past, in
nursing your children, watching by the sick-bed of
your mothers and fathers, and often following them
with tear-dimmed eyes to their graves, so in the future,
in our humble way, we shall stand by you with a devotion that no foreigner can approach, ready to lay down

our lives, if need be, in defence of yours, interlacing our
industrial, commercial, civil, and religious life with
yours in a way that shall make the interests of both
races one. In all things that are purely social we can be
as separate as the fingers, yet one as the hand in all
things essential to mutual progress.

In twenty-first-century terms, this reads like flat-out ass
kissing or, at best, cringe-inducing pragmatism. The point,
however, in reading (or rereading) this book, for young and
old, trained scholars and casual readers, is not necessarily to
become an apostle of the Booker T. Washington rhetoric, but
to take from it that which is still relevant and useful today and
can be reconciled within a contemporary context.

Washington was self-reflective, ambitious, realistic, and
hardworking. Without assigning the weight of the world or
the fate of black America to his shoulders, there is much to be
learned from his autobiography. "The individual who can do
something that the world wants done will, in the end, make
his way regardless of his race," writes Washington. In our
core, don't all of us at least want to believe that regardless of
race, black people in America will in the end make our way?
And isn't it merely fair to recognize that Booker T. Washington did?

My goal with this particular project was to find out, if possible, who Booker T. Washington was and moreover, to find
out if talking with contemporary black figures about him
might do one or all of several things: reflect the impact that
Washington has had on black people throughout history; invoke closer scrutiny of a man already quite scrutinized (by

those who actually know who he is to begin with); help a younger generation of black Americans understand the ways in which we often create and then tear down our black historical leaders all by ourselves; and simply serve as a reintroduction to Washington's classic autobiography, *Up from Slavery*, which appears in its entirety following the interview portion of the book.

The reader can decide, although if nothing else, the sharp, varied, and meditative voices herein will help in shaping the profile of a curious and fascinating black man in America who gave us one model of what it means to be up from slavery.

—Rebecca Carroll, May 2005

CHAPTER I

DR. BILL E. LAWSON,
Philosophy Scholar

Bill E. Lawson is distinguished professor of philosophy at the University of Memphis. He received his PhD from the University of North Carolina at Chapel Hill, and his professional appointments include Spelman College, West Virginia University, and the University of Delaware.

MY GENERAL SENSE of Booker T. Washington is that he was committed to the betterment of black people in the United States and that he was very forward-looking and insightful. I think people often fail to appreciate his insights, particularly with regard to race relations. People need to view Washington as a pragmatist in the John Dewey sense of pragmatism, where you're really working to solve a significant problem. Washington's problem was: How do you resolve or improve race relations between black people and white people in the South, given the history of race and racism in the United States at that particular point in history? He thought that the best way to do that was for the races to work together, and in order to accomplish that, black people had to be able to bring something to the table. That's what building Tuskegee Institute was about: bringing something to the table. Some people think that his position demeaned black people, but while Washington did acknowledge that there were blacks that deserved respect because of their accomplishments, those were not the blacks he was trying to reach. Washington never denied the humanity of black people.

I am defending Booker T. Washington because many black intellectuals seem to be against him without any knowledge of his writings or life. During the 1960s, when black nationalism became the rage, people read certain select things. Subsequently, most people know or have read only three things about Booker T. Washington at best: *Up from Slavery*, the Atlanta Exposition speech, and "Of Mr. Booker T. Washington and Others," the essay by W. E. B. Du Bois. Sometimes they know the Dudley Randall poem "Booker T. and W. E. B." If you read *Up from Slavery* in isolation from Washington's other works, then I do think that you will get a skewed view of who and what he was. But when you read *Working with the Hands, My Larger Education, The Man Farthest Down*, the biography he wrote of Frederick Douglass, or his letters and read what he wrote about his projects, you come away with a completely different view of what Washington was trying to do.

For example, Washington never said, as many have claimed, that black people should get only an industrial education. He never said that black people shouldn't participate in the political process. What he did say was, blacks should be able to secure education consistent with their ability, and if there are going to be voting requirements made for black people, the same requirements should be made for white people. He also said that the electorate should be literate; people should be able to read and write if they're going to participate in the political process. But we should consider the historical moment; it was a time when many white people were predisposed to dislike black people. Washington understood that black people had to overcome the strong dislike of some whites, while simultaneously working with the white people who were concerned with the advancement of black people. Did most white people want to have the kind of social interaction with black people that we take for granted now? No! It's not really a matter of whether black people wanted to have social interaction with white people. If you are a leader, you have a vision of how these things should play out and what programs will work best for the group you're serving. Washington's was not a consensus program. It was a program rooted in what he took to be the needs of the black southern masses at that moment in history.

I also believe that Washington's leadership had less to do with what white people thought than most people assume. In much of his work, he often says: "There shall be no unmanly cowering to the wishes of white people." But he also says you've got to bring something to the table. In the context of the lives of black people at that historical moment, a small step beyond chattel slavery, Washington had to focus on what he thought his people really needed. What they needed were skills. That was the purpose of his program: to provide black people with needed skills. With Tuskegee, Washington was able to do something that no other black person was able to do: provide an educational staging ground for literacy among southern rural blacks. It should be noted that he also thought that black men and women should be provided with the same education. There were women in the first graduating class of

Tuskegee. That's impressive and significant. But here's what I like about Washington and his approach: Not only was Tuskegee seen as an industrial training school, but it also taught people how to read and write. So Washington was able to send out into rural southern communities graduates from Tuskegee who were not just able to teach agricultural skills but were also able to set up schools to teach other black people to read and write. That in and of itself—bringing literacy to black people throughout the rural South—is exceptional. That is an important legacy!

Yet I think that one reason people tend to prefer the legacy of Du Bois over Washington is that Du Bois was so elegant and poetic in his arguments against Washington. He was seductive. But Washington was quite aware of this. In 1903 Washington wrote: "When a people are smarting under the wrongs of injustices inflicted from many quarters, it is but natural that they should look about for some individual in whom to lay the blame for their seemly misfortunes. In this case, I seem to be the one. It is not a responsibility which I have sought, but since it has come to me I'm willing to do my duty as best as I can." So he understood how some black people saw him. Within a contemporary context, it is easy to understand why or how it is that most black people cling to these negative ideas about Washington. I think that once he was branded as an Uncle Tom, the image stuck. As we know, once you get branded with a negative label it is difficult to separate yourself from that label.

When I was in college and I read Washington's Atlanta Exposition speech, it wasn't until years later that I learned the speech was not called the Atlanta Compromise. If you look up that speech in books from the sixties, where Washington is cited, it's called the Atlanta Compromise speech. But it actually should be called the Speech at the Atlanta Cotton States and International Exposition. So even in widely read and accepted books of that day there is already a bias working against Washington. This bias is at work today! If you Google "Atlanta Compromise," the exposition speech comes up. Sad.

I find, however, that when I talk to black people today about what Washington was really about, they start agreeing with me. And I think what Washington was about was making America a better place for blacks. His approach was pragmatic. As a pragmatist you have to be creative and do a real assessment of the situation. You have to have a clear understanding of the problem and be open to various options to solve problems. When Washington got to Tuskegee, he writes, "There were no students, no schools, no land, and no buildings." He got the people from Hampton to loan him money so he could buy land; he started teaching his students how to build buildings and grow their own food—he built Tuskegee from the ground up. He saw the problem, and he found a solution to the problem. Tuskegee was a place to make America work for black people.

This raises an important point in understanding the difference between Washington and Du Bois. Washington, unlike Du Bois, never expressed any feeling of twoness. Black intellectuals are drawn to Du Bois's metaphor of twoness: "One ever feels his two-ness—an American, a Negro; two souls, two thoughts, two unreconciled strivings; two warring ideals in one dark body. . . ." For Washington, on the other hand, there is no twoness; black people are human beings struggling

to make a life in this country. The question was, What was
the best way for them to make a safe and secure life in this
country? They needed skills. They needed to be able to support themselves. He knew that black people needed a place to
start building the skills needed for success in the United
States. Washington saw Tuskegee as the place to do that. Important to remember here is that he understood that there was
no history of black philanthropy. He knew, and history has
proven him correct, that you could not run a school if you
waited for black folks to give you money. If he had tried to go
that route, Tuskegee would have failed. Tuskegee was a success, but there is still dislike of Washington. Why?

Many black intellectuals are disturbed by his speech in Atlanta. But if you're talking about the part of Washington's Atlanta Exposition speech when he says, "In all things that are
purely social we can be as separate as the fingers," it's really
the same thing black nationalists were talking about. The
scholar Harold Cruse pointed this out years ago: that all black
nationalist rhetoric was just warmed-over Washington. In his
essay "Of Washington and Others," Du Bois writes about
how Washington said no higher education for the Negro, no
social integration, no involvement in politics. If you go back
and read Washington, please show me where he ever says any
of those things. Nonetheless, Du Bois's remarks became the
mantra of the young black militants in the sixties, and so once
they had that view of Washington, there was no reason to go
back and read his work.

I think what you get with most of Washington's contemporaries, Du Bois included, is what we now know as playa
hatin'. Those persons who looked at Washington in a negative

light were just playa haters. You know how black folks playa-hate on people all of the time; some playa-hate on Cornel West and Condoleezza Rice. But it's important to understand that during his lifetime it was mostly the black intellectuals who didn't like Washington. The black masses understood his message and the value of his program. Consider that the statue of Washington in Tuskegee was built from funds raised by poor black people, which shows you that on the ground level there was all this love for Washington among the black masses. This may explain why there have been so many uncles named Booker in many African American families.

People often complain about what they take to be Washington's personal failings. Was Washington the kind of person that you might want to go to dinner with? Probably not. But hell, Du Bois wouldn't want to go to dinner with you.

I think when you're considering Washington, you have to step back and look at not whether he was a megalomaniac, but at what was the nature of his project and what were the fruits of his labor. It's also important to keep in mind that when Washington came on the scene, the segregation train was well on its way. There was nothing Washington could have done to stop it. No one black man could have stopped it. One can debate whether or not he aided the segregation train, but when you look at his efforts to stop segregation in railroad cars, his efforts to get officials elected who were sympathetic to black concerns, and all his work behind the scenes to influence legislation favorable to blacks, you have to think that here was a person who was, in a very real sense, committed to the cause of black people.

If there are failings of Booker T. Washington, and there

have to be because he was a human being, they were personal. But I think his personal failings have to be, to some degree, separated from his overall project and contribution to racial uplift in the United States. People say he was an Uncle Tom and that he was a pawn of General Samuel Chapman Armstrong. I say Booker T. Washington had too much influence to be somebody's pawn. He stated very clearly that he was concerned with the race problem but that he was not a theorist. He felt theory without practice was worthless. He wrote: "I do not care to venture an opinion about the nature of knowledge in general. But it is pretty clear to anyone that reflects upon the matter, that the only kind of knowledge that has any sort of value for a race that's trying to get on its feet, is knowledge that has some definite relationship to the daily lives of the men and women who are seeking it."

I think that in a country where racism is still a problem, black people would do well to remember Washington's pragmatism—looking at the real problem and trying to solve it. For example, there is now a nationwide push to bring black kids into colleges and universities, but my position is that it may turn out that at this moment in history not all black children need to go to college. There are other vocations that are needed in the black community: plumbers, electricians, and all sorts of jobs. People are so focused on getting black kids into college, but is that what we really need right now? And this is the beauty of Washington. He always asked, What do black people need now? We needed black people who could serve in trades and start businesses in our communities then, and we need them now. Today some people will say I'm trying to stop black people from progressing, just as they said about Washington, but it's simply a realistic fact that not everyone should go to college.

I've written two papers about Washington. The first paper I wrote about five or six years ago, when I knew just a little bit about Washington; I'd read Cornel West, Bernard Boxill, and some of the works of Booker T. The second paper I wrote fairly recently. I reread the first paper a couple of days ago, and my position on Washington from the first to the second is a 180-degree shift, because I realized that I hadn't read and did not know enough about him to know what I should think about him. Washington was a true American pragmatist. He said: "In all things that are purely social we can be as separate as the fingers, yet one as the hand in all things essential to mutual progress." We can work together and still have our own.

Washington left us Tuskegee Institute. Where are the lasting institutions started by Malcolm and W. E. B.?

CHAPTER II

ELIZABETH GARDNER HINES,
Writer/Great-Grandniece of A. G. Gaston

Elizabeth Gardner Hines is coauthor with her mother, Carol Jenkins, of the biography Black Titan: A. G. Gaston and the Making of a Black American Millionaire *(Random House, 2004). Hines is a graduate of Yale, with an MA in English literature from Harvard University. She is the recipient of several academic prizes and fellowships.*

THERE IS AN intricate connection between my great-granduncle A. G. Gaston and Booker T. Washington. But even growing up in the Gaston lineage, I'm fairly certain I didn't know anything about Washington until I went to college. Even then we certainly never studied him; not in any of the classes I took at Yale did we read *Up from Slavery*. It was only when I got to graduate school at Harvard that I started to explore for myself and get a better understanding of who Washington really was.

So in my memory of growing up and throughout school, there was little attention paid to Washington, though I had certainly read Du Bois along the way. Du Bois has always been seen as the more palatable of the two—intellectually and otherwise—and I think there is a comfort blacks feel in reading and relying on Du Bois's ideology that they do not associate with Washington. I can clearly remember another black student in high school or college making a joke about "blacks like Booker T. Washington" and how everyone laughed, as if we all understood what a terrible thing that was to be.

One of the main things my mother and I felt would be important when we decided to write *Black Titan* was the idea of expanding the notion of what the black experience in this country has been about. Since the publication of the book, it's been really interesting to see how blacks respond to the idea of someone like A. G. Gaston. There are those who don't want anything to do with him, mainly because he suffers the same bad rap as Booker T. Washington for being an alleged sellout. It's crucial to understand that Gaston really, to the nth degree, bought into and believed what Booker T. Washington was saying. *Up from Slavery* was the first book Gaston ever owned, and he read it over and over again. As we write in *Black Titan*, and as he related the story to us, Gaston picked up the book one day when he was feeling really low; he had been working really hard, and nothing was happening to better his condition. On that same day Washington came to speak at the Tuggle Institute in Birmingham, where Gaston was enrolled as a student. And the story Uncle Arthur (that's what we called him) liked to tell was that when he read *Up from Slavery* again that day, after hearing Washington talk, he realized in a moment that achieving your goals was, as Washington said, all about merit and that he would have to do something meritorious if he hoped to change his life.

In doing the research for *Black Titan*, I gained a whole different view of how useful Washington's primary tenets really were and are—particularly those involving economic self-sufficiency. This is a place where something still is not connecting with us today. It's almost always the young black people who come to our readings who will say [of *Black Titan*], "This book is so important because it gives us some way of dealing with the economic disparity that still exists. And by the way, why is it that we haven't paid more attention to the economics of black culture?" It's fascinating to me to meet these eighteen- and twenty-year-olds starting their own businesses—and I've met a ton of them now—who talk to me about the very simple but untenable challenge of dealing with the economics of black life.

Since most of my substantive knowledge of Booker T. Washington has come through the research I did for *Black Titan*, I have to think my personal opinion of him is biased, as it hinges largely on the knowledge that he inspired my great-granduncle tremendously. At the same time I have to acknowledge that Washington is someone whose ideas beg for critique. So I guess my sense of him is that he is a bit of a puzzle. There is a part of me that very much wants to embrace what he put forth because it did give so much hope to so many people, but I'm still very conflicted. I think a lot of what Washington was trying to impart, and what was worth passing on to future generations, got lost during the civil rights era—mainly because during that time you had to pick your battles to a certain extent. Not every fight could be waged at once, and some, like the economic independence Washington was a proponent of, fell by the wayside in favor of other initiatives.

People often like to set Washington and W. E. B. Du Bois

against each other, as if they represented truly opposing views. I happen to think their differences have been widely exaggerated throughout history. But in any case, if you bring someone like Gaston into the equation and think about the ideologies he was presented with by these two men, the sticking point for him would have been this notion of the Talented Tenth. I think Gaston felt deeply left out of the Du Boisian circle. How would someone like him, who had only a tenth-grade education, be able to contribute by Du Bois's figuring? But what Washington offered was a kind of methodology for success that was achievable to someone like A. G. Gaston. Similarly to the Du Bois issue, the civil rights movement was largely a middle-class movement. There is plenty of evidence that shows that the people who were leading the movement had primarily middle-class interests at heart, and certainly the movement brought about great changes. Who can regret any of that? But a movement driven by a certain class often means that it speaks to certain class interests, and the question is, What are the people who are left out of that class supposed to cling to in terms of their own ideologies?

Clearly, when you are fighting for broad legislation, concessions are always going to have to be made. There is the example of Birmingham, when Martin Luther King was in town, and you had the white businessmen and the city structure, and you had the blacks who were agitating for change. The blacks came up with a list of what it was they wanted, but there were only going to be so many things that the white businessmen and city structure were going to give in on. So they compromised. And the principles that the civil rights movement ended up capitulating on, over and over again, were the business and economic needs of the black community. I think blacks in general wanted those needs to be met and knew how important they were, but clearly the prevailing belief was that if the larger social issues were addressed first, then somewhere down the line the economic issues would follow. What we've seen, of course, is that they haven't followed—not even all this time later.

My grandmother and Minnie (A. G.'s wife) were two of fifteen children. It's a very big family. Minnie was one of the oldest of the children, and she helped raise all of the rest of the children. My grandmother was one of the youngest, and Minnie and A. G. were very closely involved with her life. She would come home from Tuskegee for weekends and stay with A. G. and Minnie. Basically, through A. G. and Minnie's success together and individually, they were instrumental in the lives of all those in the family. They had forty nieces and nephews, and they made sure that each and every one of them went to college; they helped pay if necessary. Aunt Minnie sewed skirts and shirts and dresses for all those children so they had clothes to wear to school. During the summers the Gastons would take in seven or eight of the nieces and nephews at a time and take them to the business college they owned to learn shorthand and how to type, so that when they grew up, they could be qualified workers in the workplace.

The interesting thing is that even with the financial success of A. G. and Minnie, none of their nieces and nephews grew up taking money for granted. In fact, I don't think any of them ever felt like they had money growing up. I know that my mother did not, and she was one of the few cousins who grew up outside Birmingham or Montgomery. She grew up in

New York, where my grandparents owned a printing school on Park Avenue. My mother went to private schools, but I think her parents, following the lead of A. G. and Minnie, did a very good job of not being boastful and of also making it clear that everyone would have to earn her or his own way. A. G. and Minnie were very strict. They were very loving people, but they were not about instilling privilege. Everybody had to go out and get a job. They believed that their gift to their family was the privilege of being able to grow up with and witness what it was like to have things in the world, to have comfort. To go into the world with that kind of experience under your belt already puts you at an advantage. A. G. and Minnie's thought was that from there the rest would be up to us whether or not we wanted to maintain that kind of comfort, and if we did, then we would figure out how to achieve it on our own.

A. G. Gaston started out with the disadvantage of feeling as if there weren't so many examples for him to follow of black people who had succeeded at business on a really high level. There were educators—there was Booker T. Washington, and there was Du Bois—but in terms of the business world, apart from a few people in Birmingham, he had few role models. Gaston started his business life by saving nickels and dimes he had worked extremely hard for, and I really believe that for him, it wasn't so much about accumulating gobs and gobs of money as about building something that he believed in, creating jobs for blacks, and changing the perception of what black people were capable of. Gaston left most of his money to charity and some of it to his wife. When Minnie died, she left portions of the money to her siblings who were still living, and they in turn left all of us in my generation savings or savings bonds in our names. I bought my books in graduate school with that money.

If there's one lesson I learned in the process of writing my book, it's that it is incumbent upon all of us now not to be afraid to push the envelope when it comes to the importance of our financial power. We no longer stand in a place to say, as those in the civil rights era had to, that there are bigger things we're fighting for. We fought those battles then, and we may still have to fight them, but the truth of the matter is we have no excuse left. I am convinced that achieving economic parity must be *the* central concern of the black community at this stage of the game. We have to start taking work and money and our relationship to it seriously. And we need to stop counting as suspect those blacks who have found a way to economic success. To my mind, the very best thing about Booker T. Washington was that his ideology gave real hope to the people who were on the margins of the margins. And even if we can't agree with everything he said, we ought to at least be glad somebody was willing to talk candidly about the economic realities of the era. A. G. Gaston certainly appreciated it, and I'm pretty sure he wasn't alone.

CHAPTER III

RONALD WALTERS,
Director of the African American Leadership Institute

Ronald Walters is director of the African American Leadership Institute and Scholar Practitioner Program, distinguished leadership scholar at the James MacGregor Burns Academy of Leadership, and professor in government and politics at the University of Maryland. For the 2000 presidential election season, he served as senior correspondent for the National Newspaper Publishers Association and political analyst for BET's Lead Story.

Walters has also appeared on CNN's Crossfire *and the* Jim Lehrer NewsHour, *NPR's* All Things Considered, *and many other television and radio programs. He is the author of six books, including* Black Presidential Politics in America *(1989), which won the Ralph Bunche Prize from the American Political Science Association and the Best Book award from the National Conference of Black Political Scientists. A practitioner as well as a scholar, Walters has served as the senior policy staff member for Congressman Charles Diggs, Jr., Congressman William Gray, and the Jesse Jackson presidential campaign.*

I OFTEN SAY to my students, if you were Booker T. Washington after his famous speech in 1895—the Atlanta Exposition speech, which was very well received—and you were in the South, your feet were planted between two cotton rows, and someone had a gun at the back of your head and asked you to give them your philosophy, what would it be? Well, it would be Booker T. Washington's philosophy, and the reason is that he was in a situation where if he was going to make any progress at all, he had to conform to the culture and the power relationships that were dominant in the South at that time. This was the year before *Plessy v. Ferguson*; it was the era of the return of the South with a vengeance to political, economic, and social power. It was also a time of very strong rejection and exclusion of black people. Blacks were excluded from areas of common life, except for their menial labor, confirmed by a number of constitutions that were written at that time and including all sorts of things that were important in structuring racism that would last long into the twentieth century. So Booker T. Washington's time was a special period in history.

My view of Washington gives him some levity with respect to where he was and what he was confronted with in his attempt to exercise a leadership role. Where I begin to be critical of Washington is when as part of his role he attracted the attention of a number of corporate leaders in the North and in other places in the world. The evolution of the so-called Booker T. Washington model of education was one that fit the growing industrial civilization of the United States and in other parts of the world. The need to have industrial training, a compliant labor force—it's almost a universal theme for the requirements of successful industrial development. And by *compliant*, yes, I mean agreeable to work under whatever the circumstance demands. That theme still exists today; all you have to do is ask people why immigrant labor is so successful as a part of American economic development.

In an attempt to nationalize and internationalize the leadership paradigm that Booker T. Washington proposed for the South, this model of compliance was developed and exported to places such as South and West Africa. It was with respect to this that individuals such as W. E. B. Du Bois started to push back from Washington. Of course, Du Bois had a different model, and the Washington–Du Bois debate became famous. It is a very important historical paradigm; everybody who teaches African American studies teaches it, and it evokes a great deal of discussion. It's not a complex paradigm. In the beginning, the two were not opponents; there was an attempt on the part of Du Bois to work with Washington, to listen to what he had to say. And Du Bois's interest influenced some of his New York friends, including T. Thomas Fortune. So some of these black leaders of the *New York Age* tried to work with Washington. They understood he was a selected leader and people favored him, and that he had this tremendous power, that routinely, officials would pass all sorts of decisions by him, he would approve, and things would get done. They understood this and tried to work with him. It wasn't until it became clear that the aims of a southernized political culture were antithetical to where the black northern elite was going that Du Bois began to fight against Washington.

In 1905, Du Bois and William Monroe Trotter, editor of the black militant newspaper the *Boston Guardian*, founded the Niagara Movement, which was a precursor to the NAACP.

When Booker T. Washington came to Boston's Faneuil Hall to speak, Trotter confronted him and was put in jail for it. Du Bois and Trotter were representative of this paradigm of moderate to conservative forward progress for blacks in extreme deference to whites. The point of departure had started, of course, with Du Bois's *The Souls of Black Folk*, published in 1903. And then the NAACP came along in 1909 and became an even stronger platform to further this cause.

Now, during all this, Booker T. Washington was not a fool. He understood that there was strong opposition to him from these northern black elitists, and so he tried to do some things behind the scenes, not only to signal that he was not the bad guy but also to support certain initiatives. He did things that would signal that he was, for example, against lynching. In his letters from Tuskegee, he was signaling to people that he was providing financial and background support for aspects of social progress on a national level. To that extent, in terms of his public voice, he was moderate to conservative. He championed the "pull down your buckets where they are" economic approach: If you are successful in industrial education and in building economic strength, then people will respect you and can't turn you away et cetera. I don't think anybody objects to that.

However, it was not a good thing for Booker T. Washington to attempt to nationalize his philosophy. The NAACP arose in part because there was a necessity for a more aggressive voice. The Harlem Renaissance, especially in its intellectual dimension, was a direct refutation of the stereotypical Negro. This was the first-generation twentieth-century American intellectual class, many of whom were graduated from every university from Harvard to Howard. When they began to have their voice, they were almost uniformly rejecting of the stereotypical Negro of the nineteenth century, which Booker T. Washington largely represented in terms of the Negro who was maintaining a lower-rung American dream. The Harlem Renaissance was a time of throwing off the old stereotype, and the New Negro, spurred on by the nature of black oppression, became a statement that it was time to forge a new identity in the twentieth century. If you look at the period from 1890 to 1915, there was a whole series of organizations founded—the Afro American League, the Black, the National Equal Rights League, Black and Tan Society, and others—to fight back against black exclusion. Then in the early 1900s there were of course a number of riots and different manifestations of the will to fight back.

I started the African American Leadership Institute to seriously study this issue, and we have produced a couple of works as well as a number of different programs. We've settled into less of an activist role and more of a research profile, and we serve in a technical assistance role for other leadership organizations—primarily 501c3 organizations in the black community. I attend meetings for various boards and answer questions—questions about African American politics and media but generally in the areas of: How do we make progress? and What kind of strategies do we need? What I see today in my work and in our society in terms of black leadership is that it is in some ways strong, particularly because of the diversification of black leadership into a number of different fields—business, education, corporate. We have, for a relatively small community, a cadre of leaders in almost every field. So that gives us a certain strength, but it is not strong enough in terms of the financial base needed to give the kinds of initiatives to further encourage participation in the solution to our problems as a community.

There is still a very strong factor of dependence upon the majority community, as reflected in dependence upon government and private institutions for critical resources. As a result, black leadership must do two things. On the one hand, it must perform the regular task of cultural leadership of any community; on the other hand, it must also perform a crossover leadership because if the resources are someplace else, the leadership needs to be there, too. White leaders don't have the responsibility of biracial mobilization; they can stay in their community. But black people don't have that luxury because the resources are in the white community, which was of course very similar to the circumstances Booker T. Washington faced. I'm an adviser to an organization called the Booker T. Washington Institute, which actively promotes the building of black businesses. So I don't think anybody opposes what Washington was trying to do in terms of promoting economic success; it is the political aspect that came along with that success that was most objectionable.

I think the most important aspect of Washington's legacy is that he managed to exercise leadership in a critical area of the country at a critical time. He was a symbol of success for many black people and was able to affect a kind of self-determination in building Tuskegee that is very positive. But I think his focus on economic self-sufficiency is probably the strongest aspect of his legacy. And in some ways his model of industrial training runs antithetical to his position on economic self-sufficiency, because you can't be the kind of progressive business leader you need to be if at the same time you are deferential to everybody. So there is a conflict there that Booker T. Washington never resolved. Blacks owned land at that time in a number of places, and some were even very prosperous. Washington was asking blacks to emulate that ownership while at the same time fitting into and not changing southern culture. But southern culture was for most blacks, both in and outside the South, anathema, something that needed to be confronted rather than fitted into. That's where Booker T. ran afoul.

CHAPTER IV

LUCENIA WILLIAMS-DUNN,
Mayor of Tuskegee, Alabama

Lucenia Williams-Dunn is the first female mayor of Tuskegee, Alabama. She is also executive director of the Tuskegee Macon County Head Start Program and president and CEO of DDL, an international corporation that engages in economic development opportunities for communities and small businesses. As director of the Bethune Program Development Center of the National Council of Negro Women, she helped start programs in education, health, community, and business development. She received her PhD from the University of Pittsburgh's School of Education.

ONE OF THE major ideas emphasized by Booker T. Washington was personal development so that African Americans, Negroes at the time, would be able to fit into the larger social structure as individuals and be able to survive with a level of confidence. It's important to say also that the notion of survival versus excelling—assigned by Washington and W. E. B. Du Bois, respectively—is based on misinformation about the relationship between Washington and Du Bois. Much to many people's surprise, Booker T. Washington and W. E. B. Du Bois were not adversaries. In their personal relationship they were amicable, each understanding that one without the other did not complete the whole person.

Booker T. Washington used to give a lecture to his students every Sunday in chapel at Tuskegee Industrial Normal School. He spoke to them from the heart, and he emphasized that along with so many other things, like intellect and skills, there were two other important aspects of life: spirituality and character. He talked about what education means and what keeping your word means: helping your neighbor and taking all of what you learned from Tuskegee and bringing it home to teach others. It's the same idea as "each one teach one." Washington was a very strong advocate of that idea, because he felt that in order for black communities to survive—and I use that word deliberately because when you start talking about racism in this country, you cannot talk about it without talking about the word *survive*—they need to have an education. When you come out of slavery and you don't have land or the tools that the wider social system deems important to survive not only from a materialistic point of view but from an emotional point of view, you need some sort of framework to help you understand what you are facing. Today, although we may not be emerging from slavery in the immediate sense, we are still employing a mode of survival.

For me, being the mayor of a city so evocative of and perhaps synonymous with Booker T. Washington and his legacy, I am reminded of when I did my dissertation on rural southern black women as community leaders. It was a study in power and influence. I had been involved in the civil rights movement and done all those things that young people did during that era, and I thought we had really changed America and the status of my people in my community. So when I went back fifteen or twenty years later to do research for my dissertation, I went back by car, and as I was interviewing these women in the Black Belt counties of Alabama and Mississippi, I found the same things that I had found when I was a student at Tuskegee and was involved with a program called the Tuskegee Institute Community Education Program, which was a direct play, if you will, on what Booker T. Washington stood for, what he did when he put together Tuskegee Industrial and Normal School. Fifteen years later the clothes looked different, but the issues were the same.

I am governing a city that is more or less Booker T. Washington's city, and as I look around me, I see that the conditions are the same. There are still a few people that make it and a lot of people that don't. That's what Booker T. Washington found too, and I wonder: If his philosophy had not been more widespread, would we have had more major changes in the status of our community than we do? The answer to why his philosophy was not more widespread involves a more complex notion, because then we get back to the word *survival*, which then leads to the questions, Survival of what, and survival of whom? Because you see, if you are involved in a racist social system that talks about entitlement—a given privilege based on who you are, not what you earn or are capable of—it's not a level playing field. Personally, I don't believe that anyone is entitled to anything just because. But then we need to talk about the construct of capitalism and what makes capitalism operate. Capitalism always requires that someone be poor.

Booker T. Washington was saying to black folk in his time, "This is how you survive in a capitalistic society." Any criticism or disparagement of this notion had to do with the fact that society at large fostered no intention for black folks to survive at a level that would enable them to compete and participate. Washington was well aware of that lack of intention, and it's important to note that he didn't use that exact language about survival in a capitalistic society; his book *Character Building* is an important reference in terms of really understanding his philosophy and how he related to everyday people, who were mostly his students.

Criticism and disparagement are not the same as rejection. Booker T. Washington is one of the most misunderstood and slandered figures in history. Think about it, if somebody has put together a successful formula that will increase the rate of achievement among African Americans, particularly in the postslavery Reconstruction era, who's going to want that someone to survive? Of course he has been maligned not just by white people but by black people as well, but then you have to remember how many black people have gone to Tuskegee— be it the industrial school, the institute, or the university—and then you've got a whole different thing going on. Because whether they recognize it or not, they are living Booker T. Washington's philosophy, and there are graduates of Tuskegee all over the world. I've been halfway around the world, and everywhere I go, there's not one person I meet who, when I tell him where I'm from, doesn't immediately start talking about one of three things: Booker T. Washington, George Washington Carver, and the Tuskegee Airmen.

Each president of Tuskegee University carried out the philosophy of Booker T. Washington in his own way. Robert Moton, Washington's immediate successor, for example, gave acres to the VA hospital system, to do what? To accommodate black veterans after World War I. Frederick Patterson, who was president from 1935 to 1953, gave the land for the Tuskegee Airmen to come and train. The point is that each Tuskegee president blazed a trail that reemphasized Booker T. Washington's basic educational premise.

Today there are aspects of Washington's legacy in areas like the black church community, where Washington was well respected by several different denominations. But if you're talking about a sustained, all-encompassing legacy that permeates nationwide, the job was really never finished. This makes it very frustrating when you start to examine Booker T. Washington, because you know the kind of impact he had, that he was on the right track, and yet we still have slums and rural communities in the South with outdoor toilets. We still have a lot of poverty. Something didn't quite hook up all the way between then and now.

Sometime back I did a study on the development and history of black businesses in the state of Maryland from 1863 to 1993, and it was so wild, because everywhere I turned, there was Booker T. Washington. I was going through one of the first black neighborhoods there—in Prince George's County, Maryland, which was built as a place where black faculty from Howard University could buy homes—and it turned out that the architect and developer of that neighborhood was Booker T. Washington's son-in-law. Not only that, but as I was riding down the street, I saw this house that looked familiar to me, and the people I was with who were serving as guides told me that it was one of their most prized historic homes. I recognized right away that it was Tuskegee brick (Tuskegee brick, made entirely by students and faculty from clay dug on the Tuskegee farm, played a major role in the building of Tuskegee Institute). The woman I was with couldn't believe I knew that, but it's a very distinct kind of building, and I grew up with it; I know that brick. Then she told me that the man who owned the house had gone to Tuskegee Industrial and Normal School and had come back to Prince George's County to build a house for his family with bricks he made himself.

When I got into the business part of my research for the study, Booker T. Washington's influence was also there. The National Business League was formed by Booker T. Washington and is still in existence. I read the transcripts from business conventions that were held—there were three: two in Boston, the other I'm not sure where—and black folk came by train, by mule, by wagon, by horse to convene. At one of the meetings in Boston there were about six hundred and some odd black folks there to discuss the same issues that black businesses discuss today, and there were more black businesses back then.

Again, the questions become, What happened? Where did the disconnect occur? Well, I don't know. I mean, I could take some wild guesses, but it is a question that I have pondered and pondered and pondered. When I look at our black women's magazine *Essence*, for example, and see that it's no longer a black-owned magazine, I'm trying to figure out why someone would sell that magazine to a white corporation.

Was it out of greed? Why not pass it on to some young black writer or entrepreneur—or a group of young black writers or entrepreneurs? It wouldn't be hard to find a group of young folks who would rise to the call if *Essence* magazine said: "I'm tired. I don't want to do this anymore. I want to sit on Martha's Vineyard, kick my heels up, and watch the yachts go by. Y'all take it, and take it to the next level." If people had paid more attention to Booker T. Washington, would black people instead of a white corporation own *Essence*? I don't know. It's possible.

Booker T. Washington was everywhere doing all sorts of things, but there was a downside to Booker T.; there's always a downside to any human being. He was very dictatorial. He expressed his power sometimes in ways that were negative. He became so powerful that he could decide the outcome of an election in Louisiana. I'm not suggesting that the negative aspects of his personality caused any stunt in the growth of our people. He was only one man. But that doesn't stop me from asking the question, with and without Booker T. Washington in mind, What makes us do what we do?

There is a loosely organized group of people across the United States in various fields, and they are studying what we call the Maafa. The term *Maafa* is an African word that is translated to mean "the great atrocity" and has been used most notably by a sister named Dr. Marimba Ani, who wrote a book titled *Yurugu*. You see, what we as black people have not done successfully is to examine in a very open and fluid way what happened to us during slavery and the resulting generational impact. So instead of looking at our behavior in the context of our reality, we have contrite academic study or convoluted discourse.

Let me give a very simple example. One of our ways of surviving during slavery was to vent our anger by leaving the gate open as an apparent accident, so a lot of white men's cattle and hogs wandered off in the woods and got bitten by snakes and drowned in the swamp. Then the slave would say, "Oops, massa, I didn't know I left that gate open!" So then the white folks would say, "Lulu, you just lazy and you left that gate open." And then Lulu would go off somewhere and laugh about it, thinking she got her master good. The intellectual interpretation of that is that black people are lazy and slovenly and will not take care of things, but the human aspect of it is, from a slave's point of view: I'm angry with you because you beat the hell out of my sister, and you raped my mother, and you sold my father, and that's how I'm gonna get your ass back!

All this is to say that when you start examining Booker T. Washington and are trying to put him into a certain context, as I think we are doing here in this book, it's a more difficult task than taking his personality and judging it. Because he did or did not do something in the wider context of us as a race of people with damage that has been done to us, the infliction of which has carried on for several generations. William Graham Sumner, the sociologist, said that oftentimes when something starts for one reason in one generation, by the time it gets to the third generation people have forgotten why they were doing it in the first place, and it becomes inculcated in the rituals of life. That's kind of where we are as black people.

Essentially Booker T. Washington represents pride. He represents a model for success in a capitalistic society. As the first woman mayor of Tuskegee, who happens to be black, I use Booker T. Washington as my model for leadership. He has taught me that as a leader I have to be sensitive to the broader aspect of my community, not just the delivery of government services but the uplifting of my people.

CHAPTER V

CLEOPHUS THOMAS, JR.,
Chairman and CEO of A. G. Gaston Corporation, holding company for Booker T. Washington Insurance Company

Cleophus Thomas, Jr., is chairman and CEO of the A. G. Gaston Corporation and a board member of the Birmingham-based AmSouth Bancorp. Born in Sylacauga, Alabama, Thomas was educated in the public schools of Anniston, Alabama, and holds bachelor's degrees from the University of Alabama and Oxford University and a law degree from Harvard University. A former trustee of the University of Alabama, Thomas delivered the commencement address at Tuskegee University in August 2002.

I WAS INTRODUCED to Booker T. Washington in the conventional manner as a person growing up in Alabama and then later as a student of American studies and American history, which required the studying of eminent public officials in history and social studies. I have read Louis Harlan's critical two-volume biography of Booker T. Washington, and as it happens, I have a close friend who has written an unpublished manuscript about Washington that takes a much more sympathetic view of him, and I've read that as well. So my knowledge of Booker T. Washington is fairly thorough.

Booker T. Washington is a polarity in American and

African American history and African American intellectual life. In a sense, there is something generic or even emblematic about even the reference to him. When you say Booker T. Washington, it's almost like saying Kleenex as a categorical reference to any sort of tissue. Booker T. Washington has become emblematic of a kind of right-wing conservative philosophy or approach to discussion or analysis of black life in contrast with W. E. B. Du Bois. The two have become markers of factions or two opposing wings of a discussion. So you have Booker T. in theory, and then you have Booker T. the great builder, who has left a lasting monument to his philosophy in the form of Tuskegee. For me, I have never felt obliged to align myself with this side or that necessarily. I'm not an academic; I'm just a working stiff.

I don't know that there were any tenets of Washington's philosophy that did not hold. His tenets of industrial education, building, and self-reliance—those were the tenets that held. What did not hold was his bifurcation of work from civil rights and political activity. He saw the agitation for civil rights as an unhelpful diversion from a more practical commitment to economic rights and the mastery of skills. Is Booker T. Washington the spook who sat by the door? Is there something clever and duplicitous about his plea for education rather than civil rights? Because how can you develop economic skills without education, and how can you have education, public education, without civil rights? That's what *Brown v. Board of Education* was of course all about. You can't have one without the other. And you had whites who were opposed to Tuskegee because they saw that.

You may be able to own land without an education, but you

won't own it for long without some kind of education or sophistication. You're not going to own land or a house without
sophistication or pride, and then isn't that just twenty paces
away from being uppity? It goes back to this whole psychological notion of status and a place in civil society. When you talk
about property, isn't that a core principle of the Constitution—life, liberty, and property? So here we are at a place that
Booker T. Washington ostensibly forswore, which is a deep
and remote intellectual and abstract interest in being a partic-
ipant in civil society. So in terms of what is important about
Washington today, it is the idea that we should be financially
independent and involved in business. I don't think anybody
disputes that. I don't think Du Bois disputed that. The dispute
was over whether one should be concerned about financial independence to the exclusion of all else. Or that the commitment to those economic values and the Protestant work ethic
in some Max Weberian way is going to lead to the conferral of
rights or a situation just as good as having rights. I just don't
know if that's true.

One of my favorite histories of African American business
is Walter B. Weare's book on North Carolina mutual insurance companies, *Black Business in the New South: A Social History of North Carolina Mutual Life Insurance Company*, and in
that book Du Bois was very complimentary about Durham,
North Carolina's business culture, which at the turn of the
century was emblematic of the African American business
success that was launched by Booker T. Washington. So even
then I don't think anybody questioned Washington's business
values and entrepreneurial zeal and commitment.

The A. G. Gaston Corporation is a holding company for

businesses founded by A. G. Gaston. These companies were formed before the repeal of Glass-Steagall [the Banking Act of 1933, or the Glass-Steagall Act, separated investment and commercial banking activities in the wake of the 1929 stock market crash], and though there was a bank in the complex of companies that Dr. Gaston founded, it was not a part of the holding company. The primary operational company that the A. G. Gaston Corporation owns is Booker T. Washington Life Insurance Company. Glass-Steagall prohibited life insurance companies from owning banks, so the bank was a freestanding company and not a holding of Gaston but owned independently by Dr. Gaston. The companies under the Gaston Corporation are: the Booker T. Washington Life Insurance Company, A. G. Gaston Construction Company, Booker T. Washington Broadcasting Company, which owned WENN radio and WAGG FM—these radio stations have since been sold owing to the pressures of deregulation, which gave them heightened valuations that really made it prudent to sell them several years ago—a cemetery, a funeral home, also sold to family members of Dr. Gaston. The Gaston Corporation and its companies are a part of an ESOP structure [an employee stock ownership plan], and its employees own all the stock of the companies.

On the insurance company side, the policies we sell are in the range of ten to twenty thousand dollars. Many of the companies in insurance are being sold and acquired; we've acquired some ourselves. We see the challenges of small black business and financing. We see the competitiveness of the marketplace in finding bright and talented employees. We don't discriminate, but obviously the majority of our customers and the workforce in our businesses are black. During Dr. Gaston's administration when he found it difficult to find African American clerical workers—stenographers, bookkeepers, and staff accountants—he founded the Booker T. Washington Business College, which was headed by his wife. All the star students would come work for Gaston after they graduated. Even now, though the college has been closed for fifteen or twenty years, graduates are still in meaningful positions of responsibility all over the United States. My oldest child is a senior at the University of North Carolina at Chapel Hill, and when I took him to enroll four years ago, the chief staff person in the housing office was a graduate of the Booker T. Washington Business College.

Once upon a time, a company like ours would have had a monopoly on talented African Americans because of the barriers to employment in other companies, but with the advent of integration that has changed. As a matter of fact, when other companies were looking for capable employees, they would raid us, and our employees were among the first African Americans to be hired in the larger companies here— the power, gas, and phone companies. But we still have the challenges for small African American businesses: access to capital markets, and access to talent that has a choice to go and work anywhere he wants to work and demand salaries commensurate with his training and ability.

I've said that most of the greatest practitioners (of business, government, and the arts) are made, not born, which I think is a hopeful way to look at our world today. It means that there is no finite, divinely ordained group of individuals; a person with commitment and energy and a strong work ethic can master an area and achieve. There is something essentially democratic, uplifting, and perhaps Emersonian about that kind of self-reliance and ability to achieve. It also demystifies things. Many people want us to buy into a mythology of some eminent chosen people that you have to be born into in order to succeed, and if you are excluded at birth, there can be no transformation or point of entry. Either you are born into this charmed circle or you are obliged to be a servant to it. That just isn't so. There are opportunities, and as the writer Grace Paley once wrote, there can be enormous changes at the last minute. Certainly I believe that the democracy of achievement exists whether you're black or white. So many barriers are psychological; the chief barrier to achieving is the failure or inability to set a goal.

There are many things about black culture and history that have been romanticized and that need to be made less poetic and more common. For example, when Kirkwood Balton, one of my predecessors here, would speak to young people, he would often pass out his business card and say, "This is my business card—Kirkwood Balton, chairman and CEO of Booker T. Washington Insurance Company." And then he would ask them, "What do you want your business card to read five years from now? Ten years from now? Twenty years from now? Do you want to be a hairdresser? Do you want to be a teacher, a plumber, an astronaut, or a bus driver? Whatever it is, write it down on the back of my card, and once you say that, how do you become that?" So I think this sort of quotidian act, perhaps utterly lacking in lyricism but that simply states, "Write it down," gives someone a practical assignment. It's a pathway to engagement. Some imagination can be used in a quite ordinary and mechanical way that can nudge us along life's path to usefulness and fulfillment.

This is precisely the kind of practical assignment that Booker T. Washington would give. And his great legacy, Tuskegee, endures as a vehicle to help young men and women to complete this assignment.

CHAPTER VI

KAREN HUNTER,
Journalist/Radio Talk Show Personality

Karen Hunter is a Pulitzer Prize–winning journalist, radio cohost, and a former editorial board member of the New York Daily News, *for which she also wrote an op-ed column for several years. Hunter joined WWRL's* Morning Show *as cohost in June 2003. She is also an assistant visiting professor in film and media at Hunter College and a former adjunct at New York University, where she taught writing and grammar to high school students in Harlem.*

Hunter has coauthored several best-sellers, including The Wendy Williams Experience *(2004), with syndicated radio host Wendy Williams, and* Ladies First *(1999), with Oscar-nominee Queen Latifah.*

I'VE READ *Up from Slavery* twice. I first read it when I was a teen, and it didn't have much of an impact on me. I wasn't really exploring my blackness at the time. I was just an avid reader; I read everything from V. C. Andrews to Judy Blume to Stephen King. I was a real strange kid. But then after college, when I entered the workplace, I decided that it was important for me to explore myself on a deeper level. When you read things as a teenager, it's very different from when you read things as an adult. I was thirty when I read *Up from Slavery* again, and this time it had a huge impact on me.

I come from a neighborhood of two-parent households; everyone had a father, and most families were middle and upper middle class. My father had a job as a parole officer, but he also owned a store in Newark, New Jersey, where he made a lot of money and was able to pay my way through four years of college. It was a corner store that his father had owned, and when his father died, he took it over. My father, who has been working since he was five years old, was the first person in his family to graduate from college. He had a vision for his life and his family. He gave me everything that a kid could possibly want. Oddly, I don't recall ever thinking about being black during my formative years. I went to an integrated Catholic school where race was not an issue. My friends were both white and black.

When I went to college at Drew University, there were fifty-seven black students in the undergraduate school. The only reason I know that is that it was the first time that I really faced racism. There was a program, an EOF (Educational Opportunity Fund) program, that the majority of black students went through to get into Drew. I didn't go through that program, and I hung out mostly with the international students. I couldn't relate to the kids from the EOF program, most of whom were on welfare. I couldn't relate not because I was a snob but because it wasn't my experience.

Meanwhile, the white kids assumed I was from the EOF program when actually, I did well on my SATs, graduated in the top 5 percent of my class, and my parents were paying my way. But that made me think, If I did come through a program, so what? And why were they bothering me with this? What does it matter? That created in me a kind of militant desire to examine my blackness.

I came from a very noble family with a strong work ethic. For me, it was really about what it meant to be a Hunter. My father instilled in me that "Hunters never quit" and "Hunters come from a strong stock of people." "You're a Hunter," he would say, and I understood what that meant.

But being faced with something different at Drew, I decided to use the ignorance that I was met with and fight fire with fire. I made it my mission to act as ignorant as possible because then people would mistakenly underestimate me. Folks tend to underestimate you when they think you're one way, and I practically made it a business to come out of left field and prove people wrong. I think a lot of black folks come into a situation feeling inferior at the door. I never had that problem. If anything, I came in feeling superior because I was a Hunter.

What Booker T. Washington understood, and I think it's something that black folks need to understand today, is that you cannot achieve anything until you take care of your home base first. That means being the best, being the brightest, the smartest and building your infrastructure. I purposely moved into an all-black neighborhood as an adult because I know that when black folks become successful and make money, they want to run and move someplace else. But I'm not paying white folks' taxes. My mortgage and taxes are very low in the neighborhood I live in, but more important, the kids who grew up and are growing up there get to see me every day.

There are so many black neighborhoods that don't have somebody saying to these kids, "Boy, if you don't pull them pants up!" That's me in my neighborhood. I turned into Pearl from 227. I'm sure those kids can't stand me, but they listen, and they don't talk back.

Booker T. Washington didn't just build up a school; he built up a community. In my community we have a Korean hair care store, Indian folks own our major grocery store, there are half a dozen Chinese food joints. There are no black-owned businesses. There's this notion that white folks' ice water is colder. When my father owned his store, everything was top drawer because that's what he felt his community deserved. If the white folks' ice water is colder, it's not simply because it's in their home; they don't just turn on the spigot and the water is naturally colder. Black people have to make sure they have a spigot and source to allow the water to flow.

I have a Pulitzer Prize, I've written several best-selling books, and I'm not yet forty years old. I don't take anything for granted, and I never rest on my laurels. Every time I do something I always strive to be the best, because I recognize that history is going to look at what I'm doing, and I don't want history to look back and say, "Karen Hunter was a great *black* so-and-so." I want history to say, "Karen Hunter was a great columnist or writer or whatever."

I disagree that the mainstream necessarily has to mean white people. You can create your own world, your own mainstream, to say nothing of the fact that the so-called mainstream seems to be buckling under the pressure of "our" cultural influences. If you turn on television, every commercial has some sort of hip-hop flavor to it. White kids in sub-urban neighborhoods are listening to rap, piping and pimping out their rides. That's their culture now, borrowed from us.

I do media training as well, and I work a lot with Universal Records, which basically owns everybody right now. You have folks like Baby and the Cash Money Millionaires, who were making millions before they went to Universal; Master P, Nelly, and Ludacris all were doing well and had sold a lot on their own before they signed on with Universal. Now, do you think two or three of them could have gotten together and started a distribution company? Because we know that black folks buy their stuff differently from white folks. We don't necessarily go to J&R Music World or Barnes & Noble. I might have been one of three black people standing on the packed line when the fifth *Harry Potter* book went on sale at midnight in the summer 2003. Blacks primarily purchase through book clubs, pick up a book while waiting at the check-cashing place, or stop by my man Muhammad who sells on the street. We *may* go to a kiosk at the mall. The same goes for records.

And if you recognize that there is an alternative distribu-tion chain and are able to develop it so that it works the same way "mainstream" works, then why would you give your prod-uct to a company that only gives you ten cents on the dollar? It's stupid. But these hip-hop guys do it because it's easy. We as a race have become complacent and lazy, and we'd rather take a million than take the time to create something that will make a hundred million and at the same time establish some-thing for our community.

I think on some level we've been brainwashed. Money is

good. Don't get me wrong. I like money, and I like making it. But at the end of the day I'm working to create a system that will outlive me and benefit my community. I'm quiet about that mostly because as there were in Booker T. Washington's day, there are naysayers who will tell you that you can't do this and you can't do that. I see the possibilities, though. Rosewood didn't just happen, and Tulsa didn't just happen. The fact that they had to bomb and burn those places out tells you that there was something very powerful going on there. Now, you can't do it everywhere, but if all of us had that mentality about self-sufficiency, which is what Booker T. Washington was about—and have enough money with the six hundred billion dollars we spend a year as a people (more than some countries)—we would have a much stronger community.

We got lazy after Martin Luther King, Malcolm X, and Medgar Evers were murdered. We thought we overcame with the laws. We can vote; we don't have to sit at the back of the bus (even though if you look now, when blacks get on the bus they go right to the back). Everything is fine. We don't have to work so hard. To me, integration is the worst thing to ever happen to black people. I'll say it from the top of the mountain: Integration is the worst thing to ever happen to black people. It gave us a false sense of security, and it stripped us of the very foundation that made us great. The Montgomery bus boycott never would have happened if black folks weren't together in a community where your teacher, your pastor, your doctor, and your lawyer all lived on the same block with the bus drivers, the maids, and the people who cleaned toilets. The teacher had to teach your kid because she had to see you at church on Sunday. Integration meant maybe we'd get bused into white schools that didn't want you there and didn't believe you were capable of doing the work anyway. You want to live next door to white people? Okay. Maybe they'll burn a cross on your lawn; maybe they won't. But you're still going to pay twice as much as you should for that house.

When I read about Booker T. Washington's dealings with the president and other political figures at that time, I guess it might seem that he was being conciliatory, but you have to look at the Trojan horse. You can fight a system several ways, and I think Booker T. was brilliant in the ways he chose to fight. If you want people to change, calling them a racist is not going to make them change. The only way you can make them change is by forcing them to confront themselves in the most subtle of ways or by making it worth their while to change.

People who had the pleasure of sitting and talking with Booker T. Washington walked away with the feeling that they had just met with a dignified man who had a purpose. Not the N word and not someone who held his nose in the air and made you feel less important. I grapple with this a little, because I'm more on the militant side and Booker T. clearly was not. But as I get older, I recognize the wisdom of showing people they're wrong without beating them over the head. I am learning to prove my point through action and example because that's something that can't be disputed.

There are things that Booker T. said to white people that I would not say, but he was clever. Think about it. White people are in a position of power, and you want that power. There are only two ways you're going to get it. You can either take it from them (and the last I looked we don't have the might or the will or the wherewithal to do that), or sneak them. Best time to sneak someone is when his guard is down, when he has been softened. And the best way to soften someone is to compliment him. It works. I think Booker T. Washington knew exactly what he was doing the entire time. Even if he didn't, he was still clever. He chose a path to reach his goal that would get him there easier and faster.

We like to judge people based on what we think we would do in the same situation. I love it when people say, "If I lived back then, I wouldn't be no slave!" To which I say, "Your black ass would've been a slave like everyone else. You would've been picking cotton out in the field talking about 'yassah, boss,' along with every other slave."

But we wouldn't be who we are if folks like Booker T. Washington didn't do what they did. There are millions who endured the yoke of slavery just so that we could be here, so that we could survive. And we're still trying to survive. We can't move beyond sheer survival until we figure out who the hell we are.

I appreciate the idea that human beings are like water. Water is one of the strongest elements on earth, but if it's faced with an obstacle, it goes around, flows under and over. If it gets too hot, it turns into steam. It's malleable, and yet it can erode a whole car. Booker T. Washington played his game like water. He was a man who was a slave and who didn't allow slavery to define him or who he was going to become. He built something that he saw in his mind's eye when no one else believed it was possible. He made other people believe in themselves and gave them opportunities to do things that they couldn't even imagine doing. At the end of the day he went from slavery to dining with the president of the United States of America and helped to define a race of people during a time when that people was looked down upon as inferior savages. He was a great man.

CHAPTER VII

AVON KIRKLAND,
Filmmaker

Avon Kirkland is an award-winning producer, director, and writer of films and programs that have been broadcast on PBS, the BBC, the Disney Channel, and throughout the world. Programs include Up and Coming, *a black family drama series shown on PBS in the early* 1980s; Booker, *a one-hour drama about Booker T. Washington's mythic struggle for an education; and* Simple Justice, *the highly acclaimed docudrama about Thurgood Marshall's historic victory in the landmark case* Brown v. Board of Education. *Recently Kirkland produced and directed* Street Soldiers, *a documentary featuring the work of the Omega Boys Club of San Francisco, and* Ralph Ellison: An American Journey, *which premiered at the 2003 Sundance Film Festival. Kirkland is currently directing the feature-length documentary* Up from Slavery: The Triumph and Tragedy of Booker T. Washington *(working title).*

I'VE BEEN TRYING to figure out Booker T. Washington for about twenty years. The first independent film I made in 1983 is a one-hour PBS children's drama, *Booker,* the story of Booker T. Washington's boyhood struggle to learn to read and gain a sense of hope at the end of slavery. It is an inspirational film that is still being broadcast and shown in classrooms around the world. My current production is a documentary about Washington's adult career and has the working title *Up from Slavery: The Triumph and Tragedy of Booker T. Washington*. So I've been trying to answer some basic questions about the man and his legacy for some years now, questions that cause even some prominent historians great difficulty in confidently interpreting.

For example, Louis Harlan, Pulitzer Prize-winning Washington biographer. When Lou was writing the final chapter for the second volume of his two-volume biography *(Booker T. Washington: The Wizard of Tuskegee)*, he was spending a one-year sabbatical nearby in order to finish the book. I had dinner with Lou and his wife, Sadie, one evening when Lou was struggling to finish the last chapter and to arrive at some final interpretation of Washington's personality and legacy. He was having a lot of difficulty. That surprised me because although I hadn't read any of the second volume, I'd read the first one and Lou had also been an adviser on my film, *Booker*. I knew him well, and it seemed he had Washington pegged up to 1901. After dinner Lou and I had a few glasses of Jack Daniel's, and the more we drank, the easier it became to explain Booker T. At about 2:00 A.M. Sadie came out and told Lou to let me go to bed (I stayed overnight), and by that time we felt that we had the man all figured out. Unfortunately, we couldn't recall any of it the next morning. This is to say that if Lou Harlan can't do it, it ain't easy.

I think there are a lot of misconceptions about Booker T. Washington all over the place, and what drives me to seek out the truth is that I want to know for the documentary what to make of him and his life and what lessons, if any, there are to be learned. It's clear that from reading widely in the history of the era (particularly historians David Levering Lewis, James Anderson, and Fitzhugh Brundage) that there are some very obvious lessons to be learned: One, Booker T. Washington was not chosen as a leader of black people by black people; he was anointed by the certain elements of the white power structure in the United States at that time, who considered his conservative approach to racial progress convenient to their pursuit of the almighty dollar. He was welcome at a time when the South was desperate for racial peace so that it could pursue economic goals without the threat of racial turmoil and with the advantage of its cheap black labor.

Ideally, a leader has transformational capabilities; he or she can change things or at least advocate and champion a course of action that his or her followers can take to achieve their human goals in a free society. Booker T. Washington advocated trade school education, derided higher education for blacks, advocated acquiescence to disfranchisement of most blacks and social segregation of all blacks. His message was work hard, buy property, and don't give whites any cause to abuse you. Prove your worth as citizens, and all good things will come in time.

I've come to believe that Booker T. Washington is a bit overrated as a transformational leader. I didn't get there easily, but that's what I've come to believe. Although it is true that his personal success was a source of inspiration and hope for so many of us back then (he was even an early hero of Rosa Parks), his prominence was based on false impressions. For starters, Booker T. Washington was far from the first person to advocate working hard for lifting ourselves up; black uplift preceded him by a long time. At a recent conference in South Carolina I was interested to hear from Oliver Hill, one of the original lawyers in *Brown v. Board, Topeka*, who responded to the question regarding how people argue over whether *Brown* caused or catalyzed or launched the civil rights movement, and he said, "Well, look, we've had a civil rights movement in one way or another ever since we hit these shores in the 1600s." I thought that was profound, and I think the same can be said about black uplift.

Let's take a second part of what Washington's reputation is based on: pushing industrial education. It's almost as if he invented it. He didn't, of course. Industrial education was a movement before 1850. What happened was that Samuel Chapman Armstrong did such a good job at establishing Hampton Institute in Virginia and publicizing his work that he gained the avid support of Rutherford B. Hayes and various members of the American Missionary Society. Hampton was a remarkable school, but what Washington did that was remarkable when he was chosen by General Samuel Chapman Armstrong to start a separate new school was to go to Tuskegee and make something out of nothing. A chicken coop became a thriving campus. More important, and I think this is really noteworthy, was that he did it with an all-black staff—unheard of in those times—which became a source of racial pride and so has more significance than just establishing an institution from scratch.

I was born and raised in the South. My mother worked her way through high school in Tuskegee, Alabama, which back then (in the 1930s) was a part of the recently established college there. And my twin sister got her bachelor's degree from Tuskegee after she'd already earned an RN degree in Atlanta. I certainly appreciate the establishment of Tuskegee, the people Tuskegee trained, and the educational opportunities it afforded to folks who wouldn't otherwise have had them. But Washington is given credit for industrial education that he doesn't deserve. The fact that he created this institution with a black staff and thereby demonstrated black competence is a wonderful, racially validating story. In fact, I once raised close to almost a million dollars to produce that story of Tuskegee's founding as a feature film, but it wasn't quite enough money, I didn't like the script well enough, we couldn't fix it, and I wound up giving the money back.

One of the most remarkable things about Booker T. Washington was his energy and his obsession with succeeding. If you're just talking about the establishment of Tuskegee—when he started out with it, there were no students, initially no money, no buildings, no books, no nothing except a commitment on the part of the state to establish a school there—Washington had to do everything to get that school going, and he did. He also went on to grow the school well, because he was a hell of a fund-raiser. I will give him that. And like I said, it's a terrific story. But there were black people all around the country establishing schools; it went all the way back to the Civil War and the black folk who went down to the Georgia Sea Islands to teach. I'm not just playing devil's advocate here. Black people made similar efforts and progress all over the South; it's just that they never achieved the same level of fame.

John Hope of Atlanta is one instructive example that not

many people are aware of. He was of Washington's era, but unlike Washington, he had the advantage of a broad liberal arts background and knew better than to believe that black people could protect their gains without the right to vote. He never bowed to political expediency like Washington did and became president of what became Morehouse College. He, like Du Bois, would not compromise our civil rights or try to rein in black claims to full racial justice. To do so would have been to betray his black mother's humanity. Now I ask you, when you think of schools that have produced champions of racial justice, schools that insisted upon individual excellence and whose graduates challenged America to become the country it claims to be, do you think of Morehouse—and Martin Luther King, Jr., Benjamin Mays, and so on—or do you think of Tuskegee?

Black economic nationalism is, to my mind, another area where Washington gets too much credit. The truth lies elsewhere or is a lot more complicated than conservative thinkers let on. Yes, Washington founded the National Negro Business League, but what did the National Negro Business League do or change? It promoted the idea of economic self-sufficiency but was little more than a mutual support group that did not have a program to expand black business. Washington used the organization mainly as a vehicle to minimize the influence of people like Du Bois in the black community, who after all followed Frederick Douglass's final words on achieving racial progress: "Agitate, agitate, agitate."

Booker T. Washington is still a lightning rod in academia. I don't think he's an overrated lightning rod, but he's a lightning rod because he's overrated. I've been looking for somebody in academe to give me a theory of his personality, and I haven't found anyone who has done it better than Lou Harlan. At the end of Lou's Preface in volume one, he describes Booker T. Washington as an enigma. If you could put Washington on a psychoanalyst's couch and talk to him, maybe you could figure some things out, because he really was all over the place, so inconsistent, and some of the things he said to white people in public would make your skin crawl. In 1906 or 1907 he and W. E. B. Du Bois were speaking to a mostly white group in Atlanta, something about the race problem. Booker T. Washington got up and said: "Your race shows a very high standard for us to try to live up to." And he wasn't playing. He said the same thing in a hundred different ways at other times and quite seriously, too. Whether or not what he said put him in a place to better help black people doesn't matter to me. Are you willing to say, "My folks are inferior," in order to raise money or opportunities? I'm not. If it was a strategy on his part, I consider it a really corrupt one.

Ultimately, what displeases me about Washington is that he was, as Du Bois said, a politician, and I'm saying that he was so much of a politician that he was willing to please white folks by devaluing his race. There is an abundance of interstitial tissue for this argument. By contrast, Du Bois was such a defender of our basic humanity. Any leader who does not defend the basic humanity of his people is betraying his people.

There's a book called *All God's Dangers*, and it's an autobiography by a guy named Ned Cobb, who is called Nate Shaw in the book because when it was published, he didn't want his name known. Theodore Rosengarten was a young Harvard PhD student who interviewed this guy and put his "autobiography" together, so the book is in Ned Cobb's words but organized by Rosengarten—much in the way this book, *Uncle Tom or New Negro?*, is presented—and it has the most insightful estimate of Booker T. Washington that I have ever heard:

> After I become old enough to travel and go anywhere by myself, I went to them big days, the commencement days at Tuskegee in the spring of the year, and I seed Booker Washington. He was a pretty large bodied man, and he wasn't so high and he wasn't so low, just an average man, but he was an important man. He was the principal there at that school, I seed him, and I heard him talk in front of them celebration days, and I knowed he was over that school every way. And he travel yonder in them Northern states, and he'd go before them big money men, and the officials of the entire United States, he could meet with them and talk with them, and he was recognized. But I wouldn't boost him up. I wouldn't boost Booker Washington today up to everything that was industrious and right. Why? He was a nigger of this state and well known and everything, but here's what his trouble was to a great extent, he didn't feel for and didn't respect his race of people enough to go rock bottom with 'em. He leaned too much to the white people that controlled the money. He was a big man, he had authority, he had pull in life, he had a political pull anywhere he turn and he was pulling for Booker Washington. He wanted his people to do this, that,

other, but he never did get to the roots of our trouble.
Yet and still, the veil was over the nigger's eyes—
Booker Washington didn't try to pull that veil away
like he should done. He shoulda walked out full-faced
with all the courage in the world and realized: I was
born to die. What use for me to hold everything
undercover if I know it? How come I won't tell it in
favor of my own race of people? Why would I not care
who sinks just so I swim? Wrong-spirited, Booker
Washington was, quite natural. There's nobody on
earth perfect, but Booker Washington was a man got
down with his people, with his country, in the wrong
way.

To the extent that Booker T. Washington is in the contemporary American consciousness, I disagree with the notion
that he is a wrongly maligned figure. Rosa Parks—God bless
her, she's still living—is a big fan of Booker T. Washington.
People like Parks, in a sense, at one end of the political spectrum, are thinking about Washington a good deal and in a
positive light. On the other end of the spectrum, Clarence
Thomas is also a big fan of Washington, for obvious reasons.
Parks grew up in Alabama at a time when blacks were struggling, when Washington was useful as a symbol of hope. And
if Washington embodies and reflects the many African
Americans who for good or ill sought to better their lives and
struggled to navigate within the confines of the existing social
system, then that is important to remember. But in the end I
think it comes down to a question about Washington's lead-

ership, and did he mislead black people? His essential argument was: When we prove ourselves worthy, white people will accept us.

Here's the thing. Booker T. Washington gave black uplift a bad name by marrying it to acceptance of segregation and disfranchisement, putting those three things together, plus industrial education, and that is what his popularity came from. That is what he talked about in the Atlanta Compromise address, and that is what white people loved about him. Washington was very generous to white people, and he let them off the hook. He said, "We [black people] are the problem, and we have to fix it." There is no chance that we were the problem.

If you split up people's families, take away the social support system allowed every other individual born into a society, if you deny them access to anything that helps them to get to know the world, if every sign you give them is that they themselves have no value as fully human beings, how can they be the problem? What we did as a people after slavery is nearly miraculous. Booker T. Washington reinforced the collective denial on the part of white people about how bad slavery was for black people, agreed with them that slavery was a civilizing institution, so to speak, that it wasn't all that bad, that black people were loyal to their masters. And that is pernicious, because it allowed the South to go forward, without opposition from our anointed spokesperson, Washington, with perpetuating an irreparable psychological reversal. White people knew how barbaric slavery had been, but they just felt guilty and pretended that it wasn't.

One thing that Washington and Du Bois agreed on was

that there was a portion of the black population that was degenerate, hedonistic, screwed up, criminal, et cetera. Today a lot of people start from an unspoken assumption that we are somehow morally deficient, and of course some of us are. But what we needed during Washington's era was for white people to get the hell out of our way and let us grow to be the people we were capable of becoming. We're getting closer to our destiny, but the playing field is not yet level.

One reason that we are making racial progress is that we are fighting for it: using the vote, using our moral authority and an unshakable belief in our own humanity. When Du Bois and others sought to do those things, Washington secretly worked to undermine their efforts. He was working against civil rights progress at the same time he was telling black people to be patient. It's one thing to disagree; it's another to play dirty tricks on people who are courageously fighting for their rights. In my book Washington will never live that down.

Finally, I have great respect for Washington's constructive accomplishments, of which today's Tuskegee University is the most impressive example. The legacy of his economic philosophy for racial progress is, however, that he has no legacy. Black people were working hard, saving money, buying homes, and succeeding in business long before he came along. But there was a limit to what that approach could achieve. For proof, look at the economic progress we've made as a people since the Voting Rights Act of 1965. That progress alone should settle the question of Washington's economic legacy.

CHAPTER VIII

DR. JULIANNE MALVEAUX,
Author/Economist

Dr. Julianne Malveaux is a leading-edge intellectual in America, an MIT-trained economist, and a writer and syndicated columnist whose thoughts on national affairs, the American workplace, and the economy appear each week in more than twenty newspapers nationally, including the Los Angeles Times, San Francisco Examiner, *and* Detroit News. *Dr. Malveaux writes a monthly column for* USA Today *and the journal* Black Issues in Higher Education. *She appears regularly on CNN and BET and on Howard University's television show* Evening Exchange. *She is the coauthor of* Unfinished Business: The 10 Most Important Issues Women Face *(Perigee, 2003).*

I CAN'T EVEN remember when Booker T. Washington first entered my intellectual consciousness, but it was definitely early on because I'm a race person. Both my parents were race-conscious activists involved in the NAACP and other organizations, so I grew up very aware with civil rights history and with issues of justice. My grandmother was a graduate of Tuskegee, and although she did not know Booker T. Washington personally, she would often talk about him—the Tuskegee campus and some of the things that he stood for. I don't remember hearing her say anything negative about him, but then there was a tone that implied that everything about him was just not cool. I'm aware as an adult that you will encounter many folks who have less than positive things to say about Booker T. Washington. There are good reasons for that.

First let me say that whatever else he was, Booker T. Washington was a slave who made it. I think it's important to remember that first, followed by the context in which he succeeded. He was a slave who made it and who established a historically black college at a time when that was a very difficult thing to do. And he attracted white money to the mission. Unfortunately, he cut and pasted the mission. In other words, he attracted money but all this about industrial education as opposed to intellectual education, it seems to me that he told white people what they wanted to hear. If he had said, "I'm creating a mini-Harvard here," he wouldn't have gotten a red cent.

Our people had such vast needs then. You take that Dudley Randall poem "It seems to me, said Booker T." It's an entertaining poem, but such a simplistic juxtaposition, because we needed intellectuals always, but we also needed nurses and carpenters and teachers. We needed our craftspeople to have some education beyond being good craftsmen because the demands on black people were so massive.

Certainly, context is important, but it only goes so far. I think there are some things about Booker T. Washington that were purely evil. The fact that he blocked so many other black people he didn't agree with from getting positions and appointments and also tried to shut down black newspapers that didn't take the same views that he took—that was just evil.

And then there's the fact that he, Mr. Social Segregation, allegedly had an affair with a white woman at the end of his life. Let's not leave that out. A syphilitic white woman, I believe. In one of the biographies written about him, I'm not sure which, there was a mysterious occurrence toward the end of his life, and it was in all the white newspapers. He went to some brownstone in New York, in the East Sixties, and got into some altercation and got beat up. He claims he went to this house by mistake, but there was a white woman of ill repute there, and her significant other went off—I'm not getting it entirely right, but it was scandalous. It was definitely scandalous.

But to me, the real evil part of Booker T. was the blocking. He didn't have to agree with W. E. B. Du Bois and the others, but the way he tried to block people and close newspapers down—he went beyond a place of trying to help a community in whatever way he could. He went beyond "Okay, I'm gonna do it however I can. If I have to cut and paste my message, if I've gotta Tom, I'm gonna do it because I'm helping the community." He went beyond that to "I am amassing power for me. This is about me." He ate at the White House. He ate with the queen. He was the über-Negro.

In a contemporary context, I think the bad outweighs the good with Booker T. Washington. But in the time that he was living, the good of course is Tuskegee Institute and the legacy that Tuskegee Institute has left. How many people would not have had an education but for Tuskegee? He gets credit for creating an institute in Alabama when there was tremendous resistance to such an endeavor. The problem with that, though, is that I think it sparked a megalomania: "I did that, so I guess I can walk on water."

Clearly, we're at a period now in America where we're looking back at basic and foundational values, and much of what Washington was about had to do with foundational values. But again, you have to look at the venality. And you have to look at what he left out. One also wonders at some point the extent to which he contributed to the tradition of historically black college president as despot, of which there is a long tradition—where presidents get involved with everything from the quality of the food to the payment of the faculty. And some of the institutions are so small that you understand that, but there are some issues there as well around micromanagement, boundaries, and faculty governance and autonomy, to name just a few things. I understand why so many black college presidents have had to be heavy-handed. There was tremendous resistance to the very existence of some of these institutions, and any incident could be taken out of context and seen as a reflection of the campus. But there is a difference from incidents and diversity of opinion and historically, and in the tradition of Booker T. Washington, some presidents have not welcomed progressive thinking.

Booker T. Washington is an enigmatic figure. It's hard to analyze him out of context, because when you do, he comes off as a tragic buffoon. If he were living today, he *would* be a buffoon. I'm sure he would be able to find some friends— Armstrong Williams, Clarence Thomas, Ward Connelly— but his didactic authoritarianism would also probably spark all kinds of internal and intense squabbling. There is no black person today who has the power to say, "I'm going to block you from doing this or writing that." People can help you, but Washington's power was almost absolute. Basically, he was the overseer of the plantation. If white people had trouble with a recalcitrant Negro, they didn't go to that recalcitrant Negro; they went to Booker T. People could be rewarded or punished in terms of their employment, contracting opportunities, whether or not your newspaper survived. Booker T. Washington became the siphon for opinion in the black community with white people as the filter.

The black people whom we think of today as having been the most forward-thinking are people like W. E. B. Du Bois, Ida B. Wells, William Monroe Trotter. These are people that Washington did not get along with. Not only did he not get along with them, but he actively conspired to do harm against them. He was especially vicious toward W. E. B. Du Bois, perhaps because his Niagara Movement was organized in direct opposition to Booker T. and his near-absolute power. There is speculation that Washington's disapproval cost Du Bois academic appointments, as well as the opportunity to be assistant superintendent of the D.C. public schools. We do know that Washington sent "spies" to report to him on the meetings of the Niagara Movement and that he made sure the black press did not cover the historic meetings.

I think Washington chose to ignore Du Bois's criticism— that is, he never responded to it because he felt it was beneath him. But what's disconcerting is that in Washington's early life and career, it seems that his drive was motivated by utter zeal to create an institution for our people. He was admitted to

Hampton University as a provisional student; he couldn't read, he had to scramble for everything he got. And then literally he did a 180 and was training people who were coming to school just like he had. I don't question his zeal for lifting us up as a people. But I think at some point absolute power always corrupts.

Booker T. Washington's fame came from his political acumen more so than anything else. He was Machiavellian. He was able to use that Atlanta Compromise speech to launch himself into great visibility and fame. It served as the basis for the development of his national reputation. And that speech is one in which he basically tells white people what they want to hear: "We need economic integration, but you can still have social segregation." He never talked about equality. He never talked about voting. And this was at a time when violence toward black people was rising. In his mind he probably felt that much of what he was doing was for the good of Tuskegee and black people: If it's good for Booker T., it's good for black folks. He was megalomaniacal to the point where he could not hear dissent without attempting to crush people. Even Madame C. J. Walker, who had given him significant money, had to come and snatch the microphone away from him at one of the Negro Business League conferences.

The Atlanta Compromise speech was, for the most part, about us working for massa. If you look at the time period, you're looking at the issue of labor shortages and agriculture. And because of those labor shortages, the question is, How do you get the black folk to work? I don't think Booker T. was totally venal at that point. I would say that he probably felt he was prying open the minds of people to allow for not just a worker but a craftsman, too. I mean, basically, you're invited to give a humongous speech, and you can do one of two things: you can rock the boat or you can ride the boat. Booker T. rode the boat and did not advance the cause of black people in the process. To the extent that his personal fame supplied resources for Tuskegee, he did. But to the extent that black intellectuals had to hear this crap about go learn a trade, and much of what he was about was intellectual suppression, he didn't. If you believe that we belong everywhere—that our place is not just on the field and in the factory but also in the academy—then it is clear to you that Washington did not.

Back to the notion of Washington in a contemporary context, if he were here today, I think he would push for hard work, and I don't think anyone is against hard work. No one disagrees with hard work as a core value. Where Booker T. and I would clearly part is that he would probably encourage young black people to take whatever job they could find at whatever wage they could find it. I believe that work has to have dignity and that there are terms and conditions of work that you should not accept. But his thing was to take what you can get and use it to build for something else, and that is pretty much the same as the conservative position on immigrants. Very young people should take the minimum-wage jobs when they're offered, but in order to satisfy their souls, they should also do the political work to make sure that we have a living wage.

There is something called a political economy. Economics is about who gets what—when, where, and why. And so is politics. Economics does it through flows of money; politics does it through flows of access and laws. Laws can make or break or eliminate markets. It happens all the time. The two are connected, and so the pernicious part about Booker T. Washington's legacy, given that he understood economic relationships, specifically between black and white people at the bottom, is that he didn't do more to alter the terms and conditions of those relationships. His supporters may argue that he couldn't, and that may well be the case, but I don't think there's much evidence that he even tried. The evidence is that there was a major co-option of this man that took place and that he decided to go along and get along. I don't know if he ever truly befriended or respected white people, but he sure seemed happy to be around them. Again, there is the issue of context—what it was like back then—but we still have happy-to-be-there Negroes today. There are black people today who will tell you about which white people's houses they've been to.

A charitable approach to Booker T. Washington would be that he wanted to do well and create for his people and that he was co-opted during a time period and under circumstances when it would not be difficult to co-opt a black man. But then if we don't hold him accountable because of that, we ought to, at the very minimum, be clear that he wasn't all that great. He was just a man.

CHAPTER IX

BAKARI KITWANA,
Author

Bakari Kitwana is cofounder of the first National Hip-Hop Political Convention in America and author of The Hip-Hop Generation: Young Blacks and the Crisis in African American Culture *(Basic Books, 2002). Kitwana is the former executive editor of the* Source *and has been acknowledged as an expert on hip-hop politics by the* Washington Post, *the* Los Angeles Times, *CNN,* The O'Reilly Factor, *and other leading news outlets. His writings have appeared in numerous national publications, including the* New York Times, *the* Boston Globe, Savoy, *the* Nation, *and the* Village Voice.

Kitwana also writes a column on hip-hop and youth culture titled "Do the Knowledge" for the Cleveland Plain Dealer *and is a consultant on hip-hop for the Rock and Roll Hall of Fame. He has been a visiting scholar in the political science department at Kent State University and has lectured on hip-hop at colleges and universities across the country for the last decade. His other publications include* The Rap on Gangsta Rap *(Third World Press, 1994) and* Why White Kids Love Hip-Hop: Wankstas, Wiggers, Wannabes, and the New Reality of Race in America *(Basic Books, 2005). Kitwana holds master's degrees in English and education from the University of Rochester.*

I GREW UP in Bridgehampton, Long Island, and went to a public school that was about 95 percent black. Most of the affluent white families who had homes there didn't send their kids to public school. Plus, many of the homes in the Hamptons, mansions really, are seasonal, so we had this huge tax base, which made for a great public school. I read *Up from Slavery* in high school but didn't really grasp it. As a sophomore in college at the University of Rochester, though, I took an African American history class and read *Up from Slavery* again. This was 1985, and I along with many other black students on campus were involved in the antiapartheid and divestiture movements. We also had study groups in which we would read books like *The Autobiography of Malcolm X*, Carter G. Woodson's *The Miseducation of the Negro*, and Maulana Karenga's *Introduction to Black Studies*, which made it an interesting time to reread Booker T. Washington.

It was a really radical period for us, so I think the initial interpretation of Washington was, yeah, that Uncle Tom idea. But we also really valued the dialogue between Washington and W. E. B. Du Bois and were looking for ways that we could take both those viewpoints and synthesize them. What gave me an even greater appreciation of Booker T. Washington was that after I graduated from college, I moved to Chicago to work at Third World Press, which came out of the black arts movement of the late 1960s and early 1970s. One thing in particular that the black power movement emphasized was independent institution building, which of course is what Booker T. Washington was all about. At the time the Third World Press operated an independent black school—as well as a chain of bookstores that I managed for several years—that really focused on self-sufficiency. In fact, to even contemplate borrowing money from a bank to help grow the business was heart-wrenching and involved a great deal of soul-searching. And while I wasn't consciously thinking about Booker T. Washington every day—we were more tuned in to the self-help philosophy of Marcus Garvey and Elijah Muhammad—the experience of working there definitely gave me a greater appreciation, in a day-to-day practical way, for Washington's philosophy.

In the work I do now as a writer, lecturer, and media critic whose focus is in youth culture and hip-hop, the question of whether hip-hop is healthy for the black community is an interesting one that I think speaks directly to Booker T. Washington's impact on young black America today. I spoke on a panel not long ago on the subject of whether art is still a weapon of resistance as it has been historically in black music and culture: Where does hip-hop fit in the history of black music as a political and inspirational force? In the way that the corporate industry has flipped it (hip-hop), no, it's not healthy, and to a great extent, it's not a weapon of resistance. But at the same time, if hip-hop had not been commercialized, it wouldn't have the national influence that it now enjoys, and it wouldn't have become the national and international youth culture, cutting across race and class and geopolitical boundaries, that it has.

When I was a college student in the early eighties at the University of Rochester in upstate New York, just five or six hours out of New York City, young people outside a handful of Northeast urban centers for the most part had not yet been influenced by hip-hop. As a youth culture hip-hop was still a very regional, New York–centric culture. People knew the Sugar Hill Gang, Run-DMC, LL Cool Jay, but they didn't know hip-hop as a culture. Now hip-hop is a national youth culture. Everywhere in the country kids are dressing and talking the same way and tuned in to the same music and impulses, and a large part of why that's true is the commodification of hip-hop by American corporate culture, which required the willingness, on the part of both black and white America, to make a profit off blackness.

I don't think that contemporary mainstream hip-hop music, which most hip-hop aficionados agree that in its celebration of a gangsta street ethos that objectifies and degrades women is a distortion of hip-hop culture, would jive with the Booker T. Washington model—in other words, the conservative black middle-class sensibility that was true in 1900 and is true now. Let me give you an example. I used to work at the *Source* magazine, which in the beginning was founded and owned by two white guys and two black guys. By the time I went to work there in 1995, there had been a split in ownership, leaving one white owner and one black owner. In the time that I was there, the black owner decided to leave and sell his shares to the publisher because he was a Christian and felt that the way he was making his money contradicted his religious values. My sense is that Booker T. Washington would respond to hip-hop in the same way that a Christian would.

Also, for much of hip-hop's history (aside from at the local, independent level, which has been very sporadic) there's been very limited independent institution building in the hip-hop community, though you certainly have a handful of artists who

have been able to forge relationships with the mainstream industry—the major music distributors, which are essentially
corporate America and all white-owned and -operated—and
who are given a significant share of their income. I'm thinking
of the Cash Money Millionaires and Master P, who were able
to control the lion's share of the profits from their music. Then
you have a handful of groups like Rock-A-Fella, Def Jam,
Death Row, and Bad Boy, which have partnership arrangements with the major distributors, splitting the take fifty-fifty.
These are still groundbreaking arrangements for blacks in the
music industry, who have a history of being the show (the creative force) while not benefiting from the business (the profits). So in that regard, there are great strides being made in
terms of institution building, and in a very Booker T. Wash-
ingtonian way, because these guys have their own companies,
in many cases own their own masters, and have established
partnerships with the mainstream. This is historic and significant. But these are the elites. For the vast majority of rap
artists, it's more like a sharecropper situation. Wendy Day, the
founder of the Rap Coalition, a rapper advocacy group that
helps rap artists get out of bad record deals and who helped
Master P and Cash Money broker their deals, says that after
the average artist pays his manager, the label, and all other required costs, his take is only about eight cents a CD.

The other thing I would say about hip-hop relative to
Booker T. Washington's philosophy is that many rap artists,
regardless of where they fall in the food chain, have succeeded
in developing relationships outside the music industry and are
cashing in on the image of blackness in the most significant

way. Artists like Russell Simmons realize that their own image is a brand, and they use it to get into fashion, athletic wear, et cetera. Jay-Z is part owner of the New Jersey Nets and Armadale vodka and has his own footwear deal with Reebok. Ice Cube and Queen Latifah and Will Smith all came out of hip-hop, emerged as hip-hop artists, and now have formidable acting careers. So many of these individuals have a lot of other things that they are doing outside rap music to make money, and in that regard I think they are fulfilling the dream of Booker T. Washington.

By the same token, when hip-hop artists cash in on blackness by equating themselves and hip-hop with gangsta, street culture, it affects all black people negatively. Tupac, for example, had the potential to do these great revolutionary things, but the one thing that mostly stood out was this concept of thug life, which he bought into, to his own detriment. Tupac is now dead and gone, and we all still have to live with the repercussions of the character he created in the film *Juice* and perfected in his rap music persona thereafter. And it was something that we all, especially young black men, still have to live with wherever we go. That is the downside of the way blackness has been sold through hip-hop. And its effects, what Stanley Crouch calls the new black minstrel show, are both national and international.

When all is said and done, however, I think that too many hip-hop artists are less interested in achieving the more basic goals of Washington's philosophy like black self-sufficiency and more so in identifying with the idea of creating something out of nothing, the underdog who survives against all odds. This is in part the American story. The place where that seems to enter into the hip-hop narrative is in American gangster films. It's perfected with a hip-hop twist in films like *Boyz n the Hood, Menace II Society, New Jack City, Set It Off,* and *Belly*. But it's essentially the same ethos that is pushed in films like *Scarface, Carlito's Way,* and *The Godfather*—the idea of the underdog, rising to the top against the odds, wanting to live life to the fullest even if just for a moment—that is to a large extent what is celebrated in hip-hop and definitely what comes through in mainstream culture far more so than a Booker T. Washington model.

Many people—black, white, and other—perceive hip-hop as a whole separate island. But I think no more so than Robert Johnson, founder of BET. John Johnson, the founder of *Ebony* and *Jet,* is more in line with a Booker T. Washington model than Robert Johnson and too many rap artists, because he is intricately involved in the black community. John Johnson and what he does with his wealth are interrelated with the black community at large. For Robert Johnson, like many hip-hop–generation athletes and entertainers, I think, it is coincidental. BET was a good concept that happened to be one he could cash in on, which is the same as hip-hop.

The Booker T. Washington approach is more tied to a nationalistic idea of blackness, whereas the Johnson approach and too often the approach played out in hip-hop are more tied to American capitalism. If you look at someone like Damon Dash, or until very recently Russell Simmons, his push has been more about making money than promoting any cohesive sense of blackness. Read Simmons's autobiographical

Life and Def, and it's clear he's more interested in making money than in long-term institution building, which may explain why he built 360.com and then sold it, and Phat Farm and then sold it, and Def Jam and then sold it. However, now that he has ventured into the political arena, I think it has become clearer to him that young black kids are politicized by hip-hop. In the twenty-two months leading up to the 2004 election, Simmons's Hip-Hop Summit Action Network held eighteen Summits across the country. The audience in every case was over 95 percent black.

The most important aspect of Booker T. Washington's legacy in hip-hop music culture and this generation is the challenge of institution building. If we don't create institutions, how will people know we were here? Because the institutions confirm the validity of the ideas, and if the ideas are sound, then the institutions reflect that soundness. We can talk until we're blue in the face, but until you take the theory to practice, it really doesn't mean that much. I have been involved in hip-hop's recent attempt to emerge as a political force. Many of us in the hip-hop generation hope that we can translate the influence and power of hip-hop beyond only entertainment and bring it into the political arena, which was partly what my book *The Hip-Hop Generation: Young Blacks and the Crisis in African American Culture* was about. But it wasn't enough to write the book. So I got involved with a group of activists, political operatives, and artists and organized the first National Hip-Hop Political Convention, which convened in Newark, New Jersey, in June 2004. It would have been one thing to have just written the book and left it at that, but it was important to use the book as a way of mobilizing people and then to test the ideas by actually doing something on the ground (practice). Without the institution building, it's just a whole lot of talk. This, more than anything else, is the legacy this hip-hop generation inherits from Booker T. Washington.

CHAPTER X

DEBRA DICKERSON,
Writer

Debra Dickerson is an award-winning essayist and author who writes about race, gender, and poverty in such publications as the Washington Post, *the* New York Times Magazine, *the* Village Voice, *the* Nation, *the* New Republic, Slate, Salon, *and* Essence. *A former* Salon *columnist and senior editor at* U.S. News & World Report, *Dickerson offers frequent radio and television commentary; she won the 1999 New York Association of Black Journalists' award for personal commentary.*

While serving in the intelligence department of the United States Air Force, Dickerson earned a bachelor's degree from the University of Maryland and a master's degree from St. Mary's University. She earned a JD from Harvard Law School in 1995. Her memoir, An American Story, *was published in 2000, and her second book,* The End of Blackness, *in 2003.*

WHAT WOULD I tell my kids about Booker T. Washington? I guess there is an argument to be made that sometimes you have to accept one slice of bread rather than hold out for the whole loaf. It's a rationalization, but think of all the people who have come through the Tuskegee Institute. Come to think of it, I'm not sure that's something I would tell my kids.

That would be a response for when they come home dogging Booker T. To the question, Why should you respect Booker T. Washington? I'd probably say more about how his beginning did not determine his outcome. Having been born a slave running around in a little gunnysack and barefoot did not stop him from aspiring to work within his constraints. In his own way he didn't accept society's limitations for black people and succeeded in building quite the empire. He had a sense of moving forward from where he was and working his butt off. That's Booker T. Washington's legacy: You can't wait until everything is perfect to get off your ass and do what you have to do.

It's interesting, Booker T. Washington has gone through so many historical incarnations. In the first instance, unless you were very much in the know, he was seen as this great black American. From the 1960s to the 1980s, he was perceived as the ultimate Uncle Tom. Meanwhile, his nasty battle with Du Bois, which is always sort of painful to read about, has endured throughout. In the past I think people tended to only know one side of the story: Either he was the worst person in the world or the best. Now we're in a period of struggle over the role of Booker T. Washington, which I think is actually a struggle over the soul of the black community.

One of the problems is that there is a real poverty in the black imagination. You have to be either one kind of black person or the other, and there's a real resistance to allowing people their complexities. In the black psyche, for some people, figures are either an Uncle Tom or a good race person. Clearly, there has to be space for a more multidimensional perspective. And so if you apply that to Booker T. Washington, you must realize that no strictly one-dimensional person is going to stand the test of time as he has, for better or worse. And that ought to complicate things for us in the first place. How can this person we are still talking about have only been an Uncle Tom or an unmitigated genius?

What does it even mean to be an Uncle Tom? It's so easy to judge Booker T. Washington, especially that "separate as the five fingers of the hand" business. [Washington famously said in his Atlanta Compromise speech: "In all things purely social we can be as separate as the five fingers, and yet one as the hand in all things essential to mutual progress."] Basically, that just means blacks are separate but not equal to whites. And that's just, oh, my God! But at the time, in the same way that in the 1960s we needed both pre-haj Malcolm and Dr. King, we needed both Booker T. and Du Bois during postslavery Reconstruction. You know, Booker T. went the vocational tech route, advocated that there's dignity in labor, and there's something to be said for that, especially given that at the time that was basically black people's lot—to labor like mules. Unfortunately, Booker T. did not appreciate Du Bois. And that's too bad. To not have said to Du Bois, "Look, you and I fundamentally disagree, but man, you are a brother to be reckoned with. You and I have to agree to disagree on a lot of things, but I'm the vocational tech guy and you're the art intellectual guy, and isn't that great?"

But it goes back to this struggle over the soul of the black community and the notion that there are permissible ways to be black and impermissible ways to be black. How can that be true? That notion was wrong when white people limited us to the belief that we should be happy to labor in slavery: "We

take care of you, you don't need to be free." And then when
we were free, there was Jim Crow: "We know what's best. You
don't date white people, and you can't do ballet." So why is
that if white people are not allowed to limit us, it's okay for
black people to limit each other? It seems to me that we are
unwilling to follow our own moral crusades to their logical
ends. Partly, I think that's just human nature. It's the same as
feminism: Women are supposed to be free to follow their desires, but you can't be a housewife or defer to your man in any
way. But if it's wrong for men to tell us how to behave, why is
it okay for women to tell us how to behave?

I just watched a documentary about little people, dwarfs,
who opt to have that limb-lengthening surgery, and within
the disabled community they are completely judged. So I
don't think there's really anything special about that kind of
behavior; it's human nature to want to tell people how they're
supposed to be whatever it is that they are. Still, limb-
lengthening surgery hasn't been around for very long, and
slavery and racism against black people have. So I would say
that while the behavior is not unique to us, the consequences
can be more dire for us. The main consequence is that this
kind of behavior diminishes our ability to act with unity,
which sort of sounds like a contradiction, but I think it is a
form of unity to grant each other freedom to be whatever we
are. It's like the old T-shirt, "If you love something set it free."
It has to be okay that you are not so invested in a very overt
black identification—you can date interracially, talk like a valley girl, work on the environment and not on race—but then
come back home to the community when you want. That has
to be okay. Bayard Rustin, who was as gay as he wanted to

be—back in the day when he was in high school playing foot-ball, he'd knock somebody down, then stand over him and re-cite English poetry—went on to be a civil rights leader. We have always been a complicated and complex people.

Personally, my feminist and working-class consciousness really come into play before my black consciousness does, and it has to be okay for me to focus on feminist and class issues but every now and then voice the fact that I'm very upset about police brutality without people questioning my alle-giance to my race. This is about our humanity, and our black-ness has to be subsumed within that overarching humanity. If I'm a human, a sovereign entity, then I get to decide that I'm going to go to France instead of Zimbabwe for vacation or meditation.

To go back to Booker T., in his first incarnation he was the end-all because he *was* all, and he made sure that that was the case by his ruthless and sort of scary politics. But I think in his mind he was really waging war on behalf of black Amer-ica. He could have been lynched. Surely, you could argue that he was less likely to get lynched than many, many other black folks then, but still, the bravery it took to be an activist black person at that time . . . I can't imagine trying to operate in that sphere. We have to be really careful about judging folks from that time. Booker T. did what he thought was best for black people, and I don't think he was feathering his own nest first and foremost. I think he worked really, really hard. He was sort of crazy in his determination, but he was able to ac-complish a lot.

My problem with Booker T. would be that his sense of blackness was completely reactionary to what white people were thinking and doing; it didn't spring from its own well. Again, the world he was functioning in was so much more limited than our world now, but I think his blackness was all about white people. Du Bois's blackness was not; it sprang from its own source. And yes, Booker T. was an advocate of this notion, "Let's not belabor the fact that we are black; let's work alongside whites," but I think Booker T. would finish that sentence with "so we can show white people that we deserve their respect." And that's my problem with Booker. Let's be the best we can be just because that's what we should do, not so we can show white people that we deserve our freedom. We don't have to deserve anything; we're sovereign human beings.

The notion of blackness in the context of whiteness has sustained throughout time and into contemporary culture, and it's something I've fought against my entire life. Especially in the eighties, you'd see some black woman on TV with curlers in her hair, splitting infinitives. That's hard to separate from, but if one more person criticizes me for giving comfort and aid to white folks . . . George Will is going to do what George Will does no matter what I say or don't say. People see what's going on in our community, and they're going to draw their own conclusions; we can't focus on white people saying, "Uh-huh, there they go again," because that's about being embarrassed in front of white folks and trying to win their respect. I don't care what white people think about someone on television with curlers in her hair. I care that she's weeping over her son who just got shot in the street.

We have a real problem in the black community with anti-intellectualism and really low critical skills. So little has been required of us because we were born on the lowest level of this moral high ground that we often make these really unintelligent observations and arguments that are just circular. Somebody hears something negative Ann Coulter says about black people and immediately jumps to the conclusion that her comment has had a huge impact. That's just neither here nor there. We're not talking to Ann Coulter. We're not talking to George Will. They're not reachable. We're so busy focusing on and analyzing white folks that we've gotten very rusty and don't have the skills to look at ourselves and say, "What's this about?" Ooh, a white woman clutched her purse when I walked by! Why is that so significant?

The good aspect of that kind of tribal mentality is that you do live your life and make your decisions with the understanding that we are a besieged community. And even if we weren't a besieged community, we are a community that loves one another so we want to put our best foot forward. If we're coming from a place of what's best for this community, that's the positive side. If we're coming from a place of how do we continually wage war against white people and how can we prevent ourselves from looking bad in front of them, then I think that's impermissible.

There are some things that I don't write about. I have some real problems with civil rights organizations, for example. I duck producers and editors all the time who want me to write particular things about particular leaders. It's not that I'm embarrassed in front of white people, but there are just some places I'm not going to go for purely tribalistic reasons. The net gain does not in any way balance the net loss. There are a few black figures that as a matter of integrity I should really just take down. It's the same thing with anti-Americanism. I might agree with a lot of the critiques of us around the world, but at a certain point this is my damn country. I can say my brother is an idiot, but you can't. Tribalism is a perfectly justifiable, perfectly human response, but you have to be aware of when you're being tribalistic, and you have to control it.

In terms of Booker T. as an accommodationist, I don't think there's ever been a time when black leaders have not been accommodationists in one way or another; that's part of leadership. I know I have no kind of role in political leadership because I don't have the capacity to compromise. Organizations like the Congressional Black Caucus are still negotiating for what they need, and they come away with much less than they should. The problem I have with what's left of black leadership today is that just as Washington was unwilling to look outside his own vocational tech thing, so most black leaders refuse to look outside their own ranks of people who came up through the water hoses, guard dogs, and jails in order to nurture and bring up the next generation of leadership. Dr. King was tapped by the elders to lead the Montgomery bus boycott at twenty years old. That doesn't happen anymore. I think that's an unforgivable mistake. There's a litmus test, and if you don't agree with the party line, you're not just ignored, you're actively worked against.

Colin Powell is a really good example of somebody who has assessed the situation for what it is and gone forward from there. I think he's a damn Democrat and is only a Republican because he figured out he could get more done that way. I give mad props to Colin Powell. He understands the black psyche. He gets it. He gets that you can be proaffirmative action and antiabortion. A lot of black leaders today, you give them a microphone, and suddenly they forget everything they heard at the kitchen table. And they're just lying: They know and we know that we're a complicated people. It's like Booker T.: my way or the highway.

Still, having said that, in the end I wouldn't have made the choices Booker T. made, but I have to say that I'm glad he made them. I think he could have done so with less gusto, but even as he most assuredly accepted the white man's version of him, he also decided to be the best damn version of the white man's version that he could be.

CHAPTER XI

GREGORY S. BELL,
Journalist/Author

Gregory S. Bell is the son of Travers Bell, cofounder of Daniels & Bell, Inc., the firm that made history in 1971, when it became the first black-owned member of the New York Stock Exchange. Upon his father's death in 1988, he became a silent partner in Daniels & Bell, Inc. He also worked on community outreach in Harlem under the Honorable Charles Rangel. Bell is the author of In the Black: A History of African Americans on Wall Street, *published in 2001.*

I GREW UP in New York City. My father, an investment banker and cofounder of the first black-owned member firm of the New York Stock Exchange, lived on the East Side and I lived on the West Side with my mother. Because my father was always busy, I spent the majority of my time with my mother; it felt like a single-parent family, even though I had two siblings who are my father's kids from his first marriage. My brother and sister were adults when I was growing up, so I often felt like an only child. I went to private schools on the Upper East Side all my life, which was socially awkward for me. A lot of time I felt out of place with my peers and often did not relate to the material I was studying. It also didn't help that I am biracial; my mother is Filipino. When I was younger, I did feel insecure regarding my identity and my appearance but never thought much about it. It wasn't until I was about eleven years old, when I rented the movie *School Daze* (because my brother is in it), that I started to rethink my racial identity. One of the main issues the film deals with is the tension between light-skinned and dark-skinned African Americans.

In school what I learned of black history was almost nothing. In grade school I remember reading a book about Kareem Abdul Jabbar, but that was it. High school was a little better because we were reading Ralph Ellison and Richard Wright, but other than that, it was Eisenhower, Kennedy, Johnson, Nixon, and all the usual material. My teachers never said, "Booker T. Washington was so-and-so; Du Bois was this." If they did, then I don't remember, and maybe it was because it would have seemed strange coming from them. Except in gym class, I did not have one black teacher from kindergarten to senior year in high school. It is little wonder that I heard Booker T. Washington's name only in casual conversations. The first time I seriously considered him and his work was in the context of Ellison's *Invisible Man* because Ellison went to Tuskegee, and the college in the book is allegedly based on Tuskegee. I became curious about Washington and skimmed through *Up from Slavery*. I don't remember much from the book, but in talking with other people, I understood that Washington was heavily criticized as an accommodator and an Uncle Tom. That was strange, because when I was younger, I always assumed that if I was hearing about a black figure, it was because he or she was a hero, so it was odd to hear these sorts of negative things about Booker T. Washington.

I must admit that because so many people dismissed Booker T. Washington, I had spent little time trying to understand his role in the development of black capitalism and African American history. I was always interested in business history because of my father, who I always knew was a black "first," but as a child I didn't fully understand what he was a first at. My father died in 1988, when I was ten years old. Like many who experience that kind of loss, I spent countless hours trying to fill that void and often had to go to old articles written about him and other African Americans on Wall Street. In college, I started researching the history of black business more intensely. I found old articles and had all these stories in my head. Actually, it was kind of pathetic because I spent many Saturday nights looking through these articles. And in all this material Booker T. Washington was never referenced.

I understand why people dismiss him as an accommodator. I was rereading *Up from Slavery* a few weeks ago, and there's one section where he claims that the South would never tolerate the Ku Klux Klan, which of course proved to be appallingly wrong. I also do not believe his thinking that the pursuit of economic power should be fought without a struggle for social and political causes. There are definitely things about Washington that warrant dismissing, and a number of his ideas have been perplexing to me. However, I have always thought it important to consider the context and circumstances that he had to deal with and that I never had to. Growing up, I was fortunate to have a private school education and many opportunities and luxuries. I was born in 1977 and never had to deal with segregation or worry where my next meal was coming from, so it would be stupid for me to say that I could fully relate to Washington's times. The one thing I try to keep in mind when judging him is that I'll never know what it was like to be in the South during the time of lynching and Jim Crow.

Progress has been made in American business, although blacks are still woefully underrepresented in terms of the number of black-owned businesses and the percentage of African Americans at the senior levels of major corporations. Because we started centuries behind other groups, our competitive edge was a little dull. For a long time, business was not as prominent in our culture as it was for other groups. Often business was not considered a viable career alternative. Because of a lack of capital, credit, and exposure to the business world, many blacks viewed business as an inevitable avenue to broken dreams. Historically, black parents were more likely to encourage their kids to be preachers or teachers. It is here that I wish Washington's overall message about the importance of economics had been adhered to. Today it is so common to talk about diversity in the workplace and that economic equality is the final phase of social justice. If such attitudes had been as widespread decades ago, I think we'd all be better off.

Then again, maybe these attitudes could not have been as widespread before the civil rights movement because African Americans did not have a voice in America's agenda. This is where Washington's approach and predictions went wrong. I have always interpreted that his argument was if black people cast their buckets down where they were, worked hard, and proved to be dependable, white people would embrace their advancement. He also said that African Americans should not fight for political or social equality because all that would do is agitate the powers that were in charge. Well, fast-forward to the 1950s, and there were no African Americans in senior positions at the major corporations. Even though countless talented African Americans had proved themselves in lower positions, none of them had been given the opportunity to be in a management position in corporate America.

Washington's argument that equality or black advancement would have happened naturally was wrong. The first black vice-president of a major international corporation was named in 1963; the first black stockbrokers at Merrill Lynch, then Wall Street's largest brokerage, were hired in 1966; the first black member of the New York Stock Exchange arrived in 1970. In 1963 there were no black corporate directors. Eight years later there were over twenty. It is not a coincidence that these breakthroughs began happening during the civil rights era. They happened because of legislation, protests, and boy-cotts. The very actions Booker T. Washington thought would hurt the cause of black people changed America, which in turn changed corporate America. So unlike Washington, I don't think that economic power can be achieved without po-litical power. I think they fit together like pieces of a puzzle. On Wall Street, for example, black-owned investment banks had trouble getting into major deals in the 1970s. It was not until black mayors like Maynard Jackson, Harold Washing-ton, Coleman Young, and others came along and demanded that black Wall Street firms get opportunities that these firms started to prosper. Without political power, the economic cause would not have advanced.

Booker T. Washington is a complicated figure with a complicated legacy. This is no surprise because black capitalism is a complex subject. In America, black and white race relations are complicated to begin with, but when you throw green into the equation, it really gets complex and tense. The term *sellout* is in fact based on a business term. Just as Washington was viewed with a skeptical eye, so some executives in the 1960s were called Oreos and Uncle Toms simply for choosing to work in the big corporations. To some degree, this kind of skepticism endures today, especially with the recent sales of black-owned compa nies to major conglomerates. But as someone who has studied black business I think countless black capitalists have proved that it is possible to achieve one's economic dreams without sacrificing his African American identity, heritage, or culture. A person does not have to settle for anything less than equal civil rights and political power in order to achieve financial success. At the same time, all the points I have made here are in hindsight.

Although I disagree with a lot of Washington's ideas and approaches, I would never dismiss him. He was obviously an infinitely smart individual who offered some great ideas regarding self-help and the development of black-owned businesses. So rather than just completely reject him because of some of his ideas, there are many worthy aspects to his life that I will try to learn from, and I'm sure I'll be better off for it.

CHAPTER XII

CORA DANIELS,
Journalist/Author

Cora Daniels is an award-winning journalist. She is currently a staff writer for Fortune *magazine and a contributing writer to* FSB: Fortune Small Business *magazine. Her work has been published in the* New York Times, USA Today, Savoy, *and* Honey. *She has also appeared on ABC Morning News, CNN, BET, and NPR as an expert on workplace issues and minority business. In 2002 she spearheaded* Fortune's *first ever search for the fifty most powerful black executives in America. She is a graduate of Yale University with a BA in history and has a master's degree in journalism from Columbia University. Her first book,* Black Power Inc., *was published in 2004. She is working on her second book,* Ghetto Nation.

I DON'T HAVE any good anecdotes for when I first became aware of Booker T. Washington, but I definitely learned about him long before I'd heard of Du Bois, which I know is not the norm. Even though I grew up in New York and went through the New York City public school system, we didn't really even touch on Du Bois in high school. What I remember first about Washington when I was thinking about him again for this book was that he was the "pick yourself up by your bootstraps" guy. No context, just that. Washington was mentioned in school—and I didn't have any black teachers—as one of the black leaders in history. It wasn't until college (at Yale), where I was able to take black studies courses, that Booker T. Washington existed for me in any real historical context.

If we were there at the time of Booker T. Washington, I don't think anybody in my generation of black Americans would want to be recognized as being part of the Booker T. camp. And when I say "us," I mean any black folks with a sense of pride. Even if you believe in some of the things he was advocating, it's hard to get past other things about him, like how passive and silent he was about civil rights. There is no way of reading his infamous Atlanta speech without cringing when he promises the South "patient, faithful, law-abiding, and unresentful" Negroes. That is assimilation by any means necessary. But despite that silence, there are still some points to agree with.

It's my feeling that no matter how many political strides are made, those strides don't mean anything unless there is an economic base to back them up. My mom, with her 1960s ideals, will probably be horrified when I come out as the capitalist voice in this book, but what I found in writing my own book *Black Power Inc.*, which looked largely at black folks under forty going into business, was that these people went into business specifically as a civil rights action. In other words, the economic piece of the movement was missing, and these were the folks who were trying to fill in that missing link. For the generations that have come after the civil rights movement the gap between the haves and the have-nots seems larger now than before we were marching. Apart from all the hip-hop nonsense—the business of rapper labels, and fashion lines, and bling-bling, and the rest of it—there is also a contingent of very well-educated folks who are going to business school, rising up the ladder, and then ultimately starting their own companies in hopes of closing the gap by creating black wealth.

I think what brought this movement on is the disconnect between what Booker T. was promoting in terms of black ownership and where we are today: still struggling for ownership. There's this huge gap, and so even if there are a few folks that were or are able to break through, there are still only those few. Our generation has replaced "firsts" with "onlys": the only black person in such and such position. I'm the only black writer at *Fortune* magazine, and I shouldn't be in 2005. It makes you feel like something didn't work somewhere along the line, and so let's do something different. Insofar as what didn't work, I could be very pessimistic and cynical, but mainly I think people got satisfied. I think that there is a large segment of us who have decided that tomorrow is not going to be any better, so why not live for today? Once you accept that, you have failed because you have become satisfied with how things are instead of constantly fighting for something better.

For a people who aren't "there" yet, and there is no denying that black folks are not "there" yet, we can't afford to ever be satisfied. Of course now, as opposed to the 1800s, we have the luxury to focus on black wealth and economy because technically, the political fight has already been fought. We're not yet at the point where we are taking full advantage of that victory, but it's there; the victory is there. And it's up to us, our gen-

eration, to take it to the next level. So when people criticize
Booker T. Washington for weighing in too heavily on economic ownership early on, and even as I am a strong proponent of economic power, I would probably agree that you
need to establish a political framework first—on paper. Certain human equalities are necessary before you can move forward. I don't think they necessarily mean anything without
the economics, but they at least need to be written down. The
problem with Booker T., and the reason why it's so hard for
people of our generation to embrace him, are that he was doing things too quickly. He went to the second step without
accomplishing the first. If he were alive today, his approach
would be much more on point; now is when we need black
folks to care more about ownership of self and of work, more
so than of material excess.

For example, if Du Bois had come first and established his
following much earlier on, and then Booker T. had arrived on
the scene, he would seem less like an Uncle Tom because the
necessary political and philosophical framework would have
been set. And then it would be a matter of how we empower
that political movement—with an economic ownership movement. And you do that by having businesses and wealth and
money behind it. But when you concentrate on the economic
first, and it seems to others that you're sacrificing the political,
then it becomes worthless. Political gains have no power without the economic foundation holding them up. But economic
success has no value without freedom. It all sounds so idealis-
tically dramatic, doesn't it? Like when you learn about Plymouth Rock and all men being created equal in fourth-grade
history class. The thing is this country runs on money; it is

power. But it holds influence only because it can shape the political, the social, and both. Money is the force that makes all the other parts move. But Yoda, or white economic power, can control the force. So black folks have to learn to become Jedis if we want to close the gap between the few at the top and the bulk at the bottom.

I live in Bed-Stuy (Brooklyn, New York), which can be very depressing sometimes. It's depressing because I am confronted by that gap every day within my own block. I see this tremendous gap between the life that my husband and I have and the life that some of these kids on our block have. These are kids who are not going to get there. I'm pretty sure of that. It's a constant reminder that something didn't work in our history as a people, and it just feels like the gap is never going to close. Part of the reason why seeing these kids is so depressing is that the expectations for them are so low. I don't understand how black parents can raise children today and not at least hope that they get accepted into college. Anything less should be unacceptable. Do I think the economic gap would be less if black folks had taken more to heart what Booker T. Washington had to say? Maybe.

Basically, Booker T. Washington was being honest and realistic about the situation in which he was living; he was talking to and about the masses of black folks at that time. The Uncle Tom status he is given is from us looking back. If you go back to some of the things he was saying, it was all about how earning "a dollar in a factory is worth infinitely more than the opportunity to spend a dollar in an opera house." Or "No race can prosper till it learns that there is as much dignity in tilling a field as in writing a poem." These are old-

fashioned work ethic basics that we have all heard and nod-
ded our heads to at some point in our lives. Even his most famous statement about the five fingers: "In all things that are
purely social we can be as separate as the five fingers, yet one
as the hand in all things essential to mutual progress." How
are race relations very different from that today? Obviously,
he had a sense of pride and self. He cared. If he was truly an
Uncle Tom, he wouldn't have started Tuskegee or fought for
and talked about black people as a collective; he would have
been strictly out for himself.

What stands out for me now about Booker T. Washington
is how forward-thinking he actually was and how unrecog-
nized he was for that. If you read his work now, it seems as if
he could have written it a month ago. And to have written it
not a month ago but rather one hundred years ago is startling.
It's startling that what he was so narrowly concerned with—
developing basic skills, really, being able to support yourself—
is still at the center of our struggle today. Washington came
too soon.

CHAPTER XIII

EARL OFARI HUTCHINSON,
Political Analyst

Earl Ofari Hutchinson is an author, a syndicated columnist, political analyst, and commentator. His weekly syndicated column appears on AlterNet and Pacific News Service and in 150 newspapers nationally. His op-ed columns have appeared in the Los Angeles Times, Washington Post, Chicago Tribune, Newsday, Philadelphia Inquirer, San Francisco Chronicle, Christian Science Monitor, *and other major newspapers. He is the author of nine books, which include* The Assassination of the Black Male Image *(1996),* The Crisis in Black and Black *(1998), and* The Disappearance of Black Leadership, *which was published in* 2000.

Hutchinson holds a BA from California State University, Los Angeles, an MA from California State University, Dominguez Hills, and a PhD from Pacific Western University. He has conducted specialized postgraduate research at Cornell's Africana Research Center.

BOOKER T. WASHINGTON was a name spoken often within the cultural ethos that I grew up in during 1950s Chicago. Many of the folk in my family were southern born, and so I remember that Booker T. Washington and George Washing-

ton Carver were the two names we always heard in the household. Frederick Douglass, W. E. B. Du Bois—I knew nothing of them, they had no meaning, but Washington and
Carver were revered icons and looked upon as the shining
lights of black leadership in that time and place. I know now
that there was and is a great difference in perception toward
Washington depending upon whether you were from the
North or the South, but for my family there was no inherently
negative predisposition toward Washington. No one in my
world attacked him. He was an emblematic figure. As a matter of fact, my grandmother had a few Booker T. Washington
gold coins, the first coin of course to feature an African
American, minted from 1946 to 1951. They were sold off when
she passed away, but I do remember holding those coins and
the great pride my grandmother took in having them.

When I got to college in the late 1960s, everything turned
around. Booker T. Washington suddenly became the symbol
of everything that was wrong in terms of black leadership. He
was a sellout, an Uncle Tom; he held the race down. All the
negative and pejorative things that could possibly be said
about him were said. He was held in such low esteem at that
point that to be labeled a Booker T. Washington, or someone
even *like* a Booker T. Washington, was almost tantamount to
being called the *N* word. But I never bought into all that, and
I'll tell you why.

One, I actually read Booker T. Washington, and I mean
more than just *Up from Slavery*; two, I put Washington in the
context of when he lived; and three, I had the family background in which Washington was revered. Sure, I would listen to the black militants rail about Booker T. Washington,

but I knew that not only was this person of paramount importance in his time, but also many of the things that he worked for—his ideals and pragmatism in terms of self-help, personal initiative, and business development—were important for us today. I used and borrowed a lot from Booker T. Washington when I wrote my book *The Myth of Black Capitalism* and in fact dedicated a whole chapter to him and the National Negro Business League. I saw a direct link, a direct historical continuum, between what Washington did with the National Negro Business League at the turn of the century and the black capitalism movement of the late 1960s and 1970s. There's that old saying "The more things change, the more things stay the same." We always see the evolution of ideas from the past come back in the present.

Those people who are overly critical of Washington today are thinking in an ahistorical way. There's always a tendency to filter an individual, his or her work and thinking, through the prism of the present, never considering the context of the time during which that individual lived. So anytime you do that you're always going to go wrong. To understand the whole person, you have to put him in the context of the time he lived and worked. The present only counts in the sense that the ideas and the works of a particular person have modern relevance. That does count, but what I'm talking about is something else. I'm talking about when a pejorative view is taken and the denigration of an individual happens.

For example, a classic case is Abraham Lincoln. How many times have we heard that Abraham Lincoln was a racist? That's the most ridiculous thing in the world. You're talking about a man who lived circa 1860. You have to look at the surrounding ideas and politics, the culture of the times he lived. It's like expecting a caveman to master advanced technology. You can take some of the things that Abraham Lincoln said and wrote, and if you look at them through a present-day filter, you might say he was a racist—he looked at blacks as socially inferior—but then again, African Americans during that time *were* considered socially inferior. Yes, there was a core of abolitionists who were way advanced for their time. But as a rule the general population didn't think like those abolitionists. And because Abraham Lincoln was a public figure who served the general population, of course his thinking was going to be colored by that general population.

So now when we come back to Booker T. Washington, who lived and worked in turn-of-the-century America—1880 and on—what were the ideas of that era? What were the circumstances that African Americans lived in, especially in the rural South? How did the laws and public policy help shape the thinking of American society at that time and the thinking of African Americans at that time? How did those laws and that policy have an impact on the quality and content of black leadership at that time? All these things have to be taken into consideration to understand the importance of Booker T. Washington—not only then but also now, a century later.

So it's 1880, blacks are still adjusting to coming out of slavery, what is Booker T. Washington's plan? Remember we're not talking about the urban industrial North, we're talking about rural Alabama. The laws are changing. Although it is the Reconstruction era, the dominant planter class that was just defeated in the war is still trying to find its feet again politically. The laws are going to dictate a rigid, legally segregated society. Next, there is a rural agrarian economy in the South, amid which Booker T. Washington has of course grown up. And finally, there is the burning need for education and leadership. How do you prepare a people to march forward given all these factors and forces against them? Washington understood all those challenging elements. He understood that for starters, civil rights meant nothing if you couldn't feed yourself or learn some kind of industrial skill. Are you a carpenter, a bricklayer? Can you farm? These are productive skills that could move black folk along the track upward. That was Washington's basic mission: to prepare African Americans to be productive citizens, to survive, and to integrate into the changing legal milieu of that time. That's the genius of Washington: He understood all the forces that were driving against him and African Americans and used that understanding as a source to draw from.

Now, some might argue that he went too far and lost sight of his mission, particularly during his famous Atlanta Exposition speech when he talked about black and white people being as separate as the five fingers of the hand in all things social. Many have interpreted that as the condoning of segregation or the reinforcement of a mind-set among African Americans that they were in fact servile: Don't rock the boat; don't challenge or agitate the political order. That argument can be made and has been made many times over. But let's be a little counterintuitive for a minute. Again, we're talking about the American South in 1895. Segregation is virtually the law of the land. Here's a man who, for the period of time leading up to that speech starting around 1880, set out on a course to essentially build a model of industrial education for African Americans. The course ends with Tuskegee University as an established institution, which then inspired other schools and universities, today what we call historically black colleges. The Booker T. model was about preparing African Americans to operate within this very closed and narrow economy, and in that I think he did a masterful job. I think it was the proper course for him to take. In fact, he almost had no choice.

Washington was embraced by northern philanthropists. The Carnegies, the Rockefellers, the Rosenwalds poured money into his programs and essentially subsidized Booker T. Washington. Given that endorsement, could he really have stepped outside that and said, "Look, segregation is wrong. We are going to march; we're going to demonstrate, picket, and protest—use every means of political and social protest." Could he have challenged the philanthropists, none of whom were for black civil rights back then? Let's face it, Tuskegee couldn't have lasted for one second without their money and without the cooperation of state authorities in Alabama. And you might think that if he had spoken out against segregation, he would be remembered in a different light for generations to come, but he wouldn't have. You know why? Because one, if he had spoken out, he'd have been buried. Booker T. Washington would have been finished. Second, who would have even known he'd said anything in the first place? What newspaper in the rural South would have published the story of a black man attacking legal segregation in 1895? No, he would've been a buried figure, and Tuskegee would've been padlocked.

Of course there's another part to this. There was Booker T. Washington as the accommodating public figure, but he also had another side to him. Washington did secretly fund some civil rights groups and a few black newspapers that were fairly outspoken. So he did help where he could, just quietly. He wasn't an ogre. And it's not as if that sort of thing doesn't happen today: If you are dependent on certain groups and organizations for your survival, you can't take certain public stances. If you're receiving money from a foundation for a project and then turn around and attack the foundation, it's not going to keep funding your project. It's not going to work. And that's just across the board. There has to be certain diplomacy and politics involved with achieving an immediate objective. Life is a compromise, and there will always be a clash between personal idealism and pragmatism in order to get along in this world. I'm sure Booker T. Washington was probably at times very torn. To have to hear yourself being attacked by the Du Boises, the William Monroe Trotters, just raked over the coals, almost considered the worst thing since Attila the Hun, and knowing in your heart of hearts how many people you're helping—I just know that had to tear him up.

I think Booker T. Washington served black people in several ways. First, to circle back a bit, he enforced the merits of industrial skills at a time when it was necessary. He said, "Look, what good is it to be able to quote Chaucer and Shakespeare, but not be able to drive a nail through wood and make money doing it?" And he was right. I don't think he ever said that classical education should not be studied. He was merely setting priorities. Then there's Tuskegee, a shining example of what African Americans can do to help themselves by using their own resources. Booker T. Washington founded Tuskegee in 1881 when he was twenty-five years old, expanded it, and brought a great core of professors and academics to a school that is today a historical landmark.

In the end Washington provided a rallying point for African Americans, a name-identified African American who achieved and whom we could look up to, take pride in, someone who sat on the dais with important white politicians up to and including Theodore Roosevelt at the White House. Even today, as many African Americans publicly attack Condoleezza Rice and Colin Powell, privately they take pride in them. A national security adviser and a secretary of state? These are breakthroughs, firsts. No matter what their politics may be, they are shining examples of excellence and achievement. And so was Booker T. Washington. If my grandmother took pride in Booker T. Washington fifty or sixty years after his death, what do you think contemporaries of Washington were feeling about him while he was alive? That's an important point. It's always easy to take shots at people for things that we perceive to be their shortcomings or failures, but we don't know who these people really are. We don't know what Booker T. Washington was doing when he was having dinner with white politicians or Theodore Roosevelt, but simply because he was sitting there with them, he was an Uncle Tom? And that's not merely simplistic thinking; it's dangerous thinking because people who make those kinds of mindless criticisms are slipping into the monolith of race.

It's critically important for people to see Booker T. Washington not only in the context of his times but also in the context of the times we live in today. The new civil rights revolution of today is about economic development. How is that different from what Booker T. Washington was advocating a century ago? Whether or not we are where we should be or want to be with economic development in the black community, there has always been a strong emphasis throughout on business and entrepreneurship as well as on education. These themes started with Booker T. Washington.

CHAPTER XIV

RUBY SALES,
Founder and Executive Director of SpiritHouse

*A veteran of the civil rights (black freedom) movement, Ruby
Sales is founder and executive director of SpiritHouse, the Jonathan
Daniels and Samuel Younge Forum for Social Justice in
Washington, D.C. SpiritHouse uses art, education, research, action,
and reflection to build nonviolent social justice and peace
movements that repair the harm that systemic injustice does to our
lives and to the lives of others.*

I WAS SIXTEEN years old with the deep dream of becoming
a beatnik when I started at Tuskegee University in 1963. I had
bred myself on Virginia Woolf and the beat poets, and I was
going to become a beatnik and move to New York. It was the
height of the civil rights movement, and Gwen Patton was
elected student body president. Gwen was the only female
student body president in the history of Tuskegee, and she
was leading the student body toward protest in response to
Dr. King's call about the violence and beatings at the Edmund
Pettus Bridge in Selma, Alabama. Our protest took us to the
capitol. We went there in four Tuskegee-chartered buses.
Dean Phillips, the dean of students, went with us.

Now, many students like myself at that time—young, naive,

sheltered—did not understand on a firsthand basis the violence and terror of southern apartheid. Although we lived in
the South, our parents gave us an incredible gift of safety. They
made the southern landscape seem fertile and safe. So many of
us felt we were big people on campus, and it never occurred to
us that anyone would look down on us. We had been big,
smart, and respected people at our high schools, in our communities. So most of us were in shock we got to the capitol,
and there were all these state troopers with billy clubs, cattle
prods, and German shepherds as big as you could imagine.
They surrounded us. We were absolutely surrounded. By that
I mean they surrounded us and we couldn't go to the bath-
room. If you tried to break rank and leave, the troopers would
beat you up. So we had what we called the piss-in revolution,
where we literally just pissed at the capitol because we had no
other choice.

After a day of that, I guess the troopers got tired and
started charging the crowd. For the first time in my whole life
I had tangible proof in an adult way that white men were vi-
olent and that the root pillar of segregation was terrorism. I'm
sure I heard adults talking about it when I was coming up, and
I had an uncle who was killed by the Klan, but it was all abstract until that day at the capitol. Then I understood what we
were up against and what our parents and community faced
and knew: that there were people who hated you and would
kill you simply because you were black. Suddenly I had a new
religion.

I really was born again one day when I was walking down
the street with Willie Peacock, an organizer in Mississippi at
the time. We were talking about capitalism, and then right

then—zing zong, zing zong! All these bells went off in my head, and I was saying to Willie, "You're right, you're right!" I looked up in the sky, and everything looked brighter. Everything began to take on an incredible new kind of shape. Suddenly I had a language where I could talk about the disparities I had noticed growing up. I grew up in a middle-class community, but I also gave my toys away to all my friends and let them share my clothes. I fought my mother, who herself had come from a very poor environment and never wanted to go back, so her whole thing was "Nothing from nothing leaves nothing. If you associate with nothing, you're going to be nothing." I fought that, tooth and nail, because I thought she was being so unfair to judge people by what they had or didn't have. But suddenly I had a language to talk about classism. And suddenly I had a language for what it meant to be black. I read James Baldwin, Du Bois, and Sinclair Drake.

Well, you see, I had many teachers at my high school in Columbus, Georgia, who had gone to Tuskegee, so my early sense of Booker T. Washington was that he had built this incredible school and that the people who came through that school varied. My homeroom teacher, for example, was very ethnocentric. Although she was very light-skinned, she was also deeply rooted in issues of class and white supremacy. Another teacher taught civics education, and so she was very much involved in the whole citizenship question. I didn't understand Booker T. Washington as someone who thwarted black people's rights. My understanding of Washington growing up was very positive because I'm from the South and the southern understanding of Washington is very positive for a lot of good reasons.

First of all, you have to understand that in the South, black people were slaves, and we had never owned or benefited from our own work. So for a people who were enslaved, whose labor and selves belonged to someone else, it was a radical notion to argue that your work and your self should belong to you and could benefit the community. There had to be some kind of transitional conversation about the nature of work for black people in the South and to whom should their labor belong.

You can say that all blacks during the 1800 and 1900s were slaves in one form or another, but to be a theoretical slave—that you don't have certain rights in the North but do have freedom of mobility and can do all kinds of things like ride the streetcars and gain access to an education, because even in the 1800s black people were going to Harvard—is a far cry from being put in jail or killed for reading and writing. You can't compare northern oppression with southern enslavement. There's just no comparison.

Let me help dispel this notion of Booker T. Washington as an Uncle Tom because I think I can say something very critical to the argument. Even though all blacks share a common experience and history in this country of captivity and enslavement and the attempts of society to dissipate cultural roots in our community, black people's experiences were not monolithic: They differed from North to South, which is very important to understand during the period we're talking about. At that time you would definitely have a universal black agenda, but you would also have a regional black agenda.

The needs in the South were as complex as the needs in the

North. For example, while Du Bois was arguing for the Talented Tenth, the truth of the matter is tracking was an early phenomenon in northern educational history, and very few black people had access to an education that would allow them to be part of the Talented Tenth. So if you look at the argument from that perspective, it really is an argument being made for a very narrow and select group of people. But more principally, both Du Bois and Washington were talking about issues of production, Du Bois about the production and ownership of knowledge, Washington about the production and ownership of labor, both conversations put together as a whole deal with the issues that black people confronted. I don't want to see their theories as dualistic. I want to say that these differences were natural in a society where some black people had access to an education at places like Brown, Harvard, and Dartmouth.

At the heart of the Du Bois–Washington debate is leadership and who really should lead African Americans. The question of whether or not it should be the neocolonial model of white people—white people involved with the Niagara Movement and also the white abolitionist movement—was as radical as raising the question of who should own black labor. And that I think is the new optic through which we view the question of Booker T. Washington as an Uncle Tom.

The reason Du Bois's message has endured perhaps more than Washington's is that there became, based on our own experience in this country as slaves, a stigma attached to "menial work." We thought that we were the work. We didn't understand that the degradation was not in a task that was being performed but in the dehumanization that was happening while it was being performed. And so for many black people, education became an incredible hunger, and it was seen as a panacea to humanize us. But that misreading of work has generated the kind of crisis that we face today, where very few young black people are willing to see honor, as Gandhi would say, in any kind of work.

Part of the milestones that we always had for ourselves as a people is this whole thing of education and how many barriers you broke and whether you were the first person who went to Harvard, or the first this or the first that. The parents in my generation always tied their labor to our getting an education. It was essential that you got an education so that each generation could be "better than the next." That was part of the collective agenda, but I think it was predicated on some very fundamental misunderstandings.

The notion of menial labor is filled with shame: working with your hands, as a janitor, or working with the roads. Rather than do that kind of work, many black people today would rather not work or do other kind of work that has less honor, really. And the judgment of the work has to do with how much money you make. That's the part of black life and culture that is deeply materialistic and is devoid of radical critique. Although I do think that a people that are going to be sustaining independent lives must raise the fundamental, philosophical, and political question, What is the nature of work? And who is it that I work for when I work?

Let me tell you why that's critically important. The other part of that configuration says that it's more prestigious to labor in the vineyard of white institutions than it is to work in black institutions, so you've also got that paradigm. Some of the best minds in our country choose to work at white universities without ever having worked in black universities, and they give the argument that it's too bureaucratic and tiresome at black schools. But the truth of the matter is I've worked as a professor at white schools, and that's also very tiring because it's very racist. We have to make a connection between our work and survival because we've always had this consciousness that we're working for white people.

Booker T. Washington was trying to introduce a new kind of paradigm, independent workers who are using their agency to build up their own lives and the life of their community. He was not arguing that they should go be brickmasons for a white person. He was arguing that if you developed an independent business class with enough resources, that would also have an impact on the political arena.

The whole thrust in my community growing up was: I'm not doing all this work for you to become a maid. The truth of the matter is, though, everybody can't be a doctor or a lawyer. Gandhi would say that there is absolute honor and integrity in any kind of work you do. Black people in my generation did not teach this to their children; there was a great deal of shame if you graduated from high school and became a janitor. In my community, people who went north didn't want to come home without being able to say they were successful. Listen to the cultural songs that we sing: "The best things in life are free, but you can give it to the birds and bees, I want money." There is a materialistic strand that runs throughout black culture, alongside other things too, but I'm saying that materialism is an important part of our culture.

We must remember that the contemporary understanding

of Booker T. Washington has a lot to do with the ways in which principally white historians have reconstructed him in American history, particularly in relation to Du Bois, with Washington being in the camp of accommodation and Du Bois in the camp of protest. But that is really surface, because part of what always got Du Bois in trouble was that northern whites who saw themselves as liberal wanted him to be accommodating. He was always getting in trouble over the question of accommodation—in both the North and the South.

Du Bois was not willing to accommodate what he saw as the overall terrorist, debilitating, undemocratic southern society. He thought there should be no negotiation over political rights (contrary to what Booker T. Washington said in his Atlanta Exposition speech), that if we were going to be free, the power of the vote was significant. And that became a critical issue in the southern freedom movement. The power of the vote, one man, one vote, echoed from Du Bois all the way up. But you have to understand that the "vote as critical" agenda was shaped more by northerners in the movement than southerners, because black southerners were not focused on one particular thing; they were focused on a variety of things and principally on the intangible thing of being fully human in a society where they were totally degraded. Most people do not really understand the difference between living in the South and living in the North as a black person. You couldn't have a Marcus Garvey movement in the South over the question of land. Black people had their land; it would have been an irrelevant movement.

It's not fair to say that Booker T. Washington accommodated without understanding that Du Bois had to accommodate, too. Throughout history the two have been pitted against each other—by black and white people. We live in a dualistic society. Our models for seeing the world are dualistic. In other words, it is true that Booker T. Washington was an accommodationist, but it is also true that his working model offered a radical challenge to white people who still thought black people's labor belonged to them.

CHAPTER XV

JAMES CLINGMAN,
Author/Speaker

James E. Clingman is former editor of the Cincinnati Herald *newspaper. His editorials and economic columns have been featured in hundreds of newspapers, magazines, and newsletters across the United States. He is the founder of the Greater Cincinnati African American Chamber of Commerce and served as its first executive director and president. Clingman also writes a weekly syndicated newspaper column, "Blackonomics," circulated via the National Newspaper Publishers Association. He is an adjunct professor in the Department of African American Studies at the University of Cincinnati and the author of numerous books, including the new book* Black-O-Knowledge: Stuff We Need to Know *(Milligan Books,* 2004*). Clingman has been instrumental in establishing several other African American chambers of commerce around the country and continues to promote economic freedom for African Americans.*

I'VE KNOWN ABOUT Booker T. Washington's legacy for many, many years, but only in the last twenty years have I really become more deeply involved with his philosophy, reading, studying, and teaching it. Unfortunately, and fortunately, I guess, when I was going to elementary school, the only two names we ever heard were Booker T. Washington and George Washington Carver. There were never any essays or commentary given in tandem, but I knew the names. I grew up in the 1950s in Cincinnati, where my elementary school was integrated, but we didn't have any black teachers, and there wasn't a lot of black history taught at all. Because I never really got any concrete information about Booker T. Washington, I never had the opportunity to form any early opinions about him.

Later on, stemming from my interest in black economic empowerment, I was led to Washington and his papers and learned what he had accomplished—the National Negro Business League and Tuskegee, of course—and that's when I began to formulate an opinion about him. I feel that this idea of Washington as a sellout, which I find among mostly older folks, is not based on any real facts but more so on word of mouth. There is this division between the older folks—and I'm talking fifty years and up—and the younger folks on the subject of Washington, particularly in relation to Du Bois. I wrote a paper a few years ago in which I suggested that we had made a mistake in forcing ourselves to choose between these two black men. We should have taken the best from both of them. Older folks say about Washington, "Oh, he was an Uncle Tom, he was a sellout," but they don't even know the things that he did behind the scenes, particularly in regard to supporting some of the activities and strategies of Du Bois.

People get into ruts of information, just like we get into ruts of anything else. We don't seek out information—my latest book, *Black-O-Knowledge*, talks about that—we just have what we have, and then we continue to just pass it on and pass it on, instead of trying to expand our resource and information base. People don't realize that Du Bois's NAACP was started and supported by white people and had no economic empowering division for black people within it, whereas Booker T. Washington's movement, the National Negro Business League, once it really got started and it was clear that its goal was about helping black people become economically empowered, did not receive the same kind of support from white people as the NAACP did. So why did the civil rights organizations survive and get supported when the business organizations did not? It's part of the myth of Washington's incompetence. And you don't have to do anything else if that is what you believe about him. But if you believe that he was for economic empowerment and look at all the things he did, it seems to me that as a reasonable person you would react to that by saying, "Wait a minute, that was right, and I should be doing the same thing today."

Collectively, black people make a lot of money, but we are at the bottom of every economic category in this country. We are way behind where we should be. If you look back over the last forty years, since we won our so-called civil rights, we have regressed from where we were prior to 1960 in terms of ownership of income-producing assets. A lot of that I put on our shoulders. We have seven hundred billion dollars and rising every year and trillions of dollars in intellectual capital that we're not being good stewards over. If we had preserved the economic empowerment aspect of Washington's legacy rather than the Uncle Tom aspect, we would absolutely be much better off today. The disconnect, the reason the Uncle Tom myth won out, is because of the very real fact that black people in this country have been tampered with. We have been divided and conditioned to divide ourselves, to take sides and be against one another rather than for one another. The vestiges of that conditioning, which first occurred during slavery, are still with us today. People don't want to admit it, but they are, and you can see them when people start to choose between Washington and Du Bois. I call it psychological enslavement.

We have to be psychologically free if we're going to move toward true economic freedom. People say, "Oh, we're free, we can do whatever we want to do." That's not what I'm talking about. We got our physical freedom after slavery ended, but we still have the chains around our brains. My theory, Blackonomics, takes us to that reality and attempts to break those chains. Economics runs this world, and I want black people to understand the role we play in that—both globally and locally—and become smarter about how we play. But it takes work. You can't be economically free if you're lazy. And I don't think we're necessarily lazy as a people, but complacent, apathetic . . . "I got mine, and I'm okay; this is not happening to my family, I got a good job, two houses, five cars, I'm fine." That kind of attitude is easier to deal with than to say, "Wait a minute, there are other people out here suffering. They're my brothers and sisters. What can I do with my meager resources or my intellectual capacity to help us collectively?" It's very important for us to know our history, where we came from, and what our ancestors did before we got here and what our relatives did when they got here.

I always say the people who came over on the so-called slave ships were entrepreneurs. We are so taken with the slavery thing, and of course there are a lot of myths associated with that as well, but I don't look at our slave ancestors as lowly and meek. I look at them on a higher level. Without slaves this country wouldn't be what it is. We all know that. They brought skills and talents from Africa that people here did not know or have. I'm proud that we managed to live through the most horrendous treatment put upon any people, and that's how I teach: Those slave ships didn't bring slaves over here; they brought entrepreneurs. It's a matter of how we look at our history and value our past and refuse to be made to feel that we are lower human beings because our people were enslaved.

The goal is to act collectively, but the knowledge starts individually. You have to take a really good look at yourself, assess yourself honestly, and ask yourself what, if any, your obligation is to your people. Some people are going to say, "I don't have any obligation to anybody but myself." Fine. A lot of people said that to Harriet Tubman. A lot of people said it to Moses when he was trying to get the Israelites out of Egypt. Historically, that's the way people are, and we have to accept that. Some want to stay in the condition they're in. The initial enlightenment is not necessarily a group activity, but the movement is: You come to it on an individual basis, and then you find like minds and move with them. But everyone first has to make his or her own decision about his or her role in this economic empowerment that we preach about.

It may not be fair that we have to consider our circumstances as a collective more so than other groups of folks, but if that's the reality, then that's what we have to do. Black people can't change the system in the United States. I recently wrote a column called "Chasing the Illusion of Equality," because we've been off on that idea for the last forty years. That's never going to happen. And I don't want to be equal with people who are oppressing me anyway. But the illusion of equality has us chasing something we're never going to catch and taking our eyes off the things that we should be focusing on.

We have to deal with the situation the way that it is while knowing that we can't change this political system. We also can't change the economic system, but we can have a huge impact on it by working collectively. If our vote is as important as everyone says it is—the black vote this, the black vote that—then we should be using it collectively to leverage the things that we need for our people. But you don't hear that. I appreciate the black politicians who are out there doing what they're supposed to do, but all forty-three of them in Washington can't pass one law. We are not going to change the system; we can beg and scream and march and do all the things that people do, but it's not going to change the status quo. So we have to work within the system.

I really never knew where my ambition and drive to help our community came from. I just knew I had to do it. And then in 1998 I obeyed the Gospel and went into the church. Now I'm very active in the church and see what my role is. My compassion for people who were suffering and being mistreated always drove me, but I never knew why I couldn't stop. In 1996 I started the Black Chamber of Commerce and then helped to start twelve more, started an entrepreneurial high school. I did all these things, put my own family's personal resources at risk, and never knew why. But I know now. I'm driven from and sustained by a spiritual base that tells me what I'm supposed to do and the kind of steward I'm supposed to be over my resources, however meager they may be. I'm not suggesting that everyone go to church, this is not a religious crusade on my part, but it's what works for me, and if others want to be honest seekers of God, then He will let them know what they should be doing. People have to make up their own minds and seek their own purpose in life and understand that it's more than just owning a lot of bangles, baubles, and beads. Our ultimate purpose for being here is not just to be blessed but to be a blessing for somebody else.

I think a reintroduction of Booker T. Washington's values and legacy would be effective today if deployed into mainstream black culture and enforced regularly. You can't do something once a year and think you're making progress. His message has to be enforced every single day.

CHAPTER XVI

JOCK SMITH,
Attorney, Cochran, Cherry, Givens, & Smith, PC, Tuskegee

Jock M. Smith is a founder and senior partner in the national law firm of Cochran, Cherry, Givens, & Smith, PC. He received his undergraduate degree with honors from Tuskegee University and his doctor of jurisprudence from the University of Notre Dame School of Law. In 1998, along with famed O. J. Simpson attorney Johnnie L. Cochran, Jr., who died last year, J. Keith Givens, and Samuel Cherry, Smith founded the law firm of Cochran, Cherry, Givens, & Smith. The firm has offices in Tuskegee, Alabama, where Smith presides, Dothan, Alabama, Los Angeles, New York City, Chicago, and Atlanta. The firm is presently engaged in major civil tort litigation across the United States of America.

Smith is the author of Climbing Jacob's Ladder: From Queens to Tuskegee: A Trial Lawyer's Journey on Behalf of "the Least of These" *(New South Books, 2002), an autobiography about growing up the son of Jacob Smith, a lawyer and political activist who was murdered by whites in 1957.*

MY MOTHER WAS a classmate at Kansas State University with Dr. Walter Bowie, who was a professor of veterinary medicine at Tuskegee around 1965 and 1966. He came to visit us during a trip to New York, where I grew up, and he said to my mother, "Why don't you send Jock down to Tuskegee? I'll look after him." My father was murdered eight or nine years before, and my mother wanted to send me someplace where I had some guidance but was also far enough away from home so that I could grow up on my own. So I came down here to Tuskegee and entered school, and the experience was tremendous. At the time I didn't have any sense of Booker T. Washington or George Washington Carver or the work they had done. But as I got entwined with the campus culture and history, then of course I did become aware of both men, and I began to read a lot.

In high school in New York we weren't taught about black leaders. I went to a high school that was somewhat integrated, and so we didn't get that perspective, the black historical perspective. Tuskegee really helped in my growth as an individual and as a man; it really gave me a sense of wherewithal and confidence. I was in the third grade when my father was assassinated, and after that I became disjointed as a student and my grades went wayward. In the eleventh grade, I took a public speaking course amongst all the basket weaving classes they were giving me at the time because of poor academic performance, and the teacher told me I had a gift. I said, "A gift for what?" and she said, "To speak." And that was the first thing that turned the light switch back on for me. As a result of that, I was able to get up off the ground a little bit and go to Tuskegee with some expectancy of having to work hard and make up for lost time. I became a C+ student in my first semester and then became an A student the second semester and from that point on. I got grounded, I got myself together, and I got involved in student politics.

Because I was going to Tuskegee and had started to take a real interest in black history—reading *Up from Slavery, The Souls of Black Folk*, learning about the NAACP and the Niagara Movement, and of course, the battle between Du Bois and Washington over the intellectual giant versus the industrial educator—I picked up a dual appreciation for both Du Bois and Washington. I believe they both made great sacrifices for our people. Theirs was a philosophical debate, and I never relegated Washington to the basement intellectually; his contribution to the larger struggle was as significant as or more significant than anyone had made before him. He took an idea from General Samuel Chapman Armstrong and manifested it through his own efforts in an agrarian Alabama that was so racist his efforts had to have been Herculean. The idea of building an institution also had to have taken some favor with philanthropic interests, and I think Booker Washington knew that he had to say what he was saying in order for that college to remain standing and for blacks to move forward. And the business seminars that he put together also showed his understanding that blacks needed to develop businesses and gain financial independence.

Du Bois was talking about the Talented Tenth, blacks becoming educated, and I don't think Booker Washington disagreed with that. I think their argument was over what sort of use would education provide blacks, what kind of education did blacks really need, and what kind of opportunities were open to us. Du Bois and Washington were two men both

seeking the best ways for blacks to advance based on the opportunities that were available at the time; they may have had
different perspectives on those opportunities, but essentially
they wanted the same thing for blacks. If Booker T. Washington had felt that blacks could really integrate into society in
1902, he probably would have been in alignment with Du
Bois. I think the only reason Washington's philosophy was
different from Du Bois's is that he didn't feel America was
ready for integration.

Even though I was a student in the sixties—I led the Viet-
nam Moratorium March at Tuskegee, and I was involved in
the student demonstration that locked up the trustees and
prompted George Wallace to bring in the National Guard—
I never saw Booker T. Washington as a great compromiser or
an Uncle Tom. I saw him only as a great educator, which
doesn't explain why the philosophy of other black leaders has
stuck more than Washington's and, since he was such an advocate of self-reliance and ownership, why blacks own so little today.

Johnnie Cochran told me one time that the only building
that blacks own in any major downtown city is the *Ebony* and
Jet building in Chicago. There's no other large structure that
African Americans own. It's strange. I mean, the civil rights
movement, Dr. King's movement, centered on integration of
America; it never got to the point where a strategy was developed to empower blacks financially. When you think about
the poverty programs of the sixties and the LBJ administration—government gifts in an attempt to elevate and educate
a community—there was never a single focused entrepreneurial spirit in any of our black leaders. I guess you could say the

Muslims did it, but the problem with Malcolm X, Elijah Muhammad, and Farrakhan is that they were surely talking about being economically empowered and they had their own little cubbyholes, but they were never able to advance to the next level. But there are still active strands of the National Negro Business League here in Tuskegee that Booker Washington started, and the Booker T. Washington Insurance Company is still going, though I don't know how powerful it is or how fragmented it is. I suspect there isn't that much to it, but I don't know that for certain.

My own life has always been steeped in legacy. After my father's death, honoring his legacy became very important to me, and I'm often surprised that legacy in a more general sense doesn't seem as important to others around me. Johnnie Cochran was concerned about legacy; that's how we hooked up to begin with. There are other black lawyers that are rich financially and don't appear to have any concern about legacy; they're only concerned about yachts and a Rolls-Royce. I guess, though, that's pretty indicative of a lot of black professionals; many don't know or study history. I don't know if they consider themselves role models, but I like to consider myself more of a pioneer. Pioneers are people who discover a new way of doing things or bring a broader perspective on things. Johnnie Cochran and I opened sixteen offices nationwide; we represent the largest African American firm in the country. The style we use in court, how we go after people, is very upbeat, very creative.

One of the key tenets of Booker Washington's philosophy was a strong work ethic, and there is a certain disconnect today with the younger generation of black folks, particularly those who define themselves through hip-hop culture. And these young folks would probably defend themselves by saying, "Well, we got all this music going on, we making all this money, and we're trying to tell you how bad everything is. Yeah, we throw in a few things that are wrong every now and then, but if you listen to what we're really saying—take out the part where we call women bitches and hos—we're just black men who are pissed off at America." Unfortunately, you never really get to the message. But you can't tell that to the kids who follow these rappers; Puffy Combs, Master P, and all the rest have become legends to a lot of young people.

You know, I live near and work in Tuskegee, Alabama, which is a town that will always be associated with Booker T. Washington. In 2004 this town to me has not lived up to its potential: Half of the downtown area is boarded up; the leadership has been small-town and refractory. This ought to be a town of history—like Cooperstown, New York, where the Baseball Hall of Fame is housed. It ought to have little hotels and eateries and token shops. It does not. It is a town where the only thriving businesses are run by a handful of lawyers and physicians; there is a dog track, but that's out in the boonies where they still pay people below average wage. The university is a big employer, but not a well-paying employer. Still, the beauty of the town is in that campus.

The National Park Service has declared Tuskegee University a national historic landmark, and as you enter the gate, there's a Park Service guy in uniform who has to wave you through before you can even get on to the campus. The grounds have been immaculately maintained. The monument is there, the Kellogg Conference Center is there; it used to be the old Dorothy Hall, but they expanded it after they got the grant from the Kellogg Foundation, the only African American college to receive a Kellogg Foundation grant to build a conference center.

Tuskegee needs to be in more historically minded hands, and competent people who can serve in city and county positions need to come forward. Right now those positions are typically held by people with very little formal education, high school at most, some beyond and some not even that. I think this has held the town back. Now, I don't think you need a bunch of intellectual bookworms running the town, either. I'm not suggesting that you need Roscoe Pound and W. E. B. Du Bois running the town. We just need educated people who have vision and financial wherewithal.

I hope there's a future for this town, because if I don't, then I've given up, and like my father always told me, "Don't ever give up, son." The word *impossible* is the only page in the dictionary that Napoleon Hill, author of *Think and Grow Rich*, tore out. I believe in the legacy of this town and its future impact, and that started with Booker T. Washington.

CHAPTER XVII

KATHY Y. WILSON,
Author/Journalist

*Since 2001 Kathy Y. Wilson's award-winning now-defunct
column "Your Negro Tour Guide" and her National Public Radio
commentaries on* All Things Considered *put the city of
Cincinnati on notice. Wilson is a senior writer and editor for*
CityBeat, *Cincinnati's alternative newsweekly and has written for*
Newsday *and* Shelterforce. *She has won awards from the Ohio
Associated Press, the Association of Alternative Newsweeklies, the
Society of Professional Journalists, and the Knight Center for
Specialized Journalism at the University of Maryland. Wilson's
book of collected columns and commentaries,* Your Negro Tour
Guide: Truths in Black and White *(Emmis Books, 2004), is in
its second paperback printing. Her next book is a meditation on
black fathers and daughters titled* The Pimp in the Background.

BOOKER T. WASHINGTON was probably America's first
great black success story. If there had been an *Ebony* magazine
back then, he would've been all on the cover, and they
would've been all in his house looking at his furniture and his
land and his horses, because you know how *Ebony* does. And
as a great success story, Booker T. Washington can be very inspirational. It makes all the work I have to do at the office late

on a Friday night seem like a whole lot less—in the same way that my parents' stories about walking to school and getting hand-me-down books from the white schools are inspirational. It may be sentimental, but it's real.

A few months ago, prior to hearing about this project, I was at a bookstore or a yard sale, and I saw a copy of *Up from Slavery*. I flipped it open and saw that it was only twenty-five cents. I thought, well, you can't beat that. So I bought it and reread it for the first time in I can't even remember how long, but after reading it again, I started to meditate on how we as a race really continue to struggle with the perceived image and persona of Booker T. Washington every day. I was also really struck by the way he talks about his life at the beginning of the book, where he describes being born at the end of slavery, how he was always apologetic for his masters. Booker T. felt: "It was slavery, and they owned us, but they weren't that bad." He really humanized his masters and the whole slave experience in this "They could've been a lot worse, because I knew some slaves who were really going through some bullshit" sort of way. He lived in this little one-room shack with a dirt floor, the door was fucked up, his mother was always cooking for everyone else, and they slept on dirty rags and whatnot, but it wasn't that bad to him. And I believed him because part of what Booker T. Washington had going on, part of his legacy, was this pull-yourself-up-by-your-bootstraps mentality.

What resonates from his message today is that with the new black middle class and the advent of class status now among us intraracially there are camps of black people again. There are camps of black people who have been privy to education and money, jobs, and a certain kind of lifestyle, camps of those who have not and know nothing of it, and camps of those who know about education and money but have no access to it. Those black folks who have had exposure to and are enjoying a "higher standard" of living tend to be, like Washington, apologists. In other words, to other black folks the message is: Considering what we have and where we've come from, quit your bellyaching.

Washington was also a leader that was really anointed by white people. He was an ambitious and driven man to start, and this is all conjecture, of course, but I think the more that white people embraced him, the more attention he felt he was getting, the further away he got from his experience as a black man in America. It's sort of like the whole controversy around Bill Cosby's comments in recent years about the black working class. This may be a stretch, and there is so much second- and third-generation information about what Cosby has said, but basically his message is: Poor black people need to pull up their pants. Because Cosby is ambitious and perhaps thrives on the attention he gets for some of his more provocative commentary, his image and identity suffer. I think Booker T. experienced the same thing.

Black people have to be careful about being swept along in a crowd surfing kind of way—like at concerts where someone lies on top of the crowd, and they just move that person along in whatever direction. It's the same thing that happens with black people when one of us is elected spokesperson for the entire race, because there's no middle ground. You are either a spokesperson for the race or embraced by the majority culture in a way you cannot control. So we have to be careful whom we preach to and whom we allow to embrace and influence us.

I think Booker T. had a plan. Whether or not he lost sight or control of it, I don't know really. I'm not even entirely sure what the plan was, but I really believe he got drunk on the fawning of white people. He was invited to speak at important places and venues; newspaper articles were written about him. White folks were basically doing this whole Boswell thing [in 1945 the Alabama legislature adopted the Boswell Amendment in an attempt to deny black citizens the right to vote] and just monitoring him, writing down everything he said, which he in turn mistook for positive validation, and he ultimately became distracted from his original goal. And I do believe that his goal, if not a carefully orchestrated plan, was for blacks to educate themselves and cultivate basic, employable skills.

Learning employable skills is all fine and good, although I have always kind of thought that the notion of employable skills in general is a little corny. You know, even as recently as twenty years ago my father was telling me that writing is not a skill and that I'd better learn something I can fall back on, which is like saying even if it's not something you believe in, it's still a skill. And it seems that initially Booker T. Washington pushed that same sort of mentality: Let's learn how to farm. And for the time learning how to farm was fine. But times change, and people change. I don't think Booker T. moved his thinking along with the changes, and in that way his original message boomeranged back around and hit him in the ass. As black people moved forward, Booker T. was kind of working to keep them antiquated, the subtext of which became "Know your place." That's what happens when we get into any kind of mind lock that tells us to learn only certain things and better ourselves in only certain ways, because that fosters resentment, and the leader pushing that message, once seen as a hero, gets knocked down off his pedestal.

The issue of historical context for black people is very involved because it is framed by plantation thinking. If people in civilizations before us can be remembered and deemed as brilliant inventors of theories and materials we still use to this day, then why is Booker T. Washington always compartmentalized as a thinker only in the context of a certain time and set of circumstances? It's not like Plato didn't have his own set of challenging circumstances to deal with. It's plantation thinking. Whether Booker T. socialized himself that way, or if over the ages we as black people have socialized ourselves that way, to say, "Well, that brother did all right considering," it's plantation thinking. It's thinking that stops plans and ideas in their tracks for reasons that either are beyond your control or you can't put your hands on.

A lot of us do that to this day. We don't keep coming at the world with the talents and knowledge that we have, maybe because we think whatever attention or good fortune we have is good enough, or we just are not progressive enough based on whoever's definition. Of course, in this country, it's almost impossible to think about values and definitions at large without thinking about the white standard. This is how being black in America can be very much a plantation experience. I usually hate slave references, but in this instance it really works because we just don't get off the plantation. That is why we can behave in such a substandard way and then get rewarded for it, whether it's the NAACP giving R. Kelly an Image Award amidst allegations against him of statutory rape and child pornography or Robert Johnson selling Black Entertainment

Television to a corporation that has turned the network exclusively into rump shaking from morning to night. That's mainstream culture, and we seem to be satisfied with it because more of us go along with it than try to make substantive changes.

Booker T. Washington may have been as popular as 50 Cent in his day, but there had to be something about him that was more like Will Smith to have been as famous and beloved by white people as he was. And I bet the first thing was: "Oh, he speaks so well." So I'm sure he was "articulate" as hell, and unthreatening. But also the title of his autobiography, *Up from Slavery*: Those are three very powerful words to me. There's something about it that's so triumphant and resilient and even reconciliatory. It reminds me of Charlie Mingus's autobiography title, *Beneath the Underdog*. What's lower than that? *Up from Slavery*. How redemptive is that considering how insane and inhumane and deadly slavery was? There's something jovial about it, almost like there should be an exclamation point at the end, like a musical—"Up from Slavery!"

I think over the years black people have made a lot of moves based on fear and that we are operating under a fear factor unlike any other community in America, mainly because we seem to be more afraid of ourselves than even other people are afraid of us. We're afraid of the embarrassment that might come from being discovered as the worst of who we are or from being revealed as fraudulent human beings; we've come all this way, and then one person, that crazy-ass crackhead cousin, shows up, and it's all over. We are the only culture that deals with that bullshit. Do you think that when Bill Clinton was getting his dick sucked in the Oval Office, other powerful white men were going around embarrassed or afraid? It had no reflection on them. Black people need to get with that more. We are each our own person, and our individual behavior bears no reflection on the race as a whole. We need to stop being so fearful.

One thing that can be said about Booker T. Washington is that he wasn't fearful; he was more stoic than brave maybe. I'm assuming that he was more textured than what we have been told about him, simply because everyone is more textured than a general consensus would have us think. But I've never even seen any pictures of him where he doesn't look larger than life. I have a black-and-white postcard of him sitting on horseback, and he's sitting up straight and looks like he's about fifty feet tall. Of what we have been given about him, most valuable is that he thought his troubles weren't that bad, even though they were probably a million times worse than he let on. But stoicism isn't all that, and I think we as a race should learn to move away from stoicism in general.

I was watching *The Color Purple* the other night. My favorite scene is outside the general store when a white woman is trying to make Oprah Winfrey's Sofia be her maid. The woman says, "Don't you want to come home with me?" And Sofia says, "Hellllll no!" And the woman's husband, who happens to be the mayor of the town, comes over and says, "What'd you say to my wife?" And Sofia says, "I told her hellllllll no!" The mayor slaps her, and then she just knocks him on his ass. Of course they beat her down, and she loses her mind, but she didn't lose her mind from being stoic. Stoicism can drive a nigger crazy in America.

CHAPTER XVIII

JOHN McWHORTER,
Author

John McWhorter is the author of several books including
Losing the Race *(Free Press, 2000) and an anthology of race*
writings, Authentically Black *(Gotham, 2003). He has written*
on race and cultural issues for the New Republic, *the* Wall Street
Journal, *the* Washington Post, *the* Chronicle of Higher
Education, *the* National Review, *the* Los Angeles Times, *the*
American Enterprise, City Journal, *and the* New York Times.
He has appeared on Dateline NBC, Talk of the Nation, Good
Morning America, *the* NewsHour with Jim Lehrer *and does*
regular commentaries for NPR's All Things Considered. *His*
most recent book is Doing Our Own Thing: The Degradation
of Language and Music in America and Why We Should,
Like, Care *(Gotham, 2003).*

I THINK WHAT gets out on the street about Booker T.
Washington is that he said, "Turn the other cheek." And
that's it. That's all people know. We tend to forget how deeply
unknowing people are beyond the fragment of people who
went to a very good school and got a BA or beyond. The idea
is that W. E. B. Du Bois said something about the souls of
black folk—that phrase alone—and for most people that

means something very radical and forward-thinking. They don't realize that Du Bois could probably not have cared less what they thought. And Booker T. was a sellout because he said to just take it and work hard and show how good you are. That's the nut of it. Subsequently the idea that we are responsible for working hard and proving our worth is backward.

In the late 1960s an ideology permeated the black community, as well as America in general, which said that there is societal racism and societal inequity, and the response was to rail against the inequity, the implication being that until that inequity is gone, there is nothing that any black person can do to help change this inequity and others like it. At the time black people felt they shouldn't have to prove how good they are. White people should know already, and if they don't know, they're racist. That made some sense. I was five to fifteen years old during that era, and I remember hearing that sentiment spoken by several very smart and charismatic people. The problem is it doesn't work. At the end of the day the way you show people you're as good as they are is by doing it. That may not be fair, but it's true. It cannot be: Black students are as good as white students, so let them in even with lower grades and scores because if you don't think they're good enough, you're racist. What white people think when they hear that is, If you can't put up, then shut up, and Booker T. Washington probably would have agreed with them.

Today there is the business of black service that tends to be, not always, but tends to be kind of . . . you bring the chicken, I'll bring the potatoes, nothing's on time. I sense that that's because starting in the 1960s and 1970s, the main thing was black solidarity as opposed to adhering to mainstream norms. If you adhere to mainstream norms, then you are acting like the white man, so no, we're not going to try to have service as good as Wanamaker's because that takes effort, and that's what other people do. Why should we have to do what other people do? Instead here's your chicken. The mainstream is to be resisted. The mainstream is false; the mainstream is imperialist, racist, and uptight.

The idea, starting in about 1967, was that if a black person manages to make himself a decent life, he's either lucky or superman. But for the most part, the fact that the deck was stacked against us meant that black criminality was inevitable. And then you take it even further into writers like Michael Eric Dyson, and what you get from them is that the black criminal is a good thing because he's teaching America to wake up; we need these people to show that there is something really wrong. A black criminal, in a way, is doing the best he can do. He's a rebel capitalist.

I find that most people do not understand that the main change in black and white America is the cultural change that started in the late 1960s, which gives us a different sense of what is normal. And the crucial thing is that yes, the ghetto; yes, racism; yes, the factories moved away; yes, subtle biases. Now, tell me that none of those things were happening in 1930. The factories weren't moving away in 1930, but then there was a countervailing influence: People were getting lynched every four days, and you couldn't try on shoes at Sears. Okay, let's say the factories were moving away after the 1960s, but in 1930 most white people hated your guts the minute they saw you. And yet why is it that things were never as horrible in the black community until about 1970, when

suddenly leadership and activism were not judged but necessary? That is a question that is rarely asked and almost never
answered properly. Wasn't lynching in the 1930s, or in the
time of Booker T. Washington, adequately horrible?

Once the Depression hit, of course black people were going
to get hit hardest because wealth wasn't as deep in the black
community. So even if in 1915 as a black American you had
built up this beautiful business, you didn't have three generations of capital in stock. So naturally black-owned districts—
banks, funeral parlors, et cetera—started eroding. Also,
desegregation wasn't good for those districts, and although
history tells us that the big change was in the 1960s, it was already on its way starting after World War Two. Black American civil rights leaders made major inroads after World War
Two in making America realize: If we went and got shot to
fight Hitler, you have to do something for us now.

Brown v. Board of Education was a culmination that
wouldn't have happened if the country had not been ready for
it. It couldn't have happened in 1920. Even though after it
happened, things weren't perfect, *Brown v. Board* happened
because starting in about 1945, the groundwork was being
laid. There were movies made that decried segregation in a
real way. Not that they made a big change, but the fact that
you could make money on a mainstream movie even address-
ing that problem was the beginning of the crack in the dam.
And so once it got to a point where black people could shop
wherever they wanted, the sad thing was, that meant there
were going to be some problems for black businesses because
the products that white people sold were inherently more
valuable.

And probably you had more of a choice at Wanamaker's than at Mr. Delaney's, the black man's store in the black section of town. Probably the best of what you could get in the black districts was not quite as large as what you could get in the white districts, for reasons that are perfectly obvious. But most likely, once you could get the best, you didn't want to settle for pretty darn good.

Unfortunately, over the past forty years it's gotten to the point where black people have often forgotten what it's like to show that they're as good as whites, and this speaks directly to Booker T. Washington, who did believe in showing whites that blacks were as good—if only in skill set. But the backlash is that for about four of five black people, affirmative action is a reparation: "We shouldn't have to show that we're as good, because of what happened in the past. As long as we're pretty good, that should be enough." I would agree that there is probably another percentage of black people who would say, "I don't know how to be as good. I don't have the tools." But the justification is still the same: slavery and fire hoses. At the end of the day, if it's not about everybody being measured by the same standards, then we're in trouble, for this simple reason: Are we going to have a society where it's assumed that most black people in high positions are incompetent? Maybe that's okay with some people. For me, that's not a unified society.

And my sense of Booker T. Washington, whether trying to overtly impress white people in the process or not, is that he aimed for a unified society by encouraging blacks to cultivate skills and a strong work ethic.

CHAPTER XIX

SHARON MADISON POLK,
Businesswoman/Entrepreneur

Sharon Madison Polk is chairman and CEO of Madison Madison International of Michigan, Inc. Since it was founded in 1954, the company has offered architectural, engineering, and planning services. Polk joined the family business in 1978 and became company president in 1987. In 1988, under her leadership, the firm expanded its capabilities to specialize in program construction management and transportation consulting. Her outstanding leadership of this award-winning company has garnered her national acclaim. She has been named one of the Top 25 Women Business Owners by the National Association of Women Business Owners and has been recognized as an Outstanding Minority Entrepreneur in the Business of Construction as well as called one of the Top 10 to Watch for Southeastern Michigan by the Detroit Regional Chamber of Commerce. Polk was recognized by Crain's *business magazine as one of the Most Influential Women of 2002 and one of the Top 100 Black Business Leaders of 1998.*

Polk is actively involved in the Detroit community, especially in the arts and culture, serving as chairperson of Friends of African and African-American Art and as a board member of the Detroit Institute of Arts. She is also a board member of the Downtown Development Authority, the Detroit Economic

Growth Corporation, the Michigan Coalition of Human Rights, and the National Women's Business Council.

THERE HAS ALWAYS been a perceived dichotomy between Booker T. Washington and W. E. B. Du Bois. If you are in the Du Bois camp and you believe that there is a special class of black people, the Talented Tenth, then you're more likely to believe that Booker T. Washington has been rightfully maligned throughout history. In my experience, it's not accurate to suggest that Booker T. Washington was a maligned figure at all— rightfully or wrongfully. And I think it's really an issue of time and era.

Du Bois was an advocate of intellectual advancement, and Washington was more about hands-on work. In their time Washington founded and built Tuskegee as an educational resource, but it wasn't education for education's sake. It was more about economic empowerment, which I don't think black people truly understood then or now. At that time black people were still trying to deal with issues of self esteem and the negative views cast upon them as an enslaved people; they were viewed as intellectually inferior. Yet black people possessed a lot of skills. We built this country. Slaves built the United States Capitol and most of the public buildings in the South that are now over a hundred years old. But because they were an enslaved people, their skills were not valued.

Today there is a very narrow view of what education is and what it means, and I think the hip-hop generation has had a dramatic impact on that view, specifically in terms of what is the best path to success and what is the real goal behind that success. I invoke this generation because they have rejected a lot of what is considered to be the standard of success and have still managed to become quite successful in an economic sense. I see in them a generation of people who have said, "I don't have to do this the way certain people say it has to be done." Now, I don't know if these people are truly being themselves or if it's all a put-on. I look at people like Queen Latifah and LL Cool J, and I see people who have basically utilized the hip-hop genre as a route to self-expression, but also as a form of influence and self-empowerment. And they've done it differently from prior generations. There is the sense that they are doing what they are doing not only to fulfill the American dream but also to set an example of what America is supposed to be. In some ways, this echoes what Booker T. Washington was saying about working with, instead of against, white people in America. The distinction is that the hip-hop community appears to have succeeded in doing that on its own terms. That's a little different from casting your buckets down where they are, though of course, it is because of Washington and others like him, along with our history as a people, that the hip-hop generation is able to do things on its own terms.

Still, we have masses of black kids who are struggling beyond the comprehension of most people. I have friends and colleagues with kids at Harvard and elite private schools, who have done really well with their grades, in part because their parents are able to hire tutors at an additional twenty thousand dollars a year. I would say that we have really come into a class situation more than anything else right now where the really elite black people can afford to send their kids to the best schools and still supplement them with tutors. That's the exact same thing white folks do. And yet we have a public school system where kids don't have a chance and are then made to feel inferior and reprimanded because their academic scores aren't high enough. I think the same thing was happening around the time of Booker T. Washington. Only blacks were made to feel inferior for no real reason at all, and because of that, some black people then as now have rejected things that Washington said.

Clearly, a lot of the support Washington received during his time came through white people and white institutions—what we might call pandering today. And his pandering fell quickly into the context of the "house Negro" versus the "field Negro." But it's important to note that in many instances not only were the house Negroes able to keep folks alive, but they were privy to inside information that they could then pass on among the other slaves. Our situation as blacks in America up to the present is complex and very difficult to dissect. But with Washington, if you look at the essential goal, what you see is that he was trying to attain self-sufficiency for black people, and he had to go a certain route to achieve that.

Frankly, one of the problems we have as a people, and have had historically, is that we don't recognize there is more than one way to be in the world. For us to be able to progress, we need to make room for many different ways of being. Unfortunately, what tends to happen is that instead of considering a different opinion in the context of a shared goal, we criticize and tear it down when there is probably a way to understand and support that opinion either directly or indirectly that would help us all.

It's one thing to say, "I can get there from here with what I've got by utilizing what I have right now and what I know is going to work." But if you do it in such a way that causes detriment to people or can be logically explained as causing detriment to people, then there is a problem. It's not so much what Booker T. Washington was doing as *how he did it*, which by some accounts gave the outward appearance not only of embracing white people but of saying we really are an inferior people and can't do it on our own. I would say that the people who have rejected Booker T. Washington have done so less because of the content he was promoting than because of the *way* it was promoted.

I'm a third-generation business owner. My parents and grandparents on both sides were strong supporters and advocates of education and self-sufficiency. I learned that from them growing up. I'm also a child of the sixties and seventies, which was a time when there was a heightened awareness of black history. I'm sure many others of my generation feel we have a much stronger connection to our history than more recent generations. When I was growing up in Detroit, black folks all lived in the same neighborhoods, regardless of your educational background or where you worked. The kids in my neighborhood got to see my parents—my father was in business, my mother an elected official—along with the people who worked in the factories. There were different models to look at. Now, most of the people from that neighborhood who could afford to have moved out of the city, leaving these groups of kids with no exposure to any models of success, no matter what that model might be.

All these skill sets are important for our community to embrace and cultivate. This perhaps is the very best of what Booker T. Washington was trying to convey.

CHAPTER XX

JOHN BRYANT,
Founder, Chairman, and CEO of Operation HOPE

John Bryant is a national community leader cited by the past four sitting U.S. presidents for his work to empower low-wealth communities across America as well as the author of Banking on Our Future (Beacon Press, 2002), a book on youth and family financial literacy. Bryant is a businessman, a former United Nations goodwill ambassador to the United States, a partner with former President Clinton in an effort to educate every child in Harlem in financial literacy, a presidential appointee for President George W. Bush, a Young Global Leader for the World Economic Forum, and the founder of Operation HOPE. Working with HOPE spokesman Ambassador Andrew Young, he is also the creator of a new movement in America called the Silver Rights Movement.

Bryant has received more than four hundred awards and citations for his work nationwide, including a special 2001 honor from Oprah Winfrey and her Angel Network Foundation. In 2005, he received the Crystal Heart Award from the USC School of Social Work for his work in the black community, along with the establishment of the USC John Bryant Scholarship Fund, an annual scholarship for deserving low-wealth young adults seeking an advanced degree from the USC School of Social Work.

Booker T. Washington—his reputation and his work—
was never fully fleshed out for me when I was in school growing up. You heard about Dr. Martin Luther King, Jr., and
when you forgot about that, you heard about . . . Dr. Martin
Luther King, Jr., and when you forgot about that, it was Dr.
Martin Luther King, Jr. And in case you missed it, you were
given some more Dr. Martin Luther King, Jr. Because I love
Dr. King so much, I took it all in and missed almost completely the work and legacy of Booker T. Washington.

I have learned a lot in my role of leadership, which I didn't
"pick," I might add. Operation HOPE found me, thank God,
and this is God's work, I am convinced. The last thing I expected to be was the founder and CEO of a nonprofit because
by background and experience, I'm a straight-up capitalist.

People ask me what political party I belong to, and I say
pick one: I'm a capitalist with a heart, a principled pragmatist,
an optimistic realist, and I belong to the get-it-done party. I'm
not a Democrat or a Republican; I'm a *businessman*. And so I
want to know how we can "get the job done" in our communities. Plain and simple, but not so easy, I have learned. The
bottom line is my community is in crisis. . . .

It has become a bit of a popular thing of late to support
Operation HOPE, but early on a lot of those I would call tra-
ditional black political leaders didn't support our efforts. Not
only did I find this odd, but back then it hurt, too. In fact, as
quiet as it's kept, some very purportedly prestigious black
leaders tried to suppress or even hurt the work we were doing
because it was viewed by them—wrongly so—as somehow a
threat to or damaging to their own individual power bases,
which I think is just sick. And so I understand what Booker

T. Washington was dealing with when he received withering criticism from his own—some deserved and some not, in all likelihood. Two things hit me when I was thinking about Washington in this context: One, No good deed shall go unpunished, and two, I like what I'm doing much more than what other folks are not doing.

Criticism is a cheap sport; it's an easy way to do nothing. So the first thing I give Washington credit for is just rising to the occasion, in a time when you just didn't fathom the kind of fantasies he had about who he was going to become and who we could indeed be. It also had to be extraordinarily difficult to have any type of conversation about black freedom and expression in, say, 1901. Respectfully, folks were catching hell in 1960 for doing much less! As far as the support he received from white people, to do what he needed to do, if your community is in a crisis, who cares whether you're black or white, rich or poor? If someone wanted to help Booker T. Washington eradicate slavery, then come on with it. People have said to me in my own efforts to eradicate poverty, "You're trying to turn blacks into Republicans." And I've said, "I'll turn you into an orange if I think it will help me eradicate poverty." My party is not a political party; it's the get-it-done party. And I am not a Republican, by the way, as I have already said, and why does someone have to be a Republican when he is talking about wealth building and personal responsibility? Okay, another topic for another time, but a good question nonetheless. So I have a lot of compassion for folks who are trying to walk a very delicate line without bastardizing their soul, which I think is exactly what Booker T. Washington had to do.

Martin Luther King walked with Jews and had a slight theological disagreement there about a man named Christ. He talked to racists—people who were hosing down and beating black people—because he knew that if he stopped talking to them, the chances for any type of agreement and progress would be dead. And this is my gut reaction to a guy in 1901 who was probably kicking ass and taking names. Booker T. Washington probably had a lot of people jealous of him and a lot of what we would today call player haters. But he persevered, and if his idea of working our land and casting down your buckets meant getting your own forty acres and a mule, okay. If it meant sharecropping or someone else's land, not okay; that didn't work. But hindsight is also always twenty-twenty.

As I continue to say, black America is the only group of people in the world today that created a political power base before creating an economic one. Don't get me wrong. We do need to have a political base; we just needed an economic one first. Still do. And we'd better get it quick. Americans are a democracy rooted in capitalism; it's all about ownership.

By no mistake of our own, blacks have always lived our lives ready, fire, aim, so forty acres and a mule would have been the best thing that the world ever did to black America to set things right. It would have given us the immigrant work ethic that everybody else coming here had, and because that promise was not kept after Lincoln was assassinated, we got into this thing where we say to each other, "I don't like you." And I say, what does *like* have to do with it? If we'd have gotten our forty acres and a mule, we'd have had to get our little black rear ends up at six in the morning—as a family, whether we liked each other or not—get to work in the field, plant the seed, till the soil, bring in a crop, and get it to market by a specific date. Otherwise you miss the opportunity and you go broke. You have to eat, and if you don't have "a stake," you are eating beans, ladies and gentlemen.

And that would have created an environment where we would've had to work together and we'd have seen the fruits of our labor, from which we would have been able to cultivate a very healthy work ethic and build a net worth and become producers and innovators like everybody else. The reality is none of that happened.

People say today that black people don't have a work ethic, and I say, well, why should we? We were slaves and sharecroppers. Some black folks sat on their hands on principle, which is understandable. But I think this is where Booker T. Washington was trying to effect change, because after several generations blacks were still sitting on their hands, with no recognition of why their forefathers had done the same on principle.

Fast-forward to post–World War Two, when the first black middle class was created through government jobs, and our idea of middle class was a leased car, a rented apartment, and a nice suit. And what's middle class today? Black middle class has an eight-thousand-dollar net worth; white middle class, same income, has an eighty-eight-thousand-dollar net worth. There's your answer. The difference is choices.

People can disagree on Booker T. Washington's rhetoric and strategies, but from what I understand, the man was on to something.

Let's say we are back in the postslavery era, and I'm approached by a white political leader, and he asks what do we need. I would say, give us forty acres and a mule, a healthy lesson in financial literacy, and with respect, get the hell out of our way. I don't need a handout; I need a hand up. Oh, and by the way, an education for my children, too!

White people never really did get out of the way, but it was also never really personal, either. Blacks need to understand that better. In one of my speeches that I give most of the time to a black audience, I say, "Let me see if I understand this properly. Your theory is that white folks hate us so much that they brought our rear ends all the way from Africa, spent two hundred years whipping on our rear ends . . . and even today you are an afterthought even for the KKK. The average Klan member takes their raggedy rear end and goes to their raggedy ass job, from nine o'clock in the morning until five o'clock in the afternoon. They come home; they kick the dog and beat the wife. They watch TV from seven to eight, and then they go looking for you from eight-thirty to midnight. *What were you doing the rest of the day, waiting for 'em?*"

By the way, the Klan was not even the Klan in the beginning; it was a white citizens' council, which no one talks about. These were southern white businessmen in the 1950s who were afraid that the rise of black responsibility, ownership, and rights would outnumber them and drive them out of their businesses. So they whispered into the ears of ignorant whites and said, "They wanna take your stuff. They want your wife. They want your job. Go get 'em." And these ignorant whites put on hoods and went out chasing uneducated blacks who were unable to understand that behind the hoods and robes was actually a business decision. We've been fighting that shadow of an enemy for fifty years. The only reason slaves came over here in the first place was that the founders were trying to figure out how to build a country for free—another economic decision. And destroying our spirit was part of that decision, to prevent a revolt. Unfortunately, all this makes logical business sense, if not ethical business sense. So that Booker T. Washington made economic development his primary platform to move black folks ahead is both genius and common sense.

Look, I issued a pamphlet last year called *Racism and the Silver Rights Movement*, and in it I say it's not that racism doesn't exist; it's that it doesn't matter. Black folks need to stop talking about racism as if it just showed up on the eleven o'clock news last night. It's been around since the beginning of time. Get over it. As my pastor Reverend Murray would say, "It's not what they call you; it's what you *answer* to that's important. So stop answering out of your name." To argue with a fool proves there are two fools.

There's a story: a black barbershop in the South, a parrot outside, and a black father talking with his child across the street. A black guy is heading into the barbershop and walks by the parrot. The parrot says, "Nigger." Black guy turns around and looks for somebody else. Parrot says, "Dumb nigger." Black guy says, "Who you calling a dumb nigger? Ain't nobody here but me. Don't you understand I'm a PhD?" Parrot says, "Dumb nigger." So they get into it, and about this time the black father across the street says to his child, "Will you look at that dumb nigger across the street arguing with a parrot?" The man should have kept walking, but his low self-esteem required him to get into an argument with a damn parrot. That's what we're doing today as a people; we're responding to idiocy. Racism is like rain. It's either falling someplace or it's gathering, so you might as well get an umbrella in a color you like and start strolling through it, because it's not going to change anytime soon.

My ultimate answer to racism and our history of struggle is what the answer has always been; it's what the Bible suggests. Jesus says in Proverbs, to be poor is not to not have anything; to be poor is not to not *do* anything. Lazy hands make a man poor. It's always been about personal responsibility and accountability and getting yourself right. As the author Deepak Chopra has said, "We're not human beings having a spiritual experience, we're spiritual beings having a human experience." You get that right, and everything falls into place. I grew up in South Central, LA. I have a high school GED, and I'll run circles around PhDs on a regular basis. I should be a statistic.

Booker T. Washington was out there in 1901 with his shoulder against the wall, trying to do something positive. What's to criticize about that? I see in Washington a great visionary. When King was alive, we called him Martin Luther Coon, Martin Loser King, a sellout, a punk, an Uncle Tom. Malcolm X whipped on his tail for five years straight. Now King is worshiped—"We are the world, we are the future . . ." holding hands and the whole thing. I'm sure there's nobody more surprised than King himself. No good deed shall go unpunished. It just takes time to figure out whether the decisions that a King or Booker T. Washington was making really worked.

We're still talking about Booker T. Washington one hundred years later. Was he perfect? Of course not, we all have errors in judgment. We are born broken and are all sinners. But a saint is a sinner that got up. Booker T. Washington should be credited for doing what he did when he did it—for doing something when others did nothing.

ABOUT THE AUTHOR

REBECCA CARROLL is the editor in chief of the *Independent Film & Video Monthly* magazine. She is the author of *Saving the Race: Conversations on Du Bois from a Collective Memoir of Souls* and *Sugar in the Raw: Voices of Young Black Girls in America*, which won an ALA Award in 1997 as one of the Top Ten Adult Books for Young Adults. She lives in New York City with her husband and son.

UP FROM SLAVERY

EDITOR'S NOTE

BRIDGING THE GAP:
A REINTRODUCTION TO
UP FROM SLAVERY,
ONE HUNDRED YEARS LATER

WHATEVER YOUR opinion of Booker T. Washington, before and then again after reading the following text, he stood apart during postslavery Reconstruction as a man willing to confront openly the question, What do we do now? Not: How can we go to Harvard or be the next mayor of town or president of the bank? But the very basic question of what black Americans were going to do—*could* do—in the days and weeks and months following their liberation (by law) from decades of shackles and servitude and horrific torture. What do we do *now*? And *how* do we do it? You do it, Washington contended, by learning a manual skill that can be put to practice right where you are. And while this may have also conveniently coincided with what white people wanted to hear, someone needed to ask the question and then try to come up with some kind of answer. Booker T. was that someone.

An oppressed people will always look for, hope for, or help to create the illusion of a hero or some sort of savior—a light at the end of the tunnel, as it were. Although Washington may not have written *Up from Slavery* expressly for postslavery black Americans, and certainly very few read the book then, white people read it, and they read it as though they were being given reliable information *about* postslavery black Americans, which allowed black people to feel represented: Booker T. Washington as interpreter of unarticulated black demands. For a short but historic period of time that was enough.

Dr. Bill Lawson makes a very cogent point in his narrative (page 15): You might not want to have dinner with Booker T. Washington, but W. E. B. Du Bois wouldn't want to have dinner with you. Which is to say that Uncle Tom or New Negro, Washington did readily step to the plate as the savior figure black America was looking for and to some degree desperately needed, whereas Du Bois may not have cared all that much whether or not black people en masse understood his stirring and eloquent assessment of race in America. Du Bois cared that the intelligentsia—

black and white—read and discussed his work, much of which, it should be said, specifically *The Souls of Black Folk*, is brilliant and prophetic.

Ultimately, though, it is the intelligentsia that decides who is remembered, talked about, and celebrated from the annals of history. Washington's work was practical and pragmatic; Du Bois's was literary and enlightened. Intellectuals gravitate toward the latter, while a people that is actively grappling with its place in the world gravitates toward the former. I believe that today black people can be and are both. We may still be grappling with our fundamental grounding in America, but we are also enlightened intellectuals who read and write and critique literary works and regularly contribute to a national discourse about culture and commerce and politics.

To that end, assessing Booker T. Washington's contribution to American history is an imperative discussion, and black Americans are the right people to be leading it.

—*Rebecca Carroll, May 2005*

UP FROM SLAVERY

AN AUTOBIOGRAPHY

BY

BOOKER T. WASHINGTON

AUTHOR OF "THE FUTURE OF THE AMERICAN NEGRO"

NEW YORK

DOUBLEDAY, PAGE & CO.

1902

Norwood Press
J. S. Cushing & Co.—Berwick & Smith
Norwood, Mass., U.S.A.

This volume is dedicated to my Wife

MRS. MARGARET JAMES WASHINGTON

And to my Brother

MR. JOHN H. WASHINGTON

Whose patience, fidelity, and hard work have gone far

to make the work at Tuskegee successful

PREFACE

THIS VOLUME is the outgrowth of a series of articles, dealing with incidents in my life, which were published consecutively in the *Outlook*. While they were appearing in that magazine I was constantly surprised at the number of requests which came to me from all parts of the country, asking that the articles be permanently preserved in book form. I am most grateful to the *Outlook* for permission to gratify these requests.

I have tried to tell a simple, straightforward story, with no attempt at embellishment. My regret is that what I have attempted to do has been done so imperfectly. The greater part of my time and strength is required for the executive work connected with the Tuskegee Normal and Industrial Institute, and in securing the money necessary for the support of the institution. Much of what I have said has been written on board trains, or at hotels or railroad stations while

I have been waiting for trains, or during the moments that I could spare from my work while at Tuskegee. Without the painstaking and generous assistance of Mr. Max Bennett Thrasher I could not have succeeded in any satisfactory degree.

CONTENTS

UP FROM SLAVERY

CHAPTER I

A SLAVE AMONG SLAVES

I WAS born a slave on a plantation in Franklin County, Virginia. I am not quite sure of the exact place or exact date of my birth, but at any rate I suspect I must have been born somewhere and at some time. As nearly as I have been able to learn, I was born near a cross-roads post-office called Hale's Ford, and the year was 1858 or 1859.[1] I do not know the month or the day. The earliest impressions I can now recall are of the plantation and the slave quarters—the latter being the part of the plantation where the slaves had their cabins.

My life had its beginning in the midst of the most miserable, desolate, and discouraging surroundings. This was so, however, not because my owners were especially cruel, for they were not, as compared with many others. I was born in a typical log cabin, about fourteen by sixteen feet square. In this cabin I lived with my mother and a brother and sister till after the Civil War, when we were all declared free.

Of my ancestry I know almost nothing. In the slave quarters, and even later, I heard whispered conversations among the coloured people of the tortures which the slaves, including, no doubt, my ancestors on my mother's side, suffered in the middle passage of the slave ship while being conveyed from Africa to America. I have been unsuccessful in securing any information that would throw any accurate light upon the history of my family beyond my mother. She, I remember, had a half-brother and a half-sister. In the days of slavery not very much attention was given to family history and family records—that is, black family records. My mother, I suppose, attracted the attention of a purchaser who was afterward my owner and hers. Her addition to the slave family attracted about as much attention as the purchase of a new horse or cow. Of my father I know even less than of my mother. I do not even know his name. I have heard reports to the effect that he was a white man who lived on one of the near-by plantations. Whoever he was, I never heard of his taking the least interest in me or providing in any way for my rearing. But I do not find especial fault with him. He was simply another unfortunate victim of the institution which the Nation un-happily had engrafted upon it at that time.

The cabin was not only our living-place, but was also used as the kitchen for the plantation. My mother was the plantation cook. The cabin was without glass windows; it had only openings in the side which let in the light, and also the cold, chilly air of winter. There was a door to the cabin—that is, something that was called a door—but the uncertain hinges by which it was hung, and the large cracks in it, to say nothing of the fact that it was too small, made the room a very uncomfortable one. In addition to these openings there was, in the lower right-hand corner of the room, the "cat-hole,"—a contrivance which almost every mansion or cabin in Virginia possessed during the ante-bellum period. The "cat-hole" was a square opening, about seven by eight inches, provided for the purpose of letting the cat pass in and out of the house at will during the night. In the case of our particular cabin I could never understand the necessity for this convenience, since there were at least a half-dozen other places in the cabin that would have accommo-dated the cats. There was no wooden floor in our cabin, the naked earth being used as a floor. In the centre of the earthen floor there was a large, deep opening covered with boards, which was used as a place in which to store sweet potatoes during the winter. An impression of this potato-hole is very distinctly engraved upon my memory, because I recall that during the process of putting the potatoes in or taking them out I would often come into possession of one or two, which I roasted and thoroughly enjoyed. There was no cooking-stove on our plantation, and all the cooking for the whites and slaves my mother had to do over an open fireplace, mostly in pots and "skillets." While the poorly built cabin caused us to suffer with cold in the winter, the heat from the open fireplace in summer was equally trying.

The early years of my life, which were spent in the little cabin, were not very different from those of thousands of other slaves. My mother, of course, had little time in which to give attention to the training of her children during the day. She snatched a few moments for our care in the early morning before her work began, and at night after the day's work was done. One of my earliest recollections is that of my mother cooking a chicken late at night, and awakening her children for the purpose of feeding them. How or where she got it I do not know. I presume, however, it was procured from our owner's farm. Some people may call this theft. If such a thing were to happen now, I should condemn it as theft myself. But taking place at the time it did, and for the reason that it did, no one could ever make me believe that my

mother was guilty of thieving. She was simply a victim of the system of slavery. I cannot remember having slept in a bed until after our family was declared
free by the Emancipation Proclamation. Three children—John, my older brother, Amanda, my sister, and
myself—had a pallet on the dirt floor, or, to be more
correct, we slept in and on a bundle of filthy rags laid
upon the dirt floor.

I was asked not long ago to tell something about
the sports and pastimes that I engaged in during my
youth. Until that question was asked it had never occurred to me that there was no period of my life that
was devoted to play. From the time that I can remember anything, almost every day of my life has been occupied in some kind of labour; though I think I would
now be a more useful man if I had had time for sports.
During the period that I spent in slavery I was not
large enough to be of much service, still I was occupied most of the time in cleaning the yards, carrying
water to the men in the fields, or going to the mill, to
which I used to take the corn, once a week, to be
ground. The mill was about three miles from the plantation. This work I always dreaded. The heavy bag of
corn would be thrown across the back of the horse,
and the corn divided about evenly on each side; but in
some way, almost without exception, on these trips,
the corn would so shift as to become unbalanced and

would fall off the horse, and often I would fall with it. As I was not strong enough to reload the corn upon the horse, I would have to wait, sometimes for many hours, till a chance passer-by came along who would help me out of my trouble. The hours while waiting for some one were usually spent in crying. The time consumed in this way made me late in reaching the mill, and by the time I got my corn ground and reached home it would be far into the night. The road was a lonely one, and often led through dense forests. I was always frightened. The woods were said to be full of soldiers who had deserted from the army, and I had been told that the first thing a deserter did to a Negro boy when he found him alone was to cut off his ears. Besides, when I was late in getting home I knew I would always get a severe scolding or a flogging.

I had no schooling whatever while I was a slave, though I remember on several occasions I went as far as the schoolhouse door with one of my young mistresses to carry her books. The picture of several dozen boys and girls in a schoolroom engaged in study made a deep impression upon me, and I had the feeling that to get into a schoolhouse and study in this way would be about the same as getting into paradise.

So far as I can now recall, the first knowledge that I got of the fact that we were slaves, and that freedom of the slaves was being discussed, was early one morning before day, when I was awakened by my mother kneeling over her children and fervently praying that Lincoln and his armies might be successful, and that one day she and her children might be free. In this connection I have never been able to understand how the slaves throughout the South, completely ignorant as were the masses so far as books or newspapers were concerned, were able to keep themselves so accurately and completely informed about the great National questions that were agitating the country. From the time that Garrison, Lovejoy, and others began to agitate for freedom, the slaves throughout the South kept in close touch with the progress of the movement. Though I was a mere child during the preparation for the Civil War and during the war itself, I now recall the many late-at-night whispered discussions that I heard my mother and the other slaves on the plantation indulge in. These discussions showed that they understood the situation, and that they kept themselves informed of events by what was termed the "grape-vine" telegraph.

During the campaign when Lincoln was first a candidate for the Presidency, the slaves on our far-off plantation, miles from any railroad or large city or daily newspaper, knew what the issues involved were. When war was begun between the North and the South, every slave on our plantation felt and knew that, though other issues were discussed, the primal one was that of slavery. Even the most ignorant members of my race on the remote plantations felt in their hearts, with a certainty that admitted of no doubt, that the freedom of the slaves would be the one great result of the war, if the Northern armies conquered. Every success of the Federal armies and every defeat of the Confederate forces was watched with the keenest and most intense interest. Often the slaves got knowledge of the results of great battles before the white people received it. This news was usually gotten from the coloured man who was sent to the post-office for the mail. In our case the post-office was about three miles from the plantation, and the mail came once or twice a week. The man who was sent to the office would linger about the place long enough to get the drift of the conversation from the group of white people who naturally congregated there, after receiving their mail, to discuss the latest news. The mail-carrier on his way back to our master's house would as naturally retail the news that he had secured among the slaves, and in this way they often heard of important events before the white people at the "big house," as the master's house was called.

I cannot remember a single instance during my childhood or early boyhood when our entire family sat down to the table together, and God's blessing was asked, and the family ate a meal in a civilized manner. On the plantation in Virginia, and even later, meals were gotten by the children very much as dumb animals get theirs. It was a piece of bread here and a scrap of meat there. It was a cup of milk at one time and some potatoes at another. Sometimes a portion of our family would eat out of the skillet or pot, while some one else would eat from a tin plate held on the knees, and often using nothing but the hands with which to hold the food. When I had grown to sufficient size, I was required to go to the "big house" at meal-times to fan the flies from the table by means of a large set of paper fans operated by a pulley. Naturally much of the conversation of the white people turned upon the subject of freedom and the war, and I absorbed a good deal of it. I remember that at one time I saw two of my young mistresses and some lady visitors eating ginger-cakes, in the yard. At that time those cakes seemed to me to be absolutely the most tempting and desirable things that I had ever seen; and I then and there resolved that, if I ever got free, the height of my ambition would be reached if I could get to the point where I could secure and eat ginger-cakes in the way that I saw those ladies doing.

Of course as the war was prolonged the white people, in many cases, often found it difficult to secure food for themselves. I think the slaves felt the deprivation less than the whites, because the usual diet for the slaves was corn bread and pork, and these could be raised on the plantation; but coffee, tea, sugar, and other articles which the whites had been accustomed to use could not be raised on the plantation, and the conditions brought about by the war frequently made it impossible to secure these things. The whites were often in great straits. Parched corn was used for coffee, and a kind of black molasses was used instead of sugar. Many times nothing was used to sweeten the so-called tea and coffee.

The first pair of shoes that I recall wearing were wooden ones. They had rough leather on the top, but the bottoms, which were about an inch thick, were of wood. When I walked they made a fearful noise, and besides this they were very inconvenient, since there was no yielding to the natural pressure of the foot. In wearing them one presented an exceedingly awkward appearance. The most trying ordeal that I was forced to endure as a slave boy, however, was the wearing of a flax shirt. In the portion of Virginia where I lived it was common to use flax as part of the clothing for the slaves. That part of the flax from which our clothing was made was largely the refuse, which of course was the cheapest and roughest part. I can scarcely imagine any torture, except, perhaps, the pulling of a tooth, that is equal to that caused by putting on a new flax

shirt for the first time. It is almost equal to the feeling
that one would experience if he had a dozen or more
chestnut burrs, or a hundred small pin-points, in contact with his flesh. Even to this day I can recall accurately the tortures that I underwent when putting on
one of these garments. The fact that my flesh was soft
and tender added to the pain. But I had no choice. I
had to wear the flax shirt or none; and had it been left
to me to choose, I should have chosen to wear no covering. In connection with the flax shirt, my brother
John, who is several years older than I am, performed
one of the most generous acts that I ever heard of one
slave relative doing for another. On several occasions
when I was being forced to wear a new flax shirt, he
generously agreed to put it on in my stead and wear it
for several days, till it was "broken in." Until I had
grown to be quite a youth this single garment was all
that I wore.

One may get the idea, from what I have said, that
there was bitter feeling toward the white people on
the part of my race, because of the fact that most
of the white population was away fighting in a war
which would result in keeping the Negro in slavery if
the South was successful. In the case of the slaves on
our place this was not true, and it was not true of any
large portion of the slave population in the South
where the Negro was treated with anything like de-

cency. During the Civil War one of my young masters was killed, and two were severely wounded. I recall the feeling of sorrow which existed among the slaves when they heard of the death of "Mars' Billy." It was no sham sorrow, but real. Some of the slaves had nursed "Mars' Billy"; others had played with him when he was a child. "Mars' Billy" had begged for mercy in the case of others when the overseer or master was thrashing them. The sorrow in the slave quarter was only second to that in the "big house." When the two young masters were brought home wounded, the sympathy of the slaves was shown in many ways. They were just as anxious to assist in the nursing as the family relatives of the wounded. Some of the slaves would even beg for the privilege of sitting up at night to nurse their wounded masters. This tenderness and sympathy on the part of those held in bondage was a result of their kindly and generous nature. In order to defend and protect the women and children who were left on the plantations when the white males went to war, the slaves would have laid down their lives. The slave who was selected to sleep in the "big house" during the absence of the males was considered to have the place of honour. Any one attempting to harm "young Mistress" or "old Mistress" during the night would have had to cross the dead body of the slave to do so. I do not know how many have noticed it, but I think that it will be found to be true that there are few instances, either in slavery or freedom, in which a member of my race has been known to betray a specific trust.

As a rule, not only did the members of my race entertain no feelings of bitterness against the whites before and during the war, but there are many instances of Negroes tenderly caring for their former masters and mistresses who for some reason have become poor and dependent since the war. I know of instances where the former masters of slaves have for years been supplied with money by their former slaves to keep them from suffering. I have known of still other cases in which the former slaves have assisted in the education of the descendants of their former owners. I know of a case on a large plantation in the South in which a young white man, the son of the former owner of the estate, has become so reduced in purse and self-control by reason of drink that he is a pitiable creature; and yet, notwithstanding the poverty of the coloured people themselves on this plantation, they have for years supplied this young white man with the necessities of life. One sends him a little coffee or sugar, another a little meat, and so on. Nothing that the coloured people possess is too good for the son of

"old Mars' Tom," who will perhaps never be permitted
to suffer while any remain on the place who knew directly or indirectly of "old Mars' Tom."

I have said that there are few instances of a member of my race betraying a specific trust. One of the
best illustrations of this which I know of is in the case
of an ex-slave from Virginia whom I met not long ago
in a little town in the state of Ohio. I found that this
man had made a contract with his master, two or three
years previous to the Emancipation Proclamation, to
the effect that the slave was to be permitted to buy
himself, by paying so much per year for his body; and
while he was paying for himself, he was to be permitted to labour where and for whom he pleased. Finding that he could secure better wages in Ohio, he went
there. When freedom came, he was still in debt to his
master some three hundred dollars. Notwithstanding
that the Emancipation Proclamation freed him from
any obligation to his master, this black man walked
the greater portion of the distance back to where his
old master lived in Virginia, and placed the last dollar,
with interest, in his hands. In talking to me about this,
the man told me that he knew that he did not have to
pay the debt, but that he had given his word to his
master, and his word he had never broken. He felt that
he could not enjoy his freedom till he had fulfilled his
promise.

From some things that I have said one may get the idea that some of the slaves did not want freedom. This is not true. I have never seen one who did not want to be free, or one who would return to slavery.

I pity from the bottom of my heart any nation or body of people that is so unfortunate as to get entangled in the net of slavery. I have long since ceased to cherish any spirit of bitterness against the Southern white people on account of the enslavement of my race. No one section of our country was wholly responsible for its introduction, and, besides, it was recognized and protected for years by the General Government. Having once got its tentacles fastened on to the economic and social life of the Republic, it was no easy matter for the country to relieve itself of the institution. Then, when we rid ourselves of prejudice, or racial feeling, and look facts in the face, we must acknowledge that, notwithstanding the cruelty and moral wrong of slavery, the ten million Negroes inhabiting this country, who themselves or whose ancestors went through the school of American slavery, are in a stronger and more hopeful condition, materially, intellectually, morally, and religiously, than is true of an equal number of black people in any other portion of the globe. This is so to such an extent that Negroes in this country, who themselves or whose forefathers went through the school of slavery, are

constantly returning to Africa as missionaries to en-
lighten those who remained in the fatherland. This I
say, not to justify slavery—on the other hand, I condemn it as an institution, as we all know that in
America it was established for selfish and financial
reasons, and not from a missionary motive—but to
call attention to a fact, and to show how Providence so
often uses men and institutions to accomplish a purpose. When persons ask me in these days how, in the
midst of what sometimes seem hopelessly discouraging conditions, I can have such faith in the future of
my race in this country, I remind them of the wilder-
ness through which and out of which, a good Providence has already led us.

Ever since I have been old enough to think for myself, I have entertained the idea that, notwithstanding
the cruel wrongs inflicted upon us, the black man got
nearly as much out of slavery as the white man did.
The hurtful influences of the institution were not by
any means confined to the Negro. This was fully illustrated by the life upon our own plantation. The whole
machinery of slavery was so constructed as to cause
labour, as a rule, to be looked upon as a badge of
degradation, of inferiority. Hence labour was something that both races on the slave plantation sought to
escape. The slave system on our place, in a large measure, took the spirit of self-reliance and self-help out

of the white people. My old master had many boys and girls, but not one, so far as I know, ever mastered a single trade or special line of productive industry. The girls were not taught to cook, sew, or to take care of the house. All of this was left to the slaves. The slaves, of course, had little personal interest in the life of the plantation, and their ignorance prevented them from learning how to do things in the most improved and thorough manner. As a result of the system, fences were out of repair, gates were hanging half off the hinges, doors creaked, window-panes were out, plastering had fallen but was not replaced, weeds grew in the yard. As a rule, there was food for whites and blacks, but inside the house, and on the dining-room table, there was wanting that delicacy and refinement of touch and finish which can make a home the most convenient, comfortable, and attractive place in the world. Withal there was a waste of food and other materials which was sad. When freedom came, the slaves were almost as well fitted to begin life anew as the master, except in the matter of book-learning and ownership of property. The slave owner and his sons had mastered no special industry. They unconsciously had imbibed the feeling that manual labour was not the proper thing for them. On the other hand, the slaves, in many cases, had mastered some handicraft, and none were ashamed, and few unwilling, to labour.

Finally the war closed, and the day of freedom came. It was a momentous and eventful day to all upon our plantation. We had been expecting it. Freedom was in the air, and had been for months. Deserting soldiers returning to their homes were to be seen every day. Others who had been discharged, or whose regiments had been paroled, were constantly passing near our place. The "grape-vine telegraph" was kept busy night and day. The news and mutterings of great events were swiftly carried from one plantation to another. In the fear of "Yankee" invasions, the silverware and other valuables were taken from the "big house," buried in the woods, and guarded by trusted slaves. Woe be to any one who would have attempted to disturb the buried treasure. The slaves would give the Yankee soldiers food, drink, clothing—anything but that which had been specifically intrusted to their care and honour. As the great day drew nearer, there was more singing in the slave quarters than usual. It was bolder, had more ring, and lasted later into the night. Most of the verses of the plantation songs had some reference to freedom. True, they had sung those same verses before, but they had been careful to explain that the "freedom" in these songs referred to the next world, and had no connection with life in this world. Now they gradually threw off the mask, and were not afraid to let it be known that the "freedom" in their songs meant freedom of the body in this world. The night before the eventful day, word was sent to the slave quarters to the effect that something unusual was going to take place at the "big house" the next morning. There was little, if any, sleep that night. All was excitement and expectancy. Early the next morning word was sent to all the slaves, old and young, to gather at the house. In company with my mother, brother, and sister, and a large number of other slaves, I went to the master's house. All of our master's family were either standing or seated on the veranda of the house, where they could see what was to take place and hear what was said. There was a feeling of deep interest, or perhaps sadness, on their faces, but not bitterness. As I now recall the impression they made upon me, they did not at the moment seem to be sad because of the loss of property, but rather because of parting with those whom they had reared and who were in many ways very close to them. The most distinct thing that I now recall in connection with the scene was that some man who seemed to be a stranger (a United States officer, I presume) made a little speech and then read a rather long paper—the Emancipation Proclamation, I think. After the reading we were told that we were all free, and could go when and where we pleased. My mother, who was standing by my side, leaned over and kissed her children, while tears of joy ran down her cheeks. She explained to us what it all meant, that this was the day for which she had been so long praying, but fearing that she would never live to see.

For some minutes there was great rejoicing, and thanksgiving, and wild scenes of ecstasy. But there was no feeling of bitterness. In fact, there was pity among the slaves for our former owners. The wild rejoicing on the part of the emancipated coloured people lasted but for a brief period, for I noticed that by the time they returned to their cabins there was a change in their feelings. The great responsibility of being free, of having charge of themselves, of having to think and plan for themselves and their children, seemed to take possession of them. It was very much like suddenly turning a youth of ten or twelve years out into the world to provide for himself. In a few hours the great questions with which the Anglo-Saxon race had been grappling for centuries had been thrown upon these people to be solved. These were the questions of a home, a living, the rearing of children, education, citizenship, and the establishment and support of churches. Was it any wonder that within a few hours the wild rejoicing ceased and a feeling of deep gloom seemed to pervade the slave quarters? To some it seemed that, now that they were in actual possession of it, freedom was a more serious thing than they had expected to find it.

Some of the slaves were seventy or eighty years old; their best days were gone. They had no strength with which to earn a living in a strange place and among strange people, even if they had been sure where to find a new place of abode. To this class the problem seemed especially hard. Besides, deep down in their hearts there was a strange and peculiar attachment to "old Marster" and "old Missus," and to their children, which they found it hard to think of breaking off. With these they had spent in some cases nearly a half-century, and it was no light thing to think of parting. Gradually, one by one, stealthily at first, the older slaves began to wander from the slave quarters back to the "big house" to have a whispered conversation with their former owners as to the future.

CHAPTER II

BOYHOOD DAYS

After the coming of freedom there were two points upon which practically all the people on our place were agreed, and I find that this was generally true throughout the South: that they must change their names, and that they must leave the old plantation for at least a few days or weeks in order that they might really feel sure that they were free.

In some way a feeling got among the coloured people that it was far from proper for them to bear the surname of their former owners, and a great many of them took other surnames. This was one of the first signs of freedom. When they were slaves, a coloured person was simply called "John" or "Susan." There was seldom occasion for more than the use of the one name. If "John" or "Susan" belonged to a white man by the name of "Hatcher," sometimes he was called "John Hatcher," or as often "Hatcher's John." But there was a feeling that "John Hatcher" or "Hatcher's John" was not the proper title by which to denote a freeman; and so in many cases "John Hatcher" was changed to "John S. Lincoln" or "John S. Sherman," the initial "S" standing for no name, it being simply a part of what the coloured man proudly called his "entitles."

As I have stated, most of the coloured people left the old plantation for a short while at least, so as to be sure, it seemed, that they could leave and try their freedom on to see how it felt. After they had remained away for a time, many of the older slaves, especially, returned to their old homes and made some kind of contract with their former owners by which they remained on the estate.

My mother's husband, who was the stepfather of my brother John and myself, did not belong to the same owners as did my mother. In fact, he seldom came to our plantation. I remember seeing him there perhaps once a year, that being about Christmas time. In some way, during the war, by running away and following the Federal soldiers, it seems, he found his way into the new state of West Virginia. As soon as freedom was declared, he sent for my mother to come to the Kanawha Valley, in West Virginia. At that time a journey from Virginia over the mountains to West Virginia was rather a tedious and in some cases a painful undertaking. What little clothing and few household goods we had were placed in a cart, but the children walked the greater portion of the distance, which was several hundred miles.

I do not think any of us ever had been very far from the plantation, and the taking of a long journey into another state was quite an event. The parting from our former owners and the members of our own race on the plantation was a serious occasion. From the time of our parting till their death we kept up a correspondence with the older members of the family, and in later years we have kept in touch with those who were the younger members. We were several weeks making the trip, and most of the time we slept in the open air and did our cooking over a log fire out-of-doors. One night I recall that we camped near an abandoned log cabin, and my mother decided to build a fire in that for cooking, and afterward to make a "pallet" on the floor for our sleeping. Just as the fire had gotten well started a large black snake fully a yard and a half long dropped down the chimney and ran out on the floor. Of course we at once abandoned that cabin. Finally we reached our destination—a little town called Malden, which is about five miles from Charleston, the present capital of the state.

At that time salt-mining was the great industry in that part of West Virginia, and the little town of Malden was right in the midst of the salt-furnaces.

My stepfather had already secured a job at a salt-furnace, and he had also secured a little cabin for us to live in. Our new house was no better than the one we had left on the old plantation in Virginia. In fact, in one respect it was worse. Notwithstanding the poor condition of our plantation cabin, we were at all times sure of pure air. Our new home was in the midst of a cluster of cabins crowded closely together, and as there were no sanitary regulations, the filth about the cabins was often intolerable. Some of our neighbours were coloured people, and some were the poorest and most ignorant and degraded white people. It was a motley mixture. Drinking, gambling, quarrels, fights, and shockingly immoral practices were frequent. All who lived in the little town were in one way or another connected with the salt business. Though I was a mere child, my stepfather put me and my brother at work in one of the furnaces. Often I began work as early as four o'clock in the morning.

The first thing I ever learned in the way of book knowledge was while working in this salt-furnace. Each salt-packer had his barrels marked with a certain number. The number allotted to my stepfather was "18." At the close of the day's work the boss of the packers would come around and put "18" on each of our barrels, and I soon learned to recognize that fig-ure wherever I saw it, and after a while got to the point where I could make that figure, though I knew nothing about any other figures or letters.

From the time that I can remember having any thoughts about anything, I recall that I had an intense longing to learn to read. I determined, when quite a small child, that, if I accomplished nothing else in life, I would in some way get enough education to enable me to read common books and newspapers. Soon after we got settled in some manner in our new cabin in West Virginia, I induced my mother to get hold of a book for me. How or where she got it I do not know, but in some way she procured an old copy of Webster's "blue-back" spelling-book, which contained the alphabet, followed by such meaningless words as "ab," "ba," "ca," "da." I began at once to devour this book, and I think that it was the first one I ever had in my hands. I had learned from somebody that the way to begin to read was to learn the alphabet, so I tried in all the ways I could think of to learn it,—all of course without a teacher, for I could find no one to teach me. At that time there was not a single member of my race anywhere near us who could read, and I was too timid to approach any of the white people. In some way, within a few weeks, I mastered the greater portion of the alphabet. In all my efforts to learn to read my mother shared fully my ambition, and sympathized with me and aided me in every way that she could.

Though she was totally ignorant, so far as mere book knowledge was concerned, she had high ambitions for her children, and a large fund of good, hard, common sense which seemed to enable her to meet and master every situation. If I have done anything in life worth attention, I feel sure that I inherited the disposition from my mother.

In the midst of my struggles and longing for an education, a young coloured boy who had learned to read in the state of Ohio came to Malden. As soon as the coloured people found out that he could read, a newspaper was secured, and at the close of nearly every day's work this young man would be surrounded by a group of men and women who were anxious to hear him read the news contained in the papers. How I used to envy this man! He seemed to me to be the one young man in all the world who ought to be satisfied with his attainments.

About this time the question of having some kind of a school opened for the coloured children in the village began to be discussed by members of the race. As it would be the first school for Negro children that had ever been opened in that part of Virginia, it was, of course, to be a great event, and the discussion excited the widest interest. The most perplexing question was where to find a teacher. The young man from Ohio who had learned to read the papers was considered, but his age was against him. In the midst of the discussion about a teacher, another young coloured man from Ohio, who had been a soldier, in some way found his way into town. It was soon learned that he possessed considerable education, and he was engaged by the coloured people to teach their first school. As yet no free schools had been started for coloured people in that section, hence each family agreed to pay a certain amount per month, with the understanding that the teacher was to "board 'round"—that is, spend a day with each family. This was not bad for the teacher, for each family tried to provide the very best on the day the teacher was to be its guest. I recall that I looked forward with an anxious appetite to the "teacher's day" at our little cabin.

This experience of a whole race beginning to go to school for the first time, presents one of the most interesting studies that has ever occurred in connection with the development of any race. Few people who were not right in the midst of the scenes can form any exact idea of the intense desire which the people of my race showed for an education. As I have stated, it was a whole race trying to go to school. Few were too young, and none too old, to make the attempt to learn. As fast as any kind of teachers could be secured, not only were day-schools filled, but night-schools as well. The great ambition of the older people was to try to learn to read the Bible before they died. With this end in view, men and women who were fifty or seventy-five years old would often be found in the night-school. Sunday-schools were formed soon after freedom, but the principal book studied in the Sunday-school was the spelling-book. Day-school, night-school, Sunday-school, were always crowded, and often many had to be turned away for want of room.

The opening of the school in the Kanawha Valley, however, brought to me one of the keenest disappointments that I ever experienced. I had been working in a salt-furnace for several months, and my stepfather had discovered that I had a financial value, and so, when the school opened, he decided that he could not spare me from my work. This decision seemed to cloud my every ambition. The disappointment was made all the more severe by reason of the fact that my place of work was where I could see the happy children passing to and from school, mornings and afternoons. Despite this disappointment, however, I determined that I would learn something, anyway. I applied myself with greater earnestness than ever to the mastering of what was in the "blue-back" speller.

My mother sympathized with me in my disappointment, and sought to comfort me in all the ways she could, and to help me find a way to learn. After a while I succeeded in making arrangements with the teacher to give me some lessons at night, after the day's work was done. These night lessons were so welcome that I think I learned more at night than the other children did during the day. My own experiences in the night-school gave me faith in the night-school idea, with which, in after years, I had to do both at Hampton and Tuskegee. But my boyish heart was still set upon going to the day-school, and I let no opportunity slip to push my case. Finally I won, and was permitted to go to the school in the day for a few months, with the understanding that I was to rise early in the morning and work in the furnace till nine o'clock, and return immediately after school closed in the afternoon for at least two more hours of work.

The schoolhouse was some distance from the furnace, and as I had to work till nine o'clock, and the school opened at nine, I found myself in a difficulty. School would always be begun before I reached it, and sometimes my class had recited. To get around this difficulty I yielded to a temptation for which most people, I suppose, will condemn me; but since it is a fact, I might as well state it. I have great faith in the power and influence of facts. It is seldom that anything is permanently gained by holding back a fact. There was a large clock in a little office in the furnace. This clock, of course, all the hundred or more workmen depended upon to regulate their hours of beginning and ending the day's work. I got the idea that the way for me to reach school on time was to move the clock hands from half-past eight up to the nine o'clock mark. This I found myself doing morning after morning, till the furnace "boss" discovered that something was wrong, and locked the clock in a case. I did not mean to inconvenience anybody. I simply meant to reach that schoolhouse in time.

When, however, I found myself at the school for the first time, I also found myself confronted with two other difficulties. In the first place, I found that all of the other children wore hats or caps on their heads, and I had neither hat nor cap. In fact, I do not remember that up to the time of going to school I had ever worn any kind of covering upon my head, nor do I recall that either I or anybody else had even thought anything about the need of covering for my head. But, of course, when I saw how all the other boys were dressed, I began to feel quite uncomfortable. As usual, I put the case before my mother, and she explained to me that she had no money with which to buy a "store hat," which was a rather new institution at that time among the members of my race and was considered quite the thing for young and old to own, but that she would find a way to help me out of the difficulty. She accordingly got two pieces of "homespun" (jeans) and sewed them together, and I was soon the proud possessor of my first cap.

The lesson that my mother taught me in this has always remained with me, and I have tried as best I could to teach it to others. I have always felt proud, whenever I think of the incident, that my mother had strength of character enough not to be led into the temptation of seeming to be that which she was not—of trying to impress my schoolmates and others with the fact that she was able to buy me a "store hat" when she was not. I have always felt proud that she refused to go into debt for that which she did not have the money to pay for. Since that time I have owned many kinds of caps and hats, but never one of which I have felt so proud as of the cap made of the two pieces of cloth sewed together by my mother. I have noted the fact, but without satisfaction, I need not add, that several of the boys who began their careers with "store hats" and who were my schoolmates and used to join in the sport that was made of me because I had only a "homespun" cap, have ended their careers in the penitentiary, while others are not able now to buy any kind of hat.

My second difficulty was with regard to my name, or rather *a* name. From the time when I could remember anything, I had been called simply "Booker." Before going to school it had never occurred to me that it was needful or appropriate to have an additional name. When I heard the school-roll called, I noticed that all of the children had at least two names, and some of them indulged in what seemed to me the extravagance of having three. I was in deep perplexity, because I knew that the teacher would demand of me at least two names, and I had only one. By the time the occasion came for the enrolling of my name, an idea occurred to me which I thought would make me equal to the situation; and so, when the teacher asked me what my full name was, I calmly told him "Booker Washington," as if I had been called by that name all my life; and by that name I have since been known. Later in my life I found that my mother had given me the name of "Booker Taliaferro" soon after I was born, but in some way that part of my name seemed to disappear and for a long while was forgotten, but as soon as I found out about it I revived it, and made my full name "Booker Taliaferro Washington." I think there are not many men in our country who have had the privilege of naming themselves in the way that I have.

More than once I have tried to picture myself in the position of a boy or man with an honoured and distinguished ancestry which I could trace back through a period of hundreds of years, and who had not only inherited a name, but fortune and a proud family homestead; and yet I have sometimes had the feeling that if I had inherited these, and had been a member of a more popular race, I should have been inclined to yield to the temptation of depending upon my ancestry and my colour to do that for me which I should do for myself. Years ago I resolved that because I had no ancestry myself I would leave a record of which my children would be proud, and which might encourage them to still higher effort.

The world should not pass judgment upon the Negro, and especially the Negro youth, too quickly or too harshly. The Negro boy has obstacles, discouragements, and temptations to battle with that are little known to those not situated as he is. When a white boy undertakes a task, it is taken for granted that he will succeed. On the other hand, people are usually surprised if the Negro boy does not fail. In a word, the Negro youth starts out with the presumption against him.

The influence of ancestry, however, is important in helping forward any individual or race, if too much reliance is not placed upon it. Those who constantly direct attention to the Negro youth's moral weaknesses, and compare his advancement with that of white youths, do not consider the influence of the memories which cling about the old family homesteads. I have no idea, as I have stated elsewhere, who my grandmother was. I have, or have had, uncles and aunts and cousins, but I have no knowledge as to where most of them are. My case will illustrate that of hundreds of thousands of black people in every part of our country. The very fact that the white boy is conscious that, if he fails in life, he will disgrace the whole family record, extending back through many generations, is of tremendous value in helping him to resist temptations. The fact that the individual has behind and surrounding him proud family history and connection serves as a stimulus to help him to overcome obstacles when striving for success.

The time that I was permitted to attend school during the day was short, and my attendance was irregular. It was not long before I had to stop attending day-school altogether, and devote all of my time again to work. I resorted to the night-school again. In fact, the greater part of the education I secured in my boyhood was gathered through the night-school after my day's work was done. I had difficulty often in securing a satisfactory teacher. Sometimes, after I had secured some one to teach me at night, I would find, much to my disappointment, that the teacher knew but little more than I did. Often I would have to walk several miles at night in order to recite my night-school lessons. There was never a time in my youth, no matter how dark and discouraging the days might be, when one resolve did not continually remain with me, and that was a determination to secure an education at any cost.

Soon after we moved to West Virginia, my mother adopted into our family, notwithstanding our poverty, an orphan boy, to whom afterward we gave the name of James B. Washington. He has ever since remained a member of the family.

After I had worked in the salt-furnace for some time, work was secured for me in a coal-mine which was operated mainly for the purpose of securing fuel for the salt-furnace. Work in the coal-mine I always dreaded. One reason for this was that any one who worked in a coal-mine was always unclean, at least while at work, and it was a very hard job to get one's skin clean after the day's work was over. Then it was fully a mile from the opening of the coal-mine to the face of the coal, and all, of course, was in the blackest darkness. I do not believe that one ever experiences anywhere else such darkness as he does in a coal-mine. The mine was divided into a large number of different "rooms" or departments, and, as I never was able to learn the location of all these "rooms," I many times found myself lost in the mine. To add to the horror of being lost, sometimes my light would go out, and then, if I did not happen to have a match, I would wander about in the darkness until by chance I found some one to give me a light. The work was not only hard, but it was dangerous. There was always the danger of being blown to pieces by a premature explosion of powder, or of being crushed by falling slate. Accidents from one or the other of these causes were frequently occurring, and this kept me in constant fear. Many children of the tenderest years were compelled then, as is now true I fear, in most coal-mining districts, to spend a large part of their lives in these coal-mines, with little opportunity to get an education; and, what is worse, I have often noted that, as a rule, young boys who begin life in a coal-mine are often physically and mentally dwarfed. They soon lose ambition to do anything else than to continue as a coal-miner.

In those days, and later as a young man, I used to try to picture in my imagination the feelings and ambitions of a white boy with absolutely no limit placed upon his aspirations and activities. I used to envy the white boy who had no obstacles placed in the way of his becoming a Congressman, Governor, Bishop, or President by reason of the accident of his birth or race. I used to picture the way that I would act under such circumstances; how I would begin at the bottom and keep rising until I reached the highest round of success.

In later years, I confess that I do not envy the white boy as I once did. I have learned that success is to be measured not so much by the position that one has

reached in life as by the obstacles which he has overcome while trying to succeed. Looked at from this
standpoint, I almost reach the conclusion that often
the Negro boy's birth and connection with an unpop-
ular race is an advantage, so far as real life is concerned. With few exceptions, the Negro youth must
work harder and must perform his tasks even better
than a white youth in order to secure recognition. But
out of the hard and unusual struggle through which
he is compelled to pass, he gets a strength, a confidence, that one misses whose pathway is compara-
tively smooth by reason of birth and race.

From any point of view, I had rather be what I am,
a member of the Negro race, than be able to claim
membership with the most favoured of any other race.
I have always been made sad when I have heard members of any race claiming rights and privileges, or certain badges of distinction, on the ground simply that
they were members of this or that race, regardless of
their own individual worth or attainments. I have
been made to feel sad for such persons because I am
conscious of the fact that mere connection with what
is known as a superior race will not permanently carry
an individual forward unless he has individual worth,
and mere connection with what is regarded as an inferior race will not finally hold an individual back if he
possesses intrinsic, individual merit. Every persecuted

individual and race should get much consolation out of the great human law, which is universal and eternal, that merit, no matter under what skin found, is, in the long run, recognized and rewarded. This I have said here, not to call attention to myself as an individual, but to the race to which I am proud to belong.

CHAPTER III

THE STRUGGLE FOR AN EDUCATION

O NE DAY, while at work in the coal-mine, I happened to overhear two miners talking about a great school for coloured people somewhere in Virginia. This was the first time that I had ever heard anything about any kind of school or college that was more pretentious than the little coloured school in our town.

In the darkness of the mine I noiselessly crept as close as I could to the two men who were talking. I heard one tell the other that not only was the school established for the members of my race, but that opportunities were provided by which poor but worthy students could work out all or a part of the cost of board, and at the same time be taught some trade or industry.

As they went on describing the school, it seemed to me that it must be the greatest place on earth, and not even Heaven presented more attractions for me at that time than did the Hampton Normal and Agricultural Institute in Virginia, about which these men were talking. I resolved at once to go to that school, although I had no idea where it was, or how many miles away, or how I was going to reach it; I remembered only that I was on fire constantly with one ambition, and that was to go to Hampton. This thought was with me day and night.

After hearing of the Hampton Institute, I continued to work for a few months longer in the coal-mine. While at work there, I heard of a vacant position in the household of General Lewis Ruffner, the owner of the salt-furnace and coal-mine. Mrs. Viola Ruffner, the wife of General Ruffner, was a "Yankee" woman from Vermont. Mrs. Ruffner had a reputation all through the vicinity for being very strict with her servants, and especially with the boys who tried to serve her. Few of them had remained with her more than two or three weeks. They all left with the same excuse: she was too strict. I decided, however, that I would rather try Mrs. Ruffner's house than remain in the coal-mine, and so my mother applied to her for the vacant position. I was hired at a salary of $5 per month.

I had heard so much about Mrs. Ruffner's severity that I was almost afraid to see her, and trembled when I went into her presence. I had not lived with her many weeks, however, before I began to understand her. I soon began to learn that, first of all, she wanted everything kept clean about her, that she wanted things done promptly and systematically, and that at the bottom of everything she wanted absolute honesty and frankness. Nothing must be sloven or slipshod; every door, every fence, must be kept in repair.

I cannot now recall how long I lived with Mrs. Ruffner before going to Hampton, but I think it must have been a year and a half. At any rate, I here repeat what I have said more than once before, that the lessons that I learned in the home of Mrs. Ruffner were as valuable to me as any education I have ever gotten anywhere since. Even to this day I never see bits of paper scattered around a house or in the street that I do not want to pick them up at once. I never see a filthy yard that I do not want to clean it, a paling off of a fence that I do not want to put it on, an unpainted or unwhitewashed house that I do not want to paint or whitewash it, or a button off one's clothes, or a grease-spot on them or on a floor, that I do not want to call attention to it.

From fearing Mrs. Ruffner I soon learned to look upon her as one of my best friends. When she found that she could trust me she did so implicitly. During the one or two winters that I was with her she gave me an opportunity to go to school for an hour in the day during a portion of the winter months, but most of my studying was done at night, sometimes alone, sometimes under some one whom I could hire to teach me. Mrs. Ruffner always encouraged and sympathized with me in all my efforts to get an education. It was while living with her that I began to get together my first library. I secured a dry-goods box, knocked out one side of it, put some shelves in it, and began putting into it every kind of book that I could get my hands upon, and called it my "library."

Notwithstanding my success at Mrs. Ruffner's I did not give up the idea of going to the Hampton Institute. In the fall of 1872 I determined to make an effort to get there, although, as I have stated, I had no definite idea of the direction in which Hampton was, or of what it would cost to go there. I do not think that any one thoroughly sympathized with me in my ambition to go to Hampton unless it was my mother, and she was troubled with a grave fear that I was starting out on a "wild-goose chase." At any rate, I got only a half-hearted consent from her that I might start. The small amount of money that I had earned had been consumed by my stepfather and the remainder of the family, with the exception of a very few dollars, and so I had very little with which to buy clothes and pay my travelling expenses. My brother John helped me all that he could, but of course that was not a great deal, for his work was in the coal-mine, where he did not earn much, and most of what he did earn went in the direction of paying the household expenses.

Perhaps the thing that touched and pleased me most in connection with my starting for Hampton was the interest that many of the older coloured people took in the matter. They had spent the best days of their lives in slavery, and hardly expected to live to see the time when they would see a member of their race leave home to attend a boarding-school. Some of these older people would give me a nickel, others a quarter, or a handkerchief.

Finally the great day came, and I started for Hampton. I had only a small, cheap satchel that contained what few articles of clothing I could get. My mother at the time was rather weak and broken in health. I hardly expected to see her again, and thus our parting was all the more sad. She, however, was very brave through it all. At that time there were no through trains connecting that part of West Virginia with eastern Virginia. Trains ran only a portion of the way, and the remainder of the distance was travelled by stage-coaches.

The distance from Malden to Hampton is about five hundred miles. I had not been away from home many hours before it began to grow painfully evident that I did not have enough money to pay my fare to Hampton. One experience I shall long remember. I had been travelling over the mountains most of the afternoon in an old-fashioned stage-coach, when, late in the evening, the coach stopped for the night at a common, unpainted house called a hotel. All the other passengers except myself were whites. In my ignorance I supposed that the little hotel existed for the purpose of accommodating the passengers who travelled on the stage-coach. The difference that the colour of one's skin would make I had not thought anything about. After all the other passengers had been shown rooms and were getting ready for supper, I shyly presented myself before the man at the desk. It is true I had practically no money in my pocket with which to pay for bed or food, but I had hoped in some way to beg my way into the good graces of the landlord, for at that season in the mountains of Virginia the weather was cold, and I wanted to get indoors for the night. Without asking as to whether I had any money, the man at the desk firmly refused to even consider the matter of providing me with food or lodging. This was my first experience in finding out what the colour of my skin meant. In some way I managed to keep warm by walking about, and so got through the night. My whole soul was so bent upon reaching Hampton that I did not have time to cherish any bitterness toward the hotel-keeper.

By walking, begging rides both in wagons and in

the cars, in some way, after a number of days, I reached the city of Richmond, Virginia, about eighty-two miles from Hampton. When I reached there, tired, hungry, and dirty, it was late in the night. I had never been in a large city, and this rather added to my misery. When I reached Richmond, I was completely out of money. I had not a single acquaintance in the place, and, being unused to city ways, I did not know where to go. I applied at several places for lodging, but they all wanted money, and that was what I did not have. Knowing nothing else better to do, I walked the streets. In doing this I passed by many food-stands where fried chicken and half-moon apple pies were piled high and made to present a most tempting appearance. At that time it seemed to me that I would have promised all that I expected to possess in the future to have gotten hold of one of those chicken legs or one of those pies. But I could not get either of these, nor anything else to eat.

I must have walked the streets till after midnight. At last I became so exhausted that I could walk no longer. I was tired, I was hungry, I was everything but discouraged. Just about the time when I reached extreme physical exhaustion, I came upon a portion of a street where the board sidewalk was considerably elevated. I waited for a few minutes, till I was sure that no passers-by could see me, and then crept under the sidewalk and lay for the night upon the ground, with my satchel of clothing for a pillow. Nearly all night I could hear the tramp of feet over my head. The next morning I found myself somewhat refreshed, but I was extremely hungry, because it had been a long time since I had had sufficient food. As soon as it became light enough for me to see my surroundings I noticed that I was near a large ship, and that this ship seemed to be unloading a cargo of pig iron. I went at once to the vessel and asked the captain to permit me to help unload the vessel in order to get money for food. The captain, a white man, who seemed to be kind-hearted, consented. I worked long enough to earn money for my breakfast, and it seems to me, as I remember it now, to have been about the best breakfast that I have ever eaten.

My work pleased the captain so well that he told me if I desired I could continue working for a small amount per day. This I was very glad to do. I continued working on this vessel for a number of days. After buying food with the small wages I received there was not much left to add to the amount I must get to pay my way to Hampton. In order to economize in every way possible, so as to be sure to reach Hampton in a reasonable time, I continued to sleep under the same sidewalk that gave me shelter the first night I was in Richmond. Many years after that the coloured

citizens of Richmond very kindly tendered me a reception at which there must have been two thousand
people present. This reception was held not far from
the spot where I slept the first night I spent in that
city, and I must confess that my mind was more upon
the sidewalk that first gave me shelter than upon the
reception, agreeable and cordial as it was.

When I had saved what I considered enough
money with which to reach Hampton, I thanked the
captain of the vessel for his kindness, and started
again. Without any unusual occurrence I reached
Hampton, with a surplus of exactly fifty cents with
which to begin my education. To me it had been a
long, eventful journey; but the first sight of the large,
three-story, brick school building seemed to have rewarded me for all that I had undergone in order to
reach the place. If the people who gave the money to
provide that building could appreciate the influence
the sight of it had upon me, as well as upon thousands
of other youths, they would feel all the more encouraged to make such gifts. It seemed to me to be the
largest and most beautiful building I had ever seen.
The sight of it seemed to give me new life. I felt that
a new kind of existence had now begun—that life
would now have a new meaning. I felt that I had
reached the promised land, and I resolved to let no
obstacle prevent me from putting forth the highest ef-

fort to fit myself to accomplish the most good in the world.

As soon as possible after reaching the grounds of the Hampton Institute, I presented myself before the head teacher for assignment to a class. Having been so long without proper food, a bath, and change of clothing, I did not, of course, make a very favourable impression upon her, and I could see at once that there were doubts in her mind about the wisdom of admitting me as a student. I felt that I could hardly blame her if she got the idea that I was a worthless loafer or tramp. For some time she did not refuse to admit me, neither did she decide in my favour, and I continued to linger about her, and to impress her in all the ways I could with my worthiness. In the meantime I saw her admitting other students, and that added greatly to my discomfort, for I felt, deep down in my heart, that I could do as well as they, if I could only get a chance to show what was in me.

After some hours had passed, the head teacher said to me: "The adjoining recitation-room needs sweeping. Take the broom and sweep it."

It occurred to me at once that here was my chance. Never did I receive an order with more delight. I knew that I could sweep, for Mrs. Ruffner had thoroughly taught me how to do that when I lived with her.

I swept the recitation-room three times. Then I got

a dusting-cloth and I dusted it four times. All the woodwork around the walls, every bench, table, and desk, I went over four times with my dusting-cloth. Besides, every piece of furniture had been moved and every closet and corner in the room had been thoroughly cleaned. I had the feeling that in a large measure my future depended upon the impression I made upon the teacher in the cleaning of that room. When I was through, I reported to the head teacher. She was a "Yankee" woman who knew just where to look for dirt. She went into the room and inspected the floor and closets; then she took her handkerchief and rubbed it on the woodwork about the walls, and over the table and benches. When she was unable to find one bit of dirt on the floor, or a particle of dust on any of the furniture, she quietly remarked, "I guess you will do to enter this institution."

I was one of the happiest souls on earth. The sweeping of that room was my college examination, and never did any youth pass an examination for entrance into Harvard or Yale that gave him more genuine satisfaction. I have passed several examinations since then, but I have always felt that this was the best one I ever passed.

I have spoken of my own experience in entering the Hampton Institute. Perhaps few, if any, had anything like the same experience that I had, but about that same period there were hundreds who found their way to Hampton and other institutions after experiencing something of the same difficulties that I went through. The young men and women were determined to secure an education at any cost.

The sweeping of the recitation-room in the manner that I did it seems to have paved the way for me to get through Hampton. Miss Mary F. Mackie, the head teacher, offered me a position as janitor. This, of course, I gladly accepted, because it was a place where I could work out nearly all the cost of my board. The work was hard and taxing, but I stuck to it. I had a large number of rooms to care for, and had to work late into the night, while at the same time I had to rise by four o'clock in the morning, in order to build the fires and have a little time in which to prepare my lessons. In all my career at Hampton, and ever since I have been out in the world, Miss Mary F. Mackie, the head teacher to whom I have referred, proved one of my strongest and most helpful friends. Her advice and encouragement were always helpful and strengthening to me in the darkest hour.

I have spoken of the impression that was made upon me by the buildings and general appearance of the Hampton Institute, but I have not spoken of that which made the greatest and most lasting impression upon me, and that was a great man—the noblest, rarest human being that it has ever been my privilege to meet. I refer to the late General Samuel C. Armstrong.

It has been my fortune to meet personally many of what are called great characters, both in Europe and America, but I do not hesitate to say that I never met any man who, in my estimation, was the equal of General Armstrong. Fresh from the degrading influences of the slave plantation and the coal-mines, it was a rare privilege for me to be permitted to come into direct contact with such a character as General Armstrong. I shall always remember that the first time I went into his presence he made the impression upon me of being a perfect man; I was made to feel that there was something about him that was superhuman. It was my privilege to know the General personally from the time I entered Hampton till he died, and the more I saw of him the greater he grew in my estimation. One might have removed from Hampton all the buildings, class-rooms, teachers, and industries, and given the men and women there the opportunity of coming into daily contact with General Armstrong, and that alone would have been a liberal education. The older I grow, the more I am convinced that there is no education which one can get from books and costly apparatus that is equal to that which can be gotten from contact with great men and women. Instead of studying books so constantly, how I wish that our schools and colleges might learn to study men and things!

General Armstrong spent two of the last six months of his life in my home at Tuskegee. At that time he was paralyzed to the extent that he had lost control of his body and voice in a very large degree. Notwithstanding his affliction, he worked almost constantly night and day for the cause to which he had given his life. I never saw a man who so completely lost sight of himself. I do not believe he ever had a selfish thought. He was just as happy in trying to assist some other institution in the South as he was when working for Hampton. Although he fought the Southern white man in the Civil War, I never heard him utter a bitter word against him afterward. On the other hand, he was constantly seeking to find ways by which he could be of service to the Southern whites.

It would be difficult to describe the hold that he had upon the students at Hampton, or the faith they had in him. In fact, he was worshipped by his students. It never occurred to me that General Armstrong could fail in anything that he undertook. There is almost no request that he could have made that would not have been complied with. When he was a guest at my home in Alabama, and was so badly paralyzed that he had to be wheeled about in an invalid's chair, I recall that one of the General's former students had occasion to push his chair up a long, steep hill that taxed his strength to the utmost. When the top of the hill was reached, the former pupil, with a glow of happiness on his face, exclaimed, "I am so glad that I have been permitted to do something that was real hard for the General before he dies!" While I was a student at Hampton, the dormitories became so crowded that it was impossible to find room for all who wanted to be admitted. In order to help remedy the difficulty, the General conceived the plan of putting up tents to be used as rooms. As soon as it became known that General Armstrong would be pleased if some of the older students would live in the tents during the winter, nearly every student in school volunteered to go.

I was one of the volunteers. The winter that we spent in those tents was an intensely cold one, and we suffered severely—how much I am sure General Armstrong never knew, because we made no complaints. It was enough for us to know that we were pleasing General Armstrong, and that we were making it possible for an additional number of students to secure an education. More than once, during a cold night, when a stiff gale would be blowing, our tent was lifted bodily, and we would find ourselves in the open air. The General would usually pay a visit to the tents early in the morning, and his earnest, cheerful, encouraging voice would dispel any feeling of despondency.

I have spoken of my admiration for General Armstrong, and yet he was but a type of that Christlike body of men and women who went into the Negro schools at the close of the war by the hundreds to assist in lifting up my race. The history of the world fails to show a higher, purer, and more unselfish class of men and women than those who found their way into those Negro schools.

Life at Hampton was a constant revelation to me; was constantly taking me into a new world. The matter of having meals at regular hours, of eating on a tablecloth, using a napkin, the use of the bath-tub and of the tooth-brush, as well as the use of sheets upon the bed, were all new to me.

I sometimes feel that almost the most valuable lesson I got at the Hampton Institute was in the use and value of the bath. I learned there for the first time some of its value, not only in keeping the body healthy, but in inspiring self-respect and promoting virtue. In all my travels in the South and elsewhere since leaving Hampton I have always in some way sought my daily bath. To get it sometimes when I have been the guest of my own people in a single-roomed cabin has not always been easy to do, except by slipping away to some stream in the woods. I have always tried to teach my people that some provision for bathing should be a part of every house.

For some time, while a student at Hampton, I possessed but a single pair of socks, but when I had worn these till they became soiled, I would wash them at night and hang them by the fire to dry, so that I might wear them again the next morning.

The charge for my board at Hampton was ten dollars per month. I was expected to pay a part of this in cash and to work out the remainder. To meet this cash payment, as I have stated, I had just fifty cents when I reached the institution. Aside from a very few dollars that my brother John was able to send me once in a while, I had no money with which to pay my board. I was determined from the first to make my work as janitor so valuable that my services would be indispensable. This I succeeded in doing to such an extent that I was soon informed that I would be allowed the full cost of my board in return for my work. The cost of tuition was seventy dollars a year. This, of course, was wholly beyond my ability to provide. If I had been compelled to pay the seventy dollars for tuition, in addition to providing for my board, I would have been compelled to leave the Hampton school. General Armstrong, however, very kindly got Mr. S. Griffitts Morgan, of New Bedford, Mass., to defray the cost of my tuition during the whole time that I was at Hampton. After I finished the course at Hampton and had entered upon my lifework at Tuskegee, I had the pleasure of visiting Mr. Morgan several times.

After having been for a while at Hampton, I found myself in difficulty because I did not have books and clothing. Usually, however, I got around the trouble about books by borrowing from those who were more fortunate than myself. As to clothes, when I reached Hampton I had practically nothing. Everything that I possessed was in a small hand satchel. My anxiety about clothing was increased because of the fact that General Armstrong made a personal inspection of the young men in ranks, to see that their clothes were clean. Shoes had to be polished, there must be no buttons off the clothing, and no grease-spots. To wear one suit of clothes continually, while at work and in the schoolroom, and at the same time keep it clean, was rather a hard problem for me to solve. In some way I managed to get on till the teachers learned that I was in earnest and meant to succeed, and then some of them were kind enough to see that I was partly supplied with second-hand clothing that had been sent in barrels from the North. These barrels proved a blessing to hundreds of poor but deserving students. Without them I question whether I should ever have gotten through Hampton.

When I first went to Hampton I do not recall that

I had ever slept in a bed that had two sheets on it. In those days there were not many buildings there, and room was very precious. There were seven other boys in the same room with me; most of them, however, students who had been there for some time. The sheets were quite a puzzle to me. The first night I slept under both of them, and the second night I slept on top of both of them; but by watching the other boys I learned my lesson in this, and have been trying to follow it ever since and to teach it to others.

I was among the youngest of the students who were in Hampton at that time. Most of the students were men and women—some as old as forty years of age. As I now recall the scene of my first year, I do not believe that one often has the opportunity of coming into contact with three or four hundred men and women who were so tremendously in earnest as these men and women were. Every hour was occupied in study or work. Nearly all had had enough actual contact with the world to teach them the need of education. Many of the older ones were, of course, too old to master the text-books very thoroughly, and it was often sad to watch their struggles; but they made up in earnestness much of what they lacked in books. Many of them were as poor as I was, and, besides having to wrestle with their books, they had to struggle with a poverty which prevented their having the necessities of life. Many of them had aged parents who were dependent upon them, and some of them were men who had wives whose support in some way they had to provide for.

The great and prevailing idea that seemed to take possession of every one was to prepare himself to lift up the people at his home. No one seemed to think of himself. And the officers and teachers, what a rare set of human beings they were! They worked for the students night and day, in season and out of season. They seemed happy only when they were helping the students in some manner. Whenever it is written—and I hope it will be—the part that the Yankee teachers played in the education of the Negroes immediately after the war will make one of the most thrilling parts of the history of this country. The time is not far distant when the whole South will appreciate this service in a way that it has not yet been able to do.

CHAPTER IV

HELPING OTHERS

AT THE end of my first year at Hampton I was confronted with another difficulty. Most of the students went home to spend their vacation. I had no money with which to go home, but I had to go somewhere. In those days very few students were permitted to remain at the school during vacation. It made me feel very sad and homesick to see the other students preparing to leave and starting for home. I not only had no money with which to go home, but I had none with which to go anywhere.

In some way, however, I had gotten hold of an extra, second-hand coat which I thought was a pretty valuable coat. This I decided to sell, in order to get a little money for travelling expenses. I had a good deal of boyish pride, and I tried to hide, as far as I could, from the other students the fact that I had no money and nowhere to go. I made it known to a few people in the town of Hampton that I had this coat to sell,

60

and, after a good deal of persuading, one coloured man promised to come to my room to look the coat over and consider the matter of buying it. This cheered my drooping spirits considerably. Early the next morning my prospective customer appeared. After looking the garment over carefully, he asked me how much I wanted for it. I told him I thought it was worth three dollars. He seemed to agree with me as to price, but remarked in the most matter-of-fact way: "I tell you what I will do; I will take the coat, and I will pay you five cents, cash down, and pay you the rest of the money just as soon as I can get it." It is not hard to imagine what my feelings were at the time.

With this disappointment I gave up all hope of getting out of the town of Hampton for my vacation work. I wanted very much to go where I might secure work that would at least pay me enough to purchase some much-needed clothing and other necessities. In a few days practically all the students and teachers had left for their homes, and this served to depress my spirits even more.

After trying for several days in and near the town of Hampton, I finally secured work in a restaurant at Fortress Monroe. The wages, however, were very little more than my board. At night, and between meals, I found considerable time for study and reading; and in this direction I improved myself very much during the summer.

When I left school at the end of my first year, I owed the institution sixteen dollars that I had not been able to work out. It was my greatest ambition during the summer to save money enough with which to pay this debt. I felt that this was a debt of honour, and that I could hardly bring myself to the point of even trying to enter school again till it was paid. I economized in every way that I could think of—did my own washing, and went without necessary garments—but still I found my summer vacation ending and I did not have the sixteen dollars.

One day, during the last week of my stay in the restaurant, I found under one of the tables a crisp, new ten-dollar bill. I could hardly contain myself, I was so happy. As it was not my place of business I felt it to be the proper thing to show the money to the proprietor. This I did. He seemed as glad as I was, but he coolly explained to me that, as it was his place of business, he had a right to keep the money, and he proceeded to do so. This, I confess, was another pretty hard blow to me. I will not say that I became discouraged, for as I now look back over my life I do not recall that I ever became discouraged over anything that I set out to accomplish. I have begun everything with the idea that I could succeed, and I never had much patience with the multitudes of people who are always ready to explain why one cannot succeed. I have always had a high regard for the man who could tell me how to succeed. I determined to face the situation just as it was. At the end of the week I went to the treasurer of the Hampton Institute, General J. F. B. Marshall, and told him frankly my condition. To my gratification he told me that I could reënter the institution, and that he would trust me to pay the debt when I could. During the second year I continued to work as a janitor.

The education that I received at Hampton out of the text-books was but a small part of what I learned there. One of the things that impressed itself upon me deeply, the second year, was the unselfishness of the teachers. It was hard for me to understand how any individuals could bring themselves to the point where they could be so happy in working for others. Before the end of the year, I think I began learning that those who are happiest are those who do the most for others. This lesson I have tried to carry with me ever since.

I also learned a valuable lesson at Hampton by coming into contact with the best breeds of live stock and fowls. No student, I think, who has had the opportunity of doing this could go out into the world and content himself with the poorest grades.

Perhaps the most valuable thing that I got out of my second year was an understanding of the use and value of the Bible. Miss Nathalie Lord, one of the teachers, from Portland, Me., taught me how to use and love the Bible. Before this I had never cared a great deal about it, but now I learned to love to read the Bible, not only for the spiritual help which it gives, but on account of it as literature. The lessons taught me in this respect took such a hold upon me that at the present time, when I am at home, no matter how busy I am, I always make it a rule to read a chapter or a portion of a chapter in the morning, before beginning the work of the day.

Whatever ability I may have as a public speaker I owe in a measure to Miss Lord. When she found out that I had some inclination in this direction, she gave me private lessons in the matter of breathing, emphasis, and articulation. Simply to be able to talk in public for the sake of talking has never had the least attraction for me. In fact, I consider that there is nothing so empty and unsatisfactory as mere abstract public speaking; but from my early childhood I have had a desire to do something to make the world better, and then to be able to speak to the world about that thing.

The debating societies at Hampton were a constant source of delight to me. These were held on Saturday evening; and during my whole life at Hampton I do not recall that I missed a single meeting. I not only attended the weekly debating society, but was instrumental in organizing an additional society. I noticed that between the time when supper was over and the time to begin evening study there were about twenty minutes which the young men usually spent in idle gossip. About twenty of us formed a society for the purpose of utilizing this time in debate or in practice in public speaking. Few persons ever derived more happiness or benefit from the use of twenty minutes of time than we did in this way.

At the end of my second year at Hampton, by the help of some money sent me by my mother and brother John, supplemented by a small gift from one of the teachers at Hampton, I was enabled to return to my home in Malden, West Virginia, to spend my vacation. When I reached home I found that the salt-furnaces were not running, and that the coal-mine was not being operated on account of the miners being out on a "strike." This was something which, it seemed, usually occurred whenever the men got two or three months ahead in their savings. During the strike, of course, they spent all that they had saved, and would often return to work in debt at the same wages, or would move to another mine at considerable expense. In either case, my observations convinced me that the miners were worse off at the end of a strike. Before the days of strikes in that section of the country, I knew miners who had considerable money in the bank, but as soon as the professional labour agitators got control, the savings of even the more thrifty ones began disappearing.

My mother and the other members of the family were, of course, much rejoiced to see me and to note the improvement that I had made during my two years' absence. The rejoicing on the part of all classes of the coloured people, and especially the older ones, over my return, was almost pathetic. I had to pay a visit to each family and take a meal with each, and at each place tell the story of my experiences at Hampton. In addition to this I had to speak before the church and Sunday-school, and at various other places. The thing that I was most in search of, though, work, I could not find. There was no work on account of the strike. I spent nearly the whole of the first month of my vacation in an effort to find something to do by which I could earn money to pay my way back to Hampton and save a little money to use after reaching there.

Toward the end of the first month, I went to a place a considerable distance from my home, to try to find employment. I did not succeed, and it was night before I got started on my return. When I had gotten within a mile or so of my home I was so completely tired out that I could not walk any farther, and I went into an old, abandoned house to spend the remainder of the night. About three o'clock in the morning my brother John found me asleep in this house, and broke to me, as gently as he could, the sad news that our dear mother had died during the night.

This seemed to me the saddest and blankest moment in my life. For several years my mother had not been in good health, but I had no idea, when I parted from her the previous day, that I should never see her alive again. Besides that, I had always had an intense desire to be with her when she did pass away. One of the chief ambitions which spurred me on at Hampton was that I might be able to get to be in a position in which I could better make my mother comfortable and happy. She had so often expressed the wish that she might be permitted to live to see her children educated and started out into the world.

In a very short time after the death of my mother our little home was in confusion. My sister Amanda, although she tried to do the best she could, was too young to know anything about keeping house, and my stepfather was not able to hire a housekeeper. Sometimes we had food cooked for us, and sometimes we did not. I remember that more than once a can of tomatoes and some crackers constituted a meal. Our clothing went uncared for, and everything about our home was soon in a tumble-down condition. It seems to me that this was the most dismal period of my life.

My good friend Mrs. Ruffner, to whom I have already referred, always made me welcome at her home,
and assisted me in many ways during this trying period. Before the end of the vacation she gave me some
work, and this, together with work in a coal-mine at
some distance from my home, enabled me to earn a
little money.

At one time it looked as if I would have to give up
the idea of returning to Hampton, but my heart was
so set on returning that I determined not to give up
going back without a struggle. I was very anxious to
secure some clothes for the winter, but in this I was
disappointed, except for a few garments which my
brother John secured for me. Notwithstanding my
need of money and clothing, I was very happy in the
fact that I had secured enough money to pay my travelling expenses back to Hampton. Once there, I knew
that I could make myself so useful as a janitor that I
could in some way get through the school year.

Three weeks before the time for the opening of the
term at Hampton, I was pleasantly surprised to receive a letter from my good friend Miss Mary F.
Mackie, the lady principal, asking me to return to
Hampton two weeks before the opening of the
school, in order that I might assist her in cleaning the
buildings and getting things in order for the new
school year. This was just the opportunity I wanted. It

gave me a chance to secure a credit in the treasurer's office. I started for Hampton at once.

During these two weeks I was taught a lesson which I shall never forget. Miss Mackie was a member of one of the oldest and most cultured families of the North, and yet for two weeks she worked by my side cleaning windows, dusting rooms, putting beds in order, and what not. She felt that things would not be in condition for the opening of school unless every window-pane was perfectly clean, and she took the greatest satisfaction in helping to clean them herself. The work which I have described she did every year that I was at Hampton.

It was hard for me at this time to understand how a woman of her education and social standing could take such delight in performing such service, in order to assist in the elevation of an unfortunate race. Ever since then I have had no patience with any school for my race in the South which did not teach its students the dignity of labour.

During my last year at Hampton every minute of my time that was not occupied with my duties as janitor was devoted to hard study. I was determined, if possible, to make such a record in my class as would cause me to be placed on the "honour roll" of Commencement speakers. This I was successful in doing. It was June of 1875 when I finished the regular course of study at Hampton. The greatest benefits that I got out of my life at the Hampton Institute, perhaps, may be classified under two heads:—

First was contact with a great man, General S. C. Armstrong, who, I repeat, was, in my opinion, the rarest, strongest, and most beautiful character that it has ever been my privilege to meet.

Second, at Hampton, for the first time, I learned what education was expected to do for an individual. Before going there I had a good deal of the then rather prevalent idea among our people that to secure an education meant to have a good, easy time, free from all necessity for manual labour. At Hampton I not only learned that it was not a disgrace to labour, but learned to love labour, not alone for its financial value, but for labour's own sake and for the independence and self-reliance which the ability to do something which the world wants done brings. At that institution I got my first taste of what it meant to live a life of unselfishness, my first knowledge of the fact that the happiest individuals are those who do the most to make others useful and happy.

I was completely out of money when I graduated. In company with other Hampton students, I secured a place as a table waiter in a summer hotel in Connecticut, and managed to borrow enough money with which to get there. I had not been in this hotel long before I

found out that I knew practically nothing about waiting on a hotel table. The head waiter, however, supposed that I was an accomplished waiter. He soon gave
me charge of a table at which there sat four or five
wealthy and rather aristocratic people. My ignorance of
how to wait upon them was so apparent that they
scolded me in such a severe manner that I became
frightened and left their table, leaving them sitting
there without food. As a result of this I was reduced
from the position of waiter to that of a dish-carrier.

But I determined to learn the business of waiting, and
did so within a few weeks and was restored to my former position. I have had the satisfaction of being a guest
in this hotel several times since I was a waiter there.

At the close of the hotel season I returned to my
former home in Malden, and was elected to teach the
coloured school at that place. This was the beginning
of one of the happiest periods of my life. I now felt
that I had the opportunity to help the people of my
home town to a higher life. I felt from the first that
mere book education was not all that the young people of that town needed. I began my work at eight
o'clock in the morning, and, as a rule, it did not end
until ten o'clock at night. In addition to the usual routine of teaching, I taught the pupils to comb their hair,
and to keep their hands and faces clean, as well as
their clothing. I gave special attention to teaching

them the proper use of the tooth-brush and the bath. In all my teaching I have watched carefully the influence of the tooth-brush, and I am convinced that there are few single agencies of civilization that are more far-reaching.

There were so many of the older boys and girls in the town, as well as men and women, who had to work in the daytime but still were craving an opportunity for some education, that I soon opened a night-school. From the first, this was crowded every night, being about as large as the school that I taught in the day. The efforts of some of the men and women, who in many cases were over fifty years of age, to learn, were in some cases very pathetic.

My day and night school work was not all that I undertook. I established a small reading-room and a debating society. On Sundays I taught two Sunday-schools, one in the town of Malden in the afternoon, and the other in the morning at a place three miles distant from Malden. In addition to this, I gave private lessons to several young men whom I was fitting to send to the Hampton Institute. Without regard to pay and with little thought of it, I taught any one who wanted to learn anything that I could teach him. I was supremely happy in the opportunity of being able to assist somebody else. I did receive, however, a small salary from the public fund, for my work as a public-school teacher.

During the time that I was a student at Hampton my older brother, John, not only assisted me all that he could, but worked all of the time in the coal-mines in order to support the family. He willingly neglected his own education that he might help me. It was my earnest wish to help him to prepare to enter Hampton, and to save money to assist him in his expenses there. Both of these objects I was successful in accomplishing. In three years my brother finished the course at Hampton, and he is now holding the important position of Superintendent of Industries at Tuskegee. When he returned from Hampton, we both combined our efforts and savings to send our adopted brother, James, through the Hampton Institute. This we succeeded in doing, and he is now the postmaster at the Tuskegee Institute. The year 1877, which was my second year of teaching in Malden, I spent very much as I did the first.

It was while my home was at Malden that what was known as the "Ku Klux Klan" was in the height of its activity. The "Ku Klux" were bands of men who had joined themselves together for the purpose of regulating the conduct of the coloured people, especially with the object of preventing the members of the race from exercising any influence in politics. They corresponded somewhat to the "patrollers" of whom I used to hear a great deal during the days of slavery, when I was a small boy. The "patrollers" were bands of white men— usually young men—who were organized largely for the purpose of regulating the conduct of the slaves at night in such matters as preventing the slaves from going from one plantation to another without passes, and for preventing them from holding any kind of meetings without permission and without the presence at these meetings of at least one white man.

Like the "patrollers" the "Ku Klux" operated almost wholly at night. They were, however, more cruel than the "patrollers." Their objects, in the main, were to crush out the political aspirations of the Negroes, but they did not confine themselves to this, because schoolhouses as well as churches were burned by them, and many innocent persons were made to suffer. During this period not a few coloured people lost their lives.

As a young man, the acts of these lawless bands made a great impression upon me. I saw one open battle take place at Malden between some of the coloured and white people. There must have been not far from a hundred persons engaged on each side; many on both sides were seriously injured, among them being General Lewis Ruffner, the husband of my friend Mrs. Viola Ruffner. General Ruffner tried to defend the coloured people, and for this he was knocked down and so seriously wounded that he never completely recovered. It seemed to me as I watched this struggle between members of the two races, that there was no hope for our people in this country. The "Ku Klux" period was, I think, the darkest part of the Reconstruction days.

I have referred to this unpleasant part of the history of the South simply for the purpose of calling attention to the great change that has taken place since the days of the "Ku Klux." To-day there are no such organizations in the South, and the fact that such ever existed is almost forgotten by both races. There are few places in the South now where public sentiment would permit such organizations to exist.

CHAPTER V

THE RECONSTRUCTION PERIOD

THE YEARS from 1867 to 1878 I think may be called the period of Reconstruction. This included the time that I spent as a student at Hampton and as a teacher in West Virginia. During the whole of the Reconstruction period two ideas were constantly agitating the minds of the coloured people, or, at least, the minds of a large part of the race. One of these was the craze for Greek and Latin learning, and the other was a desire to hold office.

It could not have been expected that a people who had spent generations in slavery, and before that generations in the darkest heathenism, could at first form any proper conception of what an education meant. In every part of the South, during the Reconstruction period, schools, both day and night, were filled to overflowing with people of all ages and conditions, some being as far along in age as sixty and seventy years. The ambition to secure an education was most praiseworthy and encouraging. The idea, however, was too prevalent that, as soon as one secured a little education, in some unexplainable way he would be free from most of the hardships of the world, and, at any rate, could live without manual labour. There was a further feeling that a knowledge, however little, of the Greek and Latin languages would make one a very superior human being, something bordering almost on the supernatural. I remember that the first coloured man whom I saw who knew something about foreign languages impressed me at that time as being a man of all others to be envied.

Naturally, most of our people who received some little education became teachers or preachers. While among these two classes there were many capable, earnest, godly men and women, still a large proportion took up teaching or preaching as an easy way to make a living. Many became teachers who could do little more than write their names. I remember there came into our neighbourhood one of this class, who was in search of a school to teach, and the question arose while he was there as to the shape of the earth and how he would teach the children concerning this subject. He explained his position in the matter by saying that he was prepared to teach that the earth was either flat or round, according to the preference of a majority of his patrons.

The ministry was the profession that suffered most—and still suffers, though there has been great improvement—on account of not only ignorant but in many cases immoral men who claimed that they were "called to preach." In the earlier days of freedom almost every coloured man who learned to read would receive "a call to preach" within a few days after he began reading. At my home in West Virginia the process of being called to the ministry was a very interesting one. Usually the "call" came when the individual was sitting in church. Without warning the one called would fall upon the floor as if struck by a bullet, and would lie there for hours, speechless and motionless. Then the news would spread all through the neighbourhood that this individual had received a "call." If he were inclined to resist the summons, he would fall or be made to fall a second or third time. In the end he always yielded to the call. While I wanted an education badly, I confess that in my youth I had a fear that when I had learned to read and write well I would receive one of these "calls"; but, for some reason, my call never came.

When we add the number of wholly ignorant men who preached or "exhorted" to that of those who possessed something of an education, it can be seen at a glance that the supply of ministers was large. In fact, some time ago I knew a certain church that had a total membership of about two hundred, and eighteen of that number were ministers. But, I repeat, in many communities in the South the character of the ministry is being improved, and I believe that within the next two or three decades a very large proportion of the unworthy ones will have disappeared. The "calls" to preach, I am glad to say, are not nearly so numerous now as they were formerly, and the calls to some industrial occupation are growing more numerous. The improvement that has taken place in the character of the teachers is even more marked than in the case of the ministers.

During the whole of the Reconstruction period our people throughout the South looked to the Federal Government for everything, very much as a child looks to its mother. This was not unnatural. The central government gave them freedom, and the whole Nation had been enriched for more than two centuries by the labour of the Negro. Even as a youth, and later in manhood, I had the feeling that it was cruelly wrong in the central government, at the beginning of our freedom, to fail to make some provision for the general education of our people in addition to what the states might do, so that the people would be the better prepared for the duties of citizenship.

It is easy to find fault, to remark what might have been done, and perhaps, after all, and under all the circumstances, those in charge of the conduct of affairs did the only thing that could be done at the time. Still, as I look back now over the entire period of our freedom, I cannot help feeling that it would have been wiser if some plan could have been put in operation which would have made the possession of a certain amount of education or property, or both, a test for the exercise of the franchise, and a way provided by which this test should be made to apply honestly and squarely to both the white and black races.

Though I was but little more than a youth during the period of Reconstruction, I had the feeling that mistakes were being made, and that things could not remain in the condition that they were in then very long. I felt that the Reconstruction policy, so far as it related to my race, was in a large measure on a false foundation, was artificial and forced. In many cases it seemed to me that the ignorance of my race was being used as a tool with which to help white men into office, and that there was an element in the North which wanted to punish the Southern white men by forcing the Negro into positions over the heads of the Southern whites. I felt that the Negro would be the one to suffer for this in the end. Besides, the general political agitation drew the attention of our people away from the more fundamental matters of perfecting themselves in the industries at their doors and in securing property.

The temptations to enter political life were so alluring that I came very near yielding to them at one time, but I was kept from doing so by the feeling that I would be helping in a more substantial way by assisting in the laying of the foundation of the race through a generous education of the hand, head, and heart. I saw coloured men who were members of the state legislatures, and county officers, who, in some cases, could not read or write, and whose morals were as weak as their education. Not long ago, when passing through the streets of a certain city in the South, I heard some brick-masons calling out, from the top of a two-story brick building on which they were working, for the "Governor" to "hurry up and bring up some more bricks." Several times I heard the command, "Hurry up, Governor!" "Hurry up, Governor!" My curiosity was aroused to such an extent that I made inquiry as to who the "Governor" was, and soon found that he was a coloured man who at one time had held the position of Lieutenant-Governor of his state.

But not all the coloured people who were in office during Reconstruction were unworthy of their positions, by any means. Some of them, like the late Senator B. K. Bruce, Governor Pinchback, and many others, were strong, upright, useful men. Neither were all the class designated as carpetbaggers dishonourable men. Some of them, like ex-Governor Bullock, of Georgia, were men of high character and usefulness.

Of course the coloured people, so largely without education, and wholly without experience in government, made tremendous mistakes, just as any people similarly situated would have done. Many of the Southern whites have a feeling that, if the Negro is permitted to exercise his political rights now to any degree, the mistakes of the Reconstruction period will repeat themselves. I do not think this would be true, because the Negro is a much stronger and wiser man than he was thirty-five years ago, and he is fast learning the lesson that he cannot afford to act in a manner that will alienate his Southern white neighbours from him. More and more I am convinced that the final solution of the political end of our race problem will be for each state that finds it necessary to change the law bearing upon the franchise to make the law apply with absolute honesty, and without opportunity for double dealing or evasion, to both races alike. Any other course my daily observation in the South convinces me, will be unjust to the Negro, unjust to the white man, and unfair to the rest of the states in the Union, and will be, like slavery, a sin that at some time we shall have to pay for.

In the fall of 1878, after having taught school in
Malden for two years,² and after I had succeeded in
preparing several of the young men and women, besides my two brothers, to enter the Hampton Institute,
I decided to spend some months in study at Washington, D.C. I remained there for eight months. I derived
a great deal of benefit from the studies which I pursued, and I came into contact with some strong men
and women. At the institution I attended there was no
industrial training given to the students, and I had an
opportunity of comparing the influence of an institution with no industrial training with that of one like
the Hampton Institute, that emphasized the industries. At this school I found the students, in most
cases, had more money, were better dressed, wore the
latest style of all manner of clothing, and in some cases
were more brilliant mentally. At Hampton it was a
standing rule that, while the institution would be responsible for securing some one to pay the tuition for
the students, the men and women themselves must
provide for their own board, books, clothing, and room
wholly by work, or partly by work and partly in cash.
At the institution at which I now was, I found that
a large proportion of the students by some means
had their personal expenses paid for them. At Hampton the student was constantly making the effort
through the industries to help himself, and that very

effort was of immense value in character-building. The students at the other school seemed to be less self-dependent. They seemed to give more attention to mere outward appearances. In a word, they did not appear to me to be beginning at the bottom, on a real, solid foundation, to the extent that they were at Hampton. They knew more about Latin and Greek when they left school, but they seemed to know less about life and its conditions as they would meet it at their homes. Having lived for a number of years in the midst of comfortable surroundings, they were not as much inclined as the Hampton students to go into the country districts of the South, where there was little of comfort, to take up work for our people, and they were more inclined to yield to the temptation to become hotel waiters and Pullman-car porters as their life-work.

During the time I was a student in Washington the city was crowded with coloured people, many of whom had recently come from the South. A large proportion of these people had been drawn to Washington because they felt that they could lead a life of ease there. Others had secured minor government positions, and still another large class was there in the hope of securing Federal positions. A number of coloured men—some of them very strong and brilliant—were in the House of Representatives at that time, and one, the Hon. B. K. Bruce, was in the Senate. All this tended to make Washington an attractive place for members of the coloured race. Then, too, they knew that at all times they could have the protection of the law in the District of Columbia. The public schools in Washington for coloured people were better then than they were elsewhere. I took great interest in studying the life of our people there closely at that time. I found that while among them there was a large element of substantial, worthy citizens, there was also a superficiality about the life of a large class that greatly alarmed me. I saw young coloured men who were not earning more than four dollars a week spend two dollars or more for a buggy on Sunday to ride up and down Pennsylvania Avenue in, in order that they might try to convince the world that they were worth thousands. I saw other young men who received seventy-five or one hundred dollars per month from the Government, who were in debt at the end of every month. I saw men who but a few months previous were members of Congress, then without employment and in poverty. Among a large class there seemed to be a dependence upon the Government for every conceivable thing. The members of this class had little ambition to create a position for themselves, but wanted the Federal officials to create one for them. How many times I wished then, and have often wished since, that by some power of magic I might remove the great bulk of these people into the country districts and plant them upon the soil, upon the solid and never deceptive foundation of Mother Nature, where all nations and races that have ever succeeded have gotten their start,—a start that at first may be slow and toilsome, but one that nevertheless is real.

In Washington I saw girls whose mothers were earning their living by laundrying. These girls were taught by their mothers, in rather a crude way it is true, the industry of laundrying. Later, these girls entered the public schools and remained there perhaps six or eight years. When the public-school course was finally finished, they wanted more costly dresses, more costly hats and shoes. In a word, while their wants had been increased, their ability to supply their wants had not been increased in the same degree. On the other hand, their six or eight years of book education had weaned them away from the occupation of their mothers. The result of this was in too many cases that the girls went to the bad. I often thought how much wiser it would have been to give these girls the same amount of mental training—and I favour any kind of training, whether in the languages or mathematics, that gives strength and culture to the mind—but at the same time to give them the most thorough training in the latest and best methods of laundrying and other kindred occupations.

CHAPTER VI

BLACK RACE AND RED RACE

URING THE year that I spent in Washington, and for some little time before this, there had been considerable agitation in the state of West Virginia over the question of moving the capital of the state from Wheeling to some other central point. As a result of this, the Legislature designated three cities to be voted upon by the citizens of the state as the permanent seat of government. Among these cities was Charleston, only five miles from Malden, my home. At the close of my school year in Washington I was very pleasantly surprised to receive, from a committee of white people in Charleston, an invitation to canvass the state in the interests of that city. This invitation I accepted, and spent nearly three months in speaking in various parts of the state. Charleston was successful in winning the prize, and is now the permanent seat of government.

The reputation that I made as a speaker during this

campaign induced a number of persons to make an earnest effort to get me to enter political life, but I refused, still believing that I could find other service which would prove of more permanent value to my race. Even then I had a strong feeling that what our people most needed was to get a foundation in education, industry, and property, and for this I felt that they could better afford to strive than for political preferment. As for my individual self, it appeared to me to be reasonably certain that I could succeed in political life, but I had a feeling that it would be a rather selfish kind of success— individual success at the cost of failing to do my duty in assisting in laying a foundation for the masses.

At this period in the progress of our race a very large proportion of the young men who went to school or to college did so with the expressed determination to prepare themselves to be great lawyers, or Congressmen, and many of the women planned to become music teachers; but I had a reasonably fixed idea, even at that early period in my life, that there was need for something to be done to prepare the way for successful lawyers, Congressmen, and music teachers.

I felt that the conditions were a good deal like those of an old coloured man, during the days of slavery, who wanted to learn how to play on the guitar. In his desire to take guitar lessons he applied to one of his young masters to teach him; but the young man, not

having much faith in the ability of the slave to master
the guitar at his age, sought to discourage him by
telling him: "Uncle Jake, I will give you guitar lessons;
but, Jake, I will have to charge you three dollars for the
first lesson, two dollars for the second lesson, and one
dollar for the third lesson. But I will charge you only
twenty-five cents for the last lesson."

Uncle Jake answered: "All right, boss, I hires you on
dem terms. But, boss! I wants yer to be sure an' give
me dat las' lesson first."

Soon after my work in connection with the removal
of the capital was finished, I received an invitation
which gave me great joy and which at the same time
was a very pleasant surprise. This was a letter from
General Armstrong, inviting me to return to Hampton at the next Commencement to deliver what was
called the "post-graduate address." This was an honour which I had not dreamed of receiving. With much
care I prepared the best address that I was capable of.
I chose for my subject "The Force That Wins."

As I returned to Hampton for the purpose of delivering this address, I went over much of the same
ground—now, however, covered entirely by railroad—
that I had traversed nearly six years before, when I first
sought entrance into Hampton Institute as a student.
Now I was able to ride the whole distance in the train.
I was constantly contrasting this with my first journey

to Hampton. I think I may say, without seeming egotism, that it is seldom that five years have wrought such a change in the life and aspirations of an individual.

At Hampton I received a warm welcome from teachers and students. I found that during my absence from Hampton the institute each year had been getting closer to the real needs and conditions of our people; that the industrial teaching, as well as that of the academic department, had greatly improved. The plan of the school was not modelled after that of any other institution then in existence, but every improvement was made under the magnificent leadership of General Armstrong solely with the view of meeting and helping the needs of our people as they presented themselves at the time. Too often, it seems to me, in missionary and educational work among undeveloped races, people yield to the temptation of doing that which was done a hundred years before, or is being done in other communities a thousand miles away. The temptation often is to run each individual through a certain educational mould, regardless of the condition of the subject or the end to be accomplished. This was not so at Hampton Institute.

The address which I delivered on Commencement Day seems to have pleased every one, and many kind and encouraging words were spoken to me regarding it. Soon after my return to my home in West Virginia, where I had planned to continue teaching, I was again surprised to receive a letter from General Armstrong, asking me to return to Hampton partly as a teacher and partly to pursue some supplementary studies. This was in the summer of 1879. Soon after I began my first teaching in West Virginia I had picked out four of the brightest and most promising of my pupils, in addition to my two brothers, to whom I have already referred, and had given them special attention, with the view of having them go to Hampton. They had gone there, and in each case the teachers had found them so well prepared that they entered advanced classes. This fact, it seems, led to my being called back to Hampton as a teacher. One of the young men that I sent to Hampton in this way is now Dr. Samuel E. Courtney, a successful physician in Boston, and a member of the School Board of that city.

About this time the experiment was being tried for the first time, by General Armstrong, of educating Indians at Hampton. Few people then had any confidence in the ability of the Indians to receive education and to profit by it. General Armstrong was anxious to try the experiment systematically on a large scale. He secured from the reservations in the Western states over one hundred wild and for the most part perfectly ignorant Indians, the greater proportion of whom were young men. The special work which the General desired me to do was to be a sort of "house father" to the Indian young men—that is, I was to live in the building with them and have the charge of their discipline, clothing, rooms, and so on. This was a very tempting offer, but I had become so much absorbed in my work in West Virginia that I dreaded to give it up. However, I tore myself away from it. I did not know how to refuse to perform any service that General Armstrong desired of me.

On going to Hampton, I took up my residence in a building with about seventy-five Indian youths. I was the only person in the building who was not a member of their race. At first I had a good deal of doubt about my ability to succeed. I knew that the average Indian felt himself above the white man, and, of course, he felt himself far above the Negro, largely on account of the fact of the Negro having submitted to slavery—a thing which the Indian would never do. The Indians, in the Indian Territory, owned a large number of slaves during the days of slavery. Aside from this, there was a general feeling that the attempt to educate and civilize the red men at Hampton would be a failure. All this made me proceed very cautiously, for I felt keenly the great responsibility. But I was determined to succeed. It was not long before I had the complete confidence of the Indians, and not only this, but I think I am safe in saying that I had their love and respect. I found that they were about like any other human beings; that they responded to kind treatment and resented ill-treatment. They were continually planning to do something that would add to my happiness and comfort. The things that they disliked most, I think, were to have their long hair cut, to give up wearing their blankets, and to cease smoking; but no white American ever thinks that any other race is wholly civilized until he wears the white man's clothes, eats the white man's food, speaks the white man's language, and professes the white man's religion.

When the difficulty of learning the English language was subtracted, I found that in the matter of learning trades and in mastering academic studies there was little difference between the coloured and Indian students. It was a constant delight to me to note the interest which the coloured students took in trying to help the Indians in every way possible. There were a few of the coloured students who felt that the Indians ought not to be admitted to Hampton, but these were in the minority. Whenever they were asked to do so, the Negro students gladly took the Indians as room-mates, in order that they might teach them to speak English and to acquire civilized habits.

I have often wondered if there was a white institution in this country whose students would have welcomed the incoming of more than a hundred companions of another race in the cordial way that these black students at Hampton welcomed the red ones. How often I have wanted to say to white students that they lift themselves up in proportion as they help to lift others, and the more unfortunate the race, and the lower in the scale of civilization, the more does one raise one's self by giving the assistance.

This reminds me of a conversation which I once had with the Hon. Frederick Douglass. At one time Mr. Douglass was travelling in the state of Pennsylvania, and was forced, on account of his colour, to ride in the baggage-car, in spite of the fact that he had paid the same price for his passage that the other passengers had paid. When some of the white passengers went into the baggage-car to console Mr. Douglass, and one of them said to him: "I am sorry, Mr. Douglass, that you have been degraded in this manner," Mr. Douglass straightened himself up on the box upon which he was sitting, and replied: "They cannot degrade Frederick Douglass. The soul that is within me no man can degrade. I am not the one that is being degraded on account of this treatment, but those who are inflicting it upon me."

In one part of our country, where the law demands the separation of the races on the railroad trains, I saw at one time a rather amusing instance which showed how difficult it sometimes is to know where the black begins and the white ends.

There was a man who was well known in his community as a Negro, but who was so white that even an expert would have hard work to classify him as a black man. This man was riding in the part of the train set aside for the coloured passengers. When the train conductor reached him, he showed at once that he was perplexed. If the man was a Negro, the conductor did not want to send him into the white people's coach; at the same time, if he was a white man, the conductor did not want to insult him by asking him if he was a Negro. The official looked him over carefully, examining his hair, eyes, nose, and hands, but still seemed puzzled. Finally, to solve the difficulty, he stooped over and peeped at the man's feet. When I saw the conductor examining the feet of the man in question, I said to myself, "That will settle it;" and so it did, for the trainman promptly decided that the passenger was a Negro, and let him remain where he was. I congratulated myself that my race was fortunate in not losing one of its members.

My experience has been that the time to test a true gentleman is to observe him when he is in contact with individuals of a race that is less fortunate than his own. This is illustrated in no better way than by observing the conduct of the old-school type of Southern gentleman when he is in contact with his former slaves or their descendants.

An example of what I mean is shown in a story told of George Washington, who, meeting a coloured man in the road once, who politely lifted his hat, lifted his own in return. Some of his white friends who saw the incident criticised Washington for his action. In reply to their criticism George Washington said: "Do you suppose that I am going to permit a poor, ignorant, coloured man to be more polite than I am?"

While I was in charge of the Indian boys at Hampton, I had one or two experiences which illustrate the curious workings of caste in America. One of the Indian boys was taken ill, and it became my duty to take him to Washington, deliver him over to the Secretary of the Interior, and get a receipt for him, in order that he might be returned to his Western reservation. At that time I was rather ignorant of the ways of the world. During my journey to Washington, on a steamboat, when the bell rang for dinner, I was careful to wait and not enter the dining room until after the greater part of the passengers had finished their meal. Then, with my charge, I went to the dining saloon. The man in charge politely informed me that the Indian could be served, but that I could not. I never could understand how he knew just where to draw the colour line, since the Indian and I were of about the same complexion. The steward, however, seemed to be an expert in this matter. I had been directed by the authorities at Hampton to stop at a certain hotel in Washington with my charge, but when I went to this hotel the clerk stated that he would be glad to receive the Indian into the house, but said that he could not accommodate me.

An illustration of something of this same feeling came under my observation afterward. I happened to find myself in a town in which so much excitement and indignation were being expressed that it seemed likely for a time that there would be a lynching. The occasion of the trouble was that a dark-skinned man had stopped at the local hotel. Investigation, however, developed the fact that this individual was a citizen of Morocco, and that while travelling in this country he spoke the English language. As soon as it was learned that he was not an American Negro, all the signs of indignation disappeared. The man who was the innocent cause of the excitement, though, found it prudent after that not to speak English.

At the end of my first year with the Indians there came another opening for me at Hampton, which, as I look back over my life now, seems to have come providentially, to help to prepare me for my work at Tuskegee later. General Armstrong had found out that there was quite a number of young coloured men and women who were intensely in earnest in wishing to get an education, but who were prevented from entering

Hampton Institute because they were too poor to be able to pay any portion of the cost of their board, or even to supply themselves with books. He conceived the idea of starting a night-school in connection with the Institute, into which a limited number of the most promising of these young men and women would be received, on condition that they were to work for ten hours during the day, and attend school for two hours at night. They were to be paid something above the cost of their board for their work. The greater part of their earnings was to be reserved in the school's treasury as a fund to be drawn on to pay their board when they had become students in the day-school, after they had spent one or two years in the night-school. In this way they would obtain a start in their books and a knowledge of some trade or industry, in addition to the other far-reaching benefits of the institution.

General Armstrong asked me to take charge of the night-school, and I did so. At the beginning of this school there were about twelve strong, earnest men and women who entered the class. During the day the greater part of the young men worked in the school's sawmill, and the young women worked in the laundry. The work was not easy in either place, but in all my teaching I never taught pupils who gave me such genuine satisfaction as these did. They were good students, and mastered their work thoroughly. They were so much in earnest that only the ringing of the retiring-bell would make them stop studying, and often they would urge me to continue the lessons after the usual hour for going to bed had come.

These students showed so much earnestness, both in their hard work during the day, as well as in their application to their studies at night, that I gave them the name of "The Plucky Class"—a name which soon grew popular and spread throughout the institution. After a student had been in the night-school long enough to prove what was in him, I gave him a printed certificate which read something like this:—

"This is to certify that James Smith is a member of The Plucky Class of the Hampton Institute, and is in good and regular standing."

The students prized these certificates highly, and they added greatly to the popularity of the night-school. Within a few weeks this department had grown to such an extent that there were about twenty-five students in attendance. I have followed the course of many of these twenty-five men and women ever since then, and they are now holding important and useful positions in nearly every part of the South. The night-school at Hampton, which started with only twelve students, now numbers between three and four hundred, and is one of the permanent and most important features of the institution.

CHAPTER VII

EARLY DAYS AT TUSKEGEE

DURING THE time that I had charge of the Indians and the night-school at Hampton, I pursued some studies myself, under the direction of the instructors there. One of these instructors was the Rev. Dr. H. B. Frissell, the present Principal of the Hampton Institute, General Armstrong's successor.

In May, 1881, near the close of my first year in teaching the night-school, in a way that I had not dared expect, the opportunity opened for me to begin my life-work. One night in the chapel, after the usual chapel exercises were over, General Armstrong referred to the fact that he had received a letter from some gentlemen in Alabama asking him to recommend some one to take charge of what was to be a normal school for the coloured people in the little town of Tuskegee in that state. These gentlemen seemed to take it for granted that no coloured man suitable for the position could be secured, and they were expecting the General to recommend a white man for the place. The next day General Armstrong sent for me to come to his office, and, much to my surprise, asked me if I thought I could fill the position in Alabama. I told him that I would be willing to try. Accordingly, he wrote to the people who had applied to him for the information, that he did not know of any white man to suggest, but if they would be willing to take a coloured man, he had one whom he could recommend. In this letter he gave them my name.

Several days passed before anything more was heard about the matter. Some time afterward, one Sunday evening during the chapel exercises, a messenger came in and handed the General a telegram. At the end of the exercises he read the telegram to the school. In substance, these were its words: "Booker T. Washington will suit us. Send him at once."

There was a great deal of joy expressed among the students and teachers, and I received very hearty congratulations. I began to get ready at once to go to Tuskegee. I went by way of my old home in West Virginia, where I remained for several days, after which I proceeded to Tuskegee. I found Tuskegee to be a town of about two thousand inhabitants, nearly one-half of whom were coloured. It was in what was known as the Black Belt of the South. In the county in which

Tuskegee is situated the coloured people outnumbered the whites by about three to one. In some of the adjoining and near-by counties the proportion was not far from six coloured persons to one white.

I have often been asked to define the term "Black Belt." So far as I can learn, the term was first used to designate a part of the country which was distinguished by the colour of the soil. The part of the country possessing this thick, dark, and naturally rich soil was, of course, the part of the South where the slaves were most profitable, and consequently they were taken there in the largest numbers. Later, and especially since the war, the term seems to be used wholly in a political sense—that is, to designate the counties where the black people outnumber the white.

Before going to Tuskegee I had expected to find there a building and all the necessary apparatus ready for me to begin teaching. To my disappointment, I found nothing of the kind. I did find, though, that which no costly building and apparatus can supply,— hundreds of hungry, earnest souls who wanted to secure knowledge.

Tuskegee seemed an ideal place for the school. It was in the midst of the great bulk of the Negro population, and was rather secluded, being five miles from the main line of railroad, with which it was connected by a short line. During the days of slavery, and since, the town had been a centre for the education of the white people. This was an added advantage, for the reason that I found the white people possessing a degree of culture and education that is not surpassed by many localities. While the coloured people were ignorant, they had not, as a rule, degraded and weakened their bodies by vices such as are common to the lower class of people in the large cities. In general, I found the relations between the two races pleasant. For example, the largest, and I think at that time the only hardware store in the town was owned and operated jointly by a coloured man and a white man. This copartnership continued until the death of the white partner.

I found that about a year previous to my going to Tuskegee some of the coloured people who had heard something of the work of education being done at Hampton had applied to the state Legislature, through their representatives, for a small appropriation to be used in starting a normal school in Tuskegee. This request the Legislature had complied with to the extent of granting an annual appropriation of two thousand dollars. I soon learned, however, that this money could be used only for the payment of the salaries of the instructors, and that there was no provision for securing land, buildings, or apparatus. The task before me did not seem a very encouraging one. It seemed much like making bricks without straw. The coloured people were overjoyed, and were constantly offering their services in any way in which they could be of assistance in getting the school started.

My first task was to find a place in which to open the school. After looking the town over with some care, the most suitable place that could be secured seemed to be a rather dilapidated shanty near the coloured Methodist church, together with the church itself as a sort of assembly-room. Both the church and the shanty were in about as bad condition as was possible. I recall that during the first months of school that I taught in this building it was in such poor repair that, whenever it rained, one of the older students would very kindly leave his lessons and hold an umbrella over me while I heard the recitations of the others. I remember, also, that on more than one occasion my landlady held an umbrella over me while I ate breakfast.

At the time I went to Alabama the coloured people were taking considerable interest in politics, and they were very anxious that I should become one of them politically, in every respect. They seemed to have a little distrust of strangers in this regard. I recall that one man, who seemed to have been designated by the others to look after my political destiny, came to me on several occasions and said, with a good deal of earnestness: "We wants you to be sure to vote jes' like we votes. We can't read de newspapers very much, but we knows how to vote, an' we wants you to vote jes' like we votes." He added: "We watches de white man, and we keeps watching de white man till we finds out which way de white man's gwine to vote; an' when we finds out which way de white man's gwine to vote, den we votes 'xactly de other way. Den we knows we's right."

I am glad to add, however, that at the present time the disposition to vote against the white man merely because he is white is largely disappearing, and the race is learning to vote from principle, for what the voter considers to be for the best interests of both races.

I reached Tuskegee, as I have said, early in June, 1881. The first month I spent in finding accommodations for the school, and in travelling through Alabama, examining into the actual life of the people, especially in the country districts, and in getting the school advertised among the class of people that I wanted to have attend it. The most of my travelling was done over the country roads, with a mule and a cart or a mule and a buggy wagon for conveyance. I ate and slept with the people, in their little cabins. I saw their farms, their schools, their churches. Since, in the case of the most of these visits, there had been no notice given in advance that a stranger was expected, I had the advantage of seeing the real, everyday life of the people.

In the plantation districts I found that, as a rule, the

whole family slept in one room, and that in addition to the immediate family there sometimes were relatives, or others not related to the family, who slept in the same room. On more than one occasion I went outside the house to get ready for bed, or to wait until the family had gone to bed. They usually contrived some kind of a place for me to sleep, either on the floor or in a special part of another's bed. Rarely was there any place provided in the cabin where one could bathe even the face and hands, but usually some provision was made for this outside the house, in the yard.

The common diet of the people was fat pork and corn bread. At times I have eaten in cabins where they had only corn bread and "black-eye peas" cooked in plain water. The people seemed to have no other idea than to live on this fat meat and corn bread,—the meat, and the meal of which the bread was made, having been bought at a high price at a store in town, notwithstanding the fact that the land all about the cabin homes could easily have been made to produce nearly every kind of garden vegetable that is raised anywhere in the country. Their one object seemed to be to plant nothing but cotton; and in many cases cotton was planted up to the very door of the cabin.

In these cabin homes I often found sewing-machines which had been bought, or were being bought, on instalments, frequently at a cost of as

much as sixty dollars, or showy clocks for which the
occupants of the cabins had paid twelve or fourteen
dollars. I remember that on one occasion when I went
into one of these cabins for dinner, when I sat down
to the table for a meal with the four members of the
family, I noticed that, while there were five of us at the
table, there was but one fork for the five of us to use.
Naturally there was an awkward pause on my part. In
the opposite corner of that same cabin was an organ
for which the people told me they were paying sixty
dollars in monthly instalments. One fork, and a sixty-
dollar organ!

In most cases the sewing-machine was not used,
the clocks were so worthless that they did not keep
correct time—and if they had, in nine cases out of ten
there would have been no one in the family who could
have told the time of day—while the organ, of course,
was rarely used for want of a person who could play
upon it.

In the case to which I have referred, where the family sat down to the table for the meal at which I was
their guest, I could see plainly that this was an awkward
and unusual proceeding, and was done in my honour.
In most cases, when the family got up in the morning,
for example, the wife would put a piece of meat in a
frying-pan and put a lump of dough in a "skillet," as
they called it. These utensils would be placed on the

fire, and in ten or fifteen minutes breakfast would be ready. Frequently the husband would take his bread and meat in his hand and start for the field, eating as he walked. The mother would sit down in a corner and eat her breakfast, perhaps from a plate and perhaps directly from the "skillet" or frying-pan, while the children would eat their portion of the bread and meat while running about the yard. At certain seasons of the year, when meat was scarce, it was rarely that the children who were not old enough or strong enough to work in the fields would have the luxury of meat.

The breakfast over, and with practically no attention given to the house, the whole family would, as a general thing, proceed to the cotton-field. Every child that was large enough to carry a hoe was put to work, and the baby—for usually there was at least one baby—would be laid down at the end of the cotton row, so that its mother could give it a certain amount of attention when she had finished chopping her row. The noon meal and the supper were taken in much the same way as the breakfast.

All the days of the family would be spent after much this same routine, except Saturday and Sunday. On Saturday the whole family would spend at least half a day, and often a whole day, in town. The idea in going to town was, I suppose, to do shopping, but all the shopping that the whole family had money for could have been attended to in ten minutes by one person. Still, the whole family remained in town for most of the day, spending the greater part of the time in standing on the streets, the women, too often, sitting about somewhere smoking or dipping snuff. Sunday was usually spent in going to some big meeting. With few exceptions, I found that the crops were mortgaged in the counties where I went, and that the most of the coloured farmers were in debt. The state had not been able to build schoolhouses in the country districts, and, as a rule, the schools were taught in churches or in log cabins. More than once, while on my journeys, I found that there was no provision made in the house used for school purposes for heating the building during the winter, and consequently a fire had to be built in the yard, and teacher and pupils passed in and out of the house as they got cold or warm. With few exceptions, I found the teachers in these country schools to be miserably poor in preparation for their work, and poor in moral character. The schools were in session from three to five months. There was practically no apparatus in the schoolhouses, except that occasionally there was a rough blackboard. I recall that one day I went into a schoolhouse—or rather into an abandoned log cabin that was being used as a schoolhouse—and found five pupils who were studying a lesson from one book.

Two of these, on the front seat, were using the book between them; behind these were two others peeping over the shoulders of the first two, and behind the four was a fifth little fellow who was peeping over the shoulders of all four.

What I have said concerning the character of the schoolhouses and teachers will also apply quite accurately as a description of the church buildings and the ministers.

I met some very interesting characters during my travels. As illustrating the peculiar mental processes of the country people, I remember that I asked one coloured man, who was about sixty years old, to tell me something of his history. He said that he had been born in Virginia, and sold into Alabama in 1845. I asked him how many were sold at the same time. He said, "There were five of us; myself and brother and three mules."

In giving all these descriptions of what I saw during my month of travel in the country around Tuskegee, I wish my readers to keep in mind the fact that there were many encouraging exceptions to the conditions which I have described. I have stated in such plain words what I saw, mainly for the reason that later I want to emphasize the encouraging changes that have taken place in the community, not wholly by the work of the Tuskegee school, but by that of other institutions as well.

CHAPTER VIII

TEACHING SCHOOL IN A STABLE
AND A HEN-HOUSE

I CONFESS that what I saw during my month of travel and investigation left me with a very heavy heart. The work to be done in order to lift these people up seemed almost beyond accomplishing. I was only one person, and it seemed to me that the little effort which I could put forth could go such a short distance toward bringing about results. I wondered if I could accomplish anything, and if it were worth while for me to try.

Of one thing I felt more strongly convinced than ever, after spending this month in seeing the actual life of the coloured people, and that was that, in order to lift them up, something must be done more than merely to imitate New England education as it then existed. I saw more clearly than ever the wisdom of the system which General Armstrong had inaugurated at Hampton. To take the children of such people as I had been among for a month, and each day give them a few hours of mere book education, I felt would be almost a waste of time.

After consultation with the citizens of Tuskegee, I set July 4, 1881, as the day for the opening of the school in the little shanty and church which had been se-cured for its accommodation. The white people, as well as the coloured, were greatly interested in the starting of the new school, and the opening day was looked forward to with much earnest discussion. There were not a few white people in the vicinity of Tuskegee who looked with some disfavour upon the project. They questioned its value to the coloured peo-ple, and had a fear that it might result in bringing about trouble between the races. Some had the feeling that in proportion as the Negro received education, in the same proportion would his value decrease as an economic factor in the state. These people feared the result of education would be that the Negroes would leave the farms, and that it would be difficult to secure them for domestic service.

The white people who questioned the wisdom of starting this new school had in their minds pictures of what was called an educated Negro, with a high hat, imitation gold eye-glasses, a showy walking-stick, kid gloves, fancy boots, and what not—in a word, a man who was determined to live by his wits. It was difficult for these people to see how education would produce any other kind of a coloured man.

In the midst of all the difficulties which I encountered in getting the little school started, and since then through a period of nineteen years, there are two men among all the many friends of the school in Tuskegee upon whom I have depended constantly for advice and guidance; and the success of the undertaking is largely due to these men, from whom I have never sought anything in vain. I mention them simply as types. One is a white man and an ex-slaveholder, Mr. George W. Campbell; the other is a black man and an ex-slave, Mr. Lewis Adams. These were the men who wrote to General Armstrong for a teacher.

Mr. Campbell is a merchant and banker, and had had little experience in dealing with matters pertaining to education. Mr. Adams was a mechanic, and had learned the trades of shoemaking, harness-making, and tinsmithing during the days of slavery. He had never been to school a day in his life, but in some way he had learned to read and write while a slave. From the first, these two men saw clearly what my plan of education was, sympathized with me, and supported me in every effort. In the days which were darkest financially for the school, Mr. Campbell was never appealed to when he was not willing to extend all the aid in his power. I do not know two men, one an ex-

slaveholder, one an ex-slave, whose advice and judgment I would feel more like following in everything
which concerns the life and development of the
school at Tuskegee than those of these two men.

I have always felt that Mr. Adams, in a large degree,
derived his unusual power of mind from the training
given his hands in the process of mastering well three
trades during the days of slavery. If one goes to-day
into any Southern town, and asks for the leading and
most reliable coloured man in the community, I believe that in five cases out of ten he will be directed to
a Negro who learned a trade during the days of slavery.

On the morning that the school opened, thirty students reported for admission. I was the only teacher.
The students were about equally divided between the
sexes. Most of them lived in Macon County, the
county in which Tuskegee is situated, and of which it
is the county-seat. A great many more students
wanted to enter the school, but it had been decided to
receive only those who were above fifteen years of age,
and who had previously received some education. The
greater part of the thirty were public-school teachers,
and some of them were nearly forty years of age. With
the teachers came some of their former pupils, and
when they were examined it was amusing to note that
in several cases the pupil entered a higher class than
did his former teacher. It was also interesting to note

how many big books some of them had studied, and how many high-sounding subjects some of them claimed to have mastered. The bigger the book and the longer the name of the subject, the prouder they felt of their accomplishment. Some had studied Latin, and one or two Greek. This they thought entitled them to special distinction.

In fact, one of the saddest things I saw during the month of travel which I have described was a young man, who had attended some high school, sitting down in a one-room cabin, with grease on his clothing, filth all around him, and weeds in the yard and garden, engaged in studying a French grammar.

The students who came first seemed to be fond of memorizing long and complicated "rules" in grammar and mathematics, but had little thought or knowledge of applying these rules to the everyday affairs of their life. One subject which they liked to talk about, and tell me that they had mastered, in arithmetic, was "banking and discount," but I soon found out that neither they nor almost any one in the neighbourhood in which they lived had ever had a bank account. In registering the names of the students, I found that almost every one of them had one or more middle initials. When I asked what the "J" stood for, in the name of John J. Jones, it was explained to me that this was a part of his "entitles." Most of the students wanted to get an education because they thought it would enable them to earn more money as school-teachers.

Notwithstanding what I have said about them in these respects, I have never seen a more earnest and willing company of young men and women than these students were. They were all willing to learn the right thing as soon as it was shown them what was right. I was determined to start them off on a solid and thorough foundation, so far as their books were concerned. I soon learned that most of them had the merest smattering of the high-sounding things that they had studied. While they could locate the Desert of Sahara or the capital of China on an artificial globe, I found out that the girls could not locate the proper places for the knives and forks on an actual dinner-table, or the places on which the bread and meat should be set.

I had to summon a good deal of courage to take a student who had been studying cube root and "banking and discount," and explain to him that the wisest thing for him to do first was thoroughly to master the multiplication table.

The number of pupils increased each week, until by the end of the first month there were nearly fifty. Many of them, however, said that, as they could remain only for two or three months, they wanted to enter a high class and get a diploma the first year if possible.

At the end of the first six weeks a new and rare face entered the school as a co-teacher. This was Miss Olivia A. Davidson, who later became my wife. Miss Davidson was born in Ohio, and received her preparatory education in the public schools of that state. When little more than a girl, she heard of the need of teachers in the South. She went to the state of Mississippi and began teaching there. Later she taught in the city of Memphis. While teaching in Mississippi, one of her pupils became ill with smallpox. Every one in the community was so frightened that no one would nurse the boy. Miss Davidson closed her school and remained by the bedside of the boy night and day until he recovered. While she was at her Ohio home on her vacation, the worst epidemic of yellow fever broke out in Memphis, Tenn., that perhaps has ever occurred in the South. When she heard of this, she at once telegraphed the Mayor of Memphis, offering her services as a yellow-fever nurse, although she had never had the disease.

Miss Davidson's experience in the South showed her that the people needed something more than mere book-learning. She heard of the Hampton system of education, and decided that this was what she wanted in order to prepare herself for better work in the South. The attention of Mrs. Mary Hemenway, of Boston, was attracted to her rare ability. Through Mrs.

Hemenway's kindness and generosity, Miss Davidson, after graduating at Hampton, received an opportunity to complete a two years' course of training at the Massachusetts State Normal School at Framingham.

Before she went to Framingham, some one suggested to Miss Davidson that, since she was so very light in colour, she might find it more comfortable not to be known as a coloured woman in this school in Massachusetts. She at once replied that under no circumstances and for no considerations would she consent to deceive any one in regard to her racial identity.

Soon after her graduation from the Framingham institution, Miss Davidson came to Tuskegee, bringing into the school many valuable and fresh ideas as to the best methods of teaching, as well as a rare moral character and a life of unselfishness that I think has seldom been equalled. No single individual did more toward laying the foundations of the Tuskegee Institute so as to insure the successful work that has been done there than Olivia A. Davidson.

Miss Davidson and I began consulting as to the future of the school from the first. The students were making progress in learning books and in developing their minds; but it became apparent at once that, if we were to make any permanent impression upon those who had come to us for training, we must do something besides teach them mere books. The students had come from homes where they had had no opportunities for lessons which would teach them how to care for their bodies. With few exceptions, the homes in Tuskegee in which the students boarded were but little improvement upon those from which they had come. We wanted to teach the students how to bathe; how to care for their teeth and clothing. We wanted to teach them what to eat, and how to eat it properly, and how to care for their rooms. Aside from this, we wanted to give them such a practical knowledge of some one industry, together with the spirit of industry, thrift, and economy, that they would be sure of knowing how to make a living after they had left us. We wanted to teach them to study actual things instead of mere books alone.

We found that the most of our students came from the country districts, where agriculture in some form or other was the main dependence of the people. We learned that about eighty-five per cent of the coloured people in the Gulf states depended upon agriculture for their living. Since this was true, we wanted to be careful not to educate our students out of sympathy with agricultural life, so that they would be attracted from the country to the cities, and yield to the temptation of trying to live by their wits. We wanted to give them such an education as would fit a large proportion of them to be teachers, and at the same time cause them to return to the plantation districts and show the people there how to put new energy and new ideas into farming, as well as into the intellectual and moral and religious life of the people.

All these ideas and needs crowded themselves upon us with a seriousness that seemed well-nigh over-whelming. What were we to do? We had only the lit-tle old shanty and the abandoned church which the good coloured people of the town of Tuskegee had kindly loaned us for the accommodation of the classes. The number of students was increasing daily. The more we saw of them, and the more we travelled through the country districts, the more we saw that our efforts were reaching, to only a partial degree, the actual needs of the people whom we wanted to lift up through the medium of the students whom we should educate and send out as leaders.

The more we talked with the students, who were then coming to us from several parts of the state, the more we found that the chief ambition among a large proportion of them was to get an education so that they would not have to work any longer with their hands.

This is illustrated by a story told of a coloured man in Alabama, who, one hot day in July, while he was at work in a cotton-field, suddenly stopped, and, looking toward the skies, said: "O Lawd, de cotton am so grassy, de work am so hard, and the sun am so hot dat I b'lieve dis darky am called to preach!"

About three months after the opening of the school, and at the time when we were in the greatest anxiety about our work, there came into the market for sale an old and abandoned plantation which was situated about a mile from the town of Tuskegee. The mansion house—or "big house," as it would have been called—which had been occupied by the owners during slavery, had been burned. After making a careful examination of this place, it seemed to be just the location that we wanted in order to make our work effective and permanent.

But how were we to get it? The price asked for it was very little—only five hundred dollars—but we had no money, and we were strangers in the town and had no credit. The owner of the land agreed to let us occupy the place if we could make a payment of two hundred and fifty dollars down, with the understanding that the remaining two hundred and fifty dollars must be paid within a year. Although five hundred dollars was cheap for the land, it was a large sum when one did not have any part of it.

In the midst of the difficulty I summoned a great deal of courage and wrote to my friend General J. F. B. Marshall, the Treasurer of the Hampton Institute, putting the situation before him and beseeching him to lend me the two hundred and fifty dollars on my own personal responsibility. Within a few days a reply came to the effect that he had no authority to lend me money belonging to the Hampton Institute, but that he would gladly lend me the amount needed from his own personal funds.

I confess that the securing of this money in this way was a great surprise to me, as well as a source of gratification. Up to that time I never had had in my possession so much money as one hundred dollars at a time, and the loan which I had asked General Marshall for seemed a tremendously large sum to me. The fact of my being responsible for the repaying of such a large amount of money weighed very heavily upon me.

I lost no time in getting ready to move the school on to the new farm. At the time we occupied the place there were standing upon it a cabin, formerly used as the dining room, an old kitchen, a stable, and an old hen-house. Within a few weeks we had all of these structures in use. The stable was repaired and used as a recitation-room, and very presently the hen-house was utilized for the same purpose.

I recall that one morning, when I told an old coloured man who lived near, and who sometimes helped me, that our school had grown so large that it would be necessary for us to use the hen-house for school purposes, and that I wanted him to help me give it a thorough cleaning out the next day, he replied, in the most earnest manner: "What you mean, boss? You sholy ain't gwine clean out de hen-house in de *day*-time?"

Nearly all the work of getting the new location ready for school purposes was done by the students after school was over in the afternoon. As soon as we got the cabins in condition to be used, I determined to clear up some land so that we could plant a crop. When I explained my plan to the young men, I noticed that they did not seem to take to it very kindly. It was hard for them to see the connection between clearing land and an education. Besides, many of them had been school-teachers, and they questioned whether or not clearing land would be in keeping with their dignity. In order to relieve them from any embarrassment, each afternoon after school I took my axe and led the way to the woods. When they saw that I was not afraid or ashamed to work, they began to assist with more enthusiasm. We kept at the work each afternoon, until we had cleared about twenty acres and had planted a crop.

In the meantime Miss Davidson was devising plans to repay the loan. Her first effort was made by holding festivals, or "suppers." She made a personal canvass among the white and coloured families in the town of

Tuskegee, and got them to agree to give something, like a cake, a chicken, bread, or pies, that could be sold at the festival. Of course the coloured people were glad to give anything that they could spare, but I want to add that Miss Davidson did not apply to a single white family, so far as I now remember, that failed to donate something; and in many ways the white families showed their interest in the school.

Several of these festivals were held, and quite a little sum of money was raised. A canvass was also made among the people of both races for direct gifts of money, and most of those applied to gave small sums. It was often pathetic to note the gifts of the older coloured people, most of whom had spent their best days in slavery. Sometimes they would give five cents, sometimes twenty-five cents. Sometimes the contribution was a quilt, or a quantity of sugarcane. I recall one old coloured woman, who was about seventy years of age, who came to see me when we were raising money to pay for the farm. She hobbled into the room where I was, leaning on a cane. She was clad in rags; but they were clean. She said: "Mr. Washin'ton, God knows I spent de bes' days of my life in slavery. God knows I's ignorant an' poor; but," she added, "I knows what you an' Miss Davidson is tryin' to do. I knows you is tryin' to make better men an' better women for de coloured race. I ain't got no money, but I wants you to take dese six eggs, what I's been savin' up, an' I wants you to put dese six eggs into de eddication of dese boys an' gals."

Since the work at Tuskegee started, it has been my privilege to receive many gifts for the benefit of the institution, but never any, I think, that touched me so deeply as this one.

CHAPTER IX

ANXIOUS DAYS AND SLEEPLESS NIGHTS

THE COMING of Christmas, that first year of our residence in Alabama, gave us an opportunity to get a farther insight into the real life of the people. The first thing that reminded us that Christmas had arrived was the "foreday" visits of scores of children rapping at our doors, asking for "Chris'mus gifts! Chris'mus gifts!" Between the hours of two o'clock and five o'clock in the morning I presume that we must have had a half-hundred such calls. This custom prevails throughout this portion of the South to-day.

During the days of slavery it was a custom quite generally observed throughout all the Southern states to give the coloured people a week of holiday at Christmas, or to allow the holiday to continue as long as the "yule log" lasted. The male members of the race, and often the female members, were expected to get drunk. We found that for a whole week the coloured people in and around Tuskegee dropped work the day before Christmas, and that it was difficult to get any one to perform any service from the time they stopped work until after the New Year. Persons who at other times did not use strong drink thought it quite the proper thing to indulge in it rather freely during the Christmas week. There was a widespread hilarity, and a free use of guns, pistols, and gunpowder generally. The sacredness of the season seemed to have been almost wholly lost sight of.

During this first Christmas vacation I went some distance from the town to visit the people on one of the large plantations. In their poverty and ignorance it was pathetic to see their attempts to get joy out of the season that in most parts of the country is so sacred and so dear to the heart. In one cabin I noticed that all that the five children had to remind them of the coming of Christ was a single bunch of firecrackers, which they had divided among them. In another cabin, where there were at least a half-dozen persons, they had only ten cents' worth of ginger-cakes, which had been bought in the store the day before. In another family they had only a few pieces of sugarcane. In still another cabin I found nothing but a new jug of cheap, mean whiskey, which the husband and wife were making free use of, notwithstanding the fact that the husband was one of the local ministers. In a few instances I found that the people had gotten hold of some bright-coloured cards that had been designed for advertising purposes, and were making the most of those. In other homes some member of the family had bought a new pistol. In the majority of cases there was nothing to be seen in the cabin to remind one of the coming of the Saviour, except that the people had ceased work in the fields and were lounging about their homes. At night, during Christmas week, they usually had what they called a "frolic," in some cabin on the plantation. This meant a kind of rough dance, where there was likely to be a good deal of whiskey used, and where there might be some shooting or cutting with razors.

While I was making this Christmas visit I met an old coloured man who was one of the numerous local preachers, who tried to convince me, from the experience Adam had in the Garden of Eden, that God had cursed all labour, and that, therefore, it was a sin for any man to work. For that reason this man sought to do as little work as possible. He seemed at that time to be supremely happy, because he was living, as he expressed it, through one week that was free from sin.

In the school we made a special effort to teach our students the meaning of Christmas, and to give them lessons in its proper observance. In this we have been successful to a degree that makes me feel safe in saying that the season now has a new meaning, not only through all that immediate region, but, in a measure, wherever our graduates have gone.

At the present time one of the most satisfactory features of the Christmas and Thanksgiving seasons at Tuskegee is the unselfish and beautiful way in which our graduates and students spend their time in administering to the comfort and happiness of others, especially the unfortunate. Not long ago some of our young men spent a holiday in rebuilding a cabin for a helpless coloured woman who is about seventy-five years old. At another time I remember that I made it known in chapel, one night, that a very poor student was suffering from cold, because he needed a coat. The next morning two coats were sent to my office for him.

I have referred to the disposition on the part of the white people in the town of Tuskegee and vicinity to help the school. From the first, I resolved to make the school a real part of the community in which it was located. I was determined that no one should have the feeling that it was a foreign institution, dropped down in the midst of the people, for which they had no responsibility and in which they had no interest. I noticed that the very fact that they had been asked to contribute toward the purchase of the land made them begin to feel as if it was going to be their school, to a large degree. I noted that just in proportion as we made the white people feel that the institution was a part of the life of the community, and that, while we wanted to make friends in Boston, for example, we also wanted to make white friends in Tuskegee, and that we wanted to make the school of real service to all the people, their attitude toward the school became favourable.

Perhaps I might add right here, what I hope to demonstrate later, that, so far as I know, the Tuskegee school at the present time has no warmer and more enthusiastic friends anywhere than it has among the white citizens of Tuskegee and throughout the state of Alabama and the entire South. From the first, I have advised our people in the South to make friends in every straightforward, manly way with their next-door neighbour, whether he be a black man or a white man. I have also advised them, where no principle is at stake, to consult the interests of their local communities, and to advise with their friends in regard to their voting.

For several months the work of securing the money with which to pay for the farm went on without ceasing. At the end of three months enough was secured to repay the loan of two hundred and fifty dollars to General Marshall, and within two months more we had secured the entire five hundred dollars and had received a deed of the one hundred acres of land. This gave us a great deal of satisfaction. It was not only a source of satisfaction to secure a permanent location for the school, but it was equally satisfactory to know that the greater part of the money with which it was paid for had been gotten from the white and coloured people in the town of Tuskegee. The most of this money was obtained by holding festivals and concerts, and from small individual donations.

Our next effort was in the direction of increasing the cultivation of the land, so as to secure some return from it, and at the same time give the students training in agriculture. All the industries at Tuskegee have been started in natural and logical order, growing out of the needs of a community settlement. We began with farming, because we wanted something to eat.

Many of the students, also, were able to remain in school but a few weeks at a time, because they had so little money with which to pay their board. Thus another object which made it desirable to get an industrial system started was in order to make it available as a means of helping the students to earn money enough so that they might be able to remain in school during the nine months' session of the school year.

The first animal that the school came into possession of was an old blind horse given us by one of the white citizens of Tuskegee. Perhaps I may add here that at the present time the school owns over two hundred horses, colts, mules, cows, calves, and oxen, and about seven hundred hogs and pigs, as well as a large number of sheep and goats.

The school was constantly growing in numbers, so much so that, after we had got the farm paid for, the cultivation of the land begun, and the old cabins which we had found on the place somewhat repaired, we turned our attention toward providing a large, substantial building. After having given a good deal of thought to the subject, we finally had the plans drawn for a building that was estimated to cost about six thousand dollars. This seemed to us a tremendous sum, but we knew that the school must go backward or forward, and that our work would mean little unless we could get hold of the students in their home life.

One incident which occurred about this time gave me a great deal of satisfaction as well as surprise. When it became known in the town that we were discussing the plans for a new, large building, a Southern white man who was operating a sawmill not far from Tuskegee came to me and said that he would gladly put all the lumber necessary to erect the building on the grounds, with no other guarantee for payment than my word that it would be paid for when we secured some money. I told the man frankly that at the time we did not have in our hands one dollar of the money needed. Notwithstanding this, he insisted on being allowed to put the lumber on the grounds. After we had secured some portion of the money we permitted him to do this.

Miss Davidson again began the work of securing in various ways small contributions for the new building from the white and coloured people in and near Tuskegee. I think I never saw a community of people so happy over anything as were the coloured people over the prospect of this new building. One day, when we were holding a meeting to secure funds for its erection, an old, ante-bellum coloured man came a distance of twelve miles and brought in his ox-cart a large hog. When the meeting was in progress, he rose in the midst of the company and said that he had no money which he could give, but that he had raised two fine hogs, and that he had brought one of them as a contribution toward the expenses of the building. He closed his announcement by saying: "Any nigger that's got any love for his race, or any respect for himself, will bring a hog to the next meeting." Quite a number of men in the community also volunteered to give several days' work, each, toward the erection of the building.

After we had secured all the help that we could in Tuskegee, Miss Davidson decided to go North for the purpose of securing additional funds. For weeks she

visited individuals and spoke in churches and before
Sunday schools and other organizations. She found
this work quite trying, and often embarrassing. The
school was not known, but she was not long in winning her way into the confidence of the best people in
the North.

The first gift from any Northern person was received from a New York lady whom Miss Davidson
met on the boat that was bringing her North. They fell
into a conversation, and the Northern lady became so
much interested in the effort being made at Tuskegee
that before they parted Miss Davidson was handed a
check for fifty dollars. For some time before our marriage, and also after it, Miss Davidson kept up the
work of securing money in the North and in the South
by interesting people by personal visits and through
correspondence. At the same time she kept in close
touch with the work at Tuskegee, as lady principal and
classroom teacher. In addition to this, she worked
among the older people in and near Tuskegee, and
taught a Sunday school class in the town. She was
never very strong, but never seemed happy unless she
was giving all of her strength to the cause which she
loved. Often, at night, after spending the day in going
from door to door trying to interest persons in the
work at Tuskegee, she would be so exhausted that
she could not undress herself. A lady upon whom she

called, in Boston, afterward told me that at one time when Miss Davidson called to see her and sent up her card the lady was detained a little before she could see Miss Davidson, and when she entered the parlour she found Miss Davidson so exhausted that she had fallen asleep.

While putting up our first building, which was named Porter Hall, after Mr. A. H. Porter, of Brooklyn, N.Y., who gave a generous sum toward its erection, the need for money became acute. I had given one of our creditors a promise that upon a certain day he should be paid four hundred dollars. On the morning of that day we did not have a dollar. The mail arrived at the school at ten o'clock, and in this mail there was a check sent by Miss Davidson for exactly four hundred dollars. I could relate many instances of almost the same character. This four hundred dollars was given by two ladies in Boston. Two years later, when the work at Tuskegee had grown considerably, and when we were in the midst of a season when we were so much in need of money that the future looked doubtful and gloomy, the same two Boston ladies sent us six thousand dollars. Words cannot describe our surprise, or the encouragement that the gift brought to us. Perhaps I might add here that for fourteen years these same friends have sent us six thousand dollars each year.

As soon as the plans were drawn for the new building, the students began digging out the earth where the foundations were to be laid, working after the regular classes were over. They had not fully outgrown the idea that it was hardly the proper thing for them to use their hands, since they had come there, as one of them expressed it, "to be educated, and not to work." Gradually, though, I noted with satisfaction that a sentiment in favour of work was gaining ground. After a few weeks of hard work the foundations were ready, and a day was appointed for the laying of the corner-stone.

When it is considered that the laying of this corner-stone took place in the heart of the South, in the "Black Belt," in the centre of that part of our country that was most devoted to slavery; that at that time slavery had been abolished only about sixteen years; that only sixteen years before that no Negro could be taught from books without the teacher receiving the condemnation of the law or of public sentiment—when all this is considered, the scene that was witnessed on that spring day at Tuskegee was a remarkable one. I believe there are few places in the world where it could have taken place.

The principal address was delivered by the Hon. Waddy Thompson, the Superintendent of Education for the county. About the corner-stone were gathered the teachers, the students, their parents and friends, the county officials—who were white—and all the leading white men in that vicinity, together with many of the black men and women whom these same white people but a few years before had held a title to as property. The members of both races were anxious to exercise the privilege of placing under the corner-stone some memento.

Before the building was completed we passed through some very trying seasons. More than once our hearts were made to bleed, as it were, because bills were falling due that we did not have the money to meet. Perhaps no one who has not gone through the experience, month after month, of trying to erect buildings and provide equipment for a school when no one knew where the money was to come from, can properly appreciate the difficulties under which we laboured. During the first years at Tuskegee I recall that night after night I would roll and toss on my bed, without sleep, because of the anxiety and uncertainty which we were in regarding money. I knew that, in a large degree, we were trying an experiment—that of testing whether or not it was possible for Negroes to build up and control the affairs of a large educational institution. I knew that if we failed it would injure the whole race. I knew that the presumption was against us. I knew that in the case of white people beginning such an enterprise it would be taken for granted that they were going to succeed, but in our case I felt that people would be surprised if we succeeded. All this made a burden which pressed down on us, sometimes, it seemed, at the rate of a thousand pounds to the square inch.

In all our difficulties and anxieties, however, I never went to a white or a black person in the town of Tuskegee for any assistance that was in their power to render, without being helped according to their means. More than a dozen times, when bills figuring up into the hundreds of dollars were falling due, I applied to the white men of Tuskegee for small loans, often borrowing small amounts from as many as a half-dozen persons, to meet our obligations. One thing I was determined to do from the first, and that was to keep the credit of the school high; and this, I think I can say without boasting, we have done all through these years.

I shall always remember a bit of advice given me by Mr. George W. Campbell, the white man to whom I have referred as the one who induced General Armstrong to send me to Tuskegee. Soon after I entered upon the work Mr. Campbell said to me, in his fatherly way: "Washington, always remember that credit is capital."

At one time when we were in the greatest distress for money that we ever experienced, I placed the situation frankly before General Armstrong. Without hesitation he gave me his personal check for all the money which he had saved for his own use. This was not the only time that General Armstrong helped Tuskegee in this way. I do not think I have ever made this fact public before.

During the summer of 1882, at the end of the first year's work of the school, I was married to Miss Fannie N. Smith, of Malden, W. Va. We began keeping house in Tuskegee early in the fall. This made a home for our teachers, who now had been increased to four in number. My wife was also a graduate of the Hampton Institute. After earnest and constant work in the interests of the school, together with her housekeeping duties, my wife passed away in May, 1884. One child, Portia M. Washington, was born during our marriage.

From the first, my wife most earnestly devoted her thoughts and time to the work of the school, and was completely one with me in every interest and ambition. She passed away, however, before she had an opportunity of seeing what the school was designed to be.

CHAPTER X

A HARDER TASK THAN MAKING
BRICKS WITHOUT STRAW

FROM THE very beginning, at Tuskegee, I was determined to have the students do not only the agricultural and domestic work, but to have them erect their own buildings. My plan was to have them, while performing this service, taught the latest and best methods of labour, so that the school would not only get the benefit of their efforts, but the students themselves would be taught to see not only utility in labour, but beauty and dignity; would be taught, in fact, how to lift labour up from mere drudgery and toil, and would learn to love work for its own sake. My plan was not to teach them to work in the old way, but to show them how to make the forces of nature—air, water, steam, electricity, horse-power—assist them in their labour.

At first many advised against the experiment of having the buildings erected by the labour of the students, but I was determined to stick to it. I told those who doubted the wisdom of the plan that I knew that our first buildings would not be so comfortable or so complete in their finish as buildings erected by the experienced hands of outside workmen, but that in the teaching of civilization, self-help, and self-reliance, the erection of the buildings by the students themselves would more than compensate for any lack of comfort or fine finish.

I further told those who doubted the wisdom of this plan, that the majority of our students came to us in poverty, from the cabins of the cotton, sugar, and rice plantations of the South, and that while I knew it would please the students very much to place them at once in finely constructed buildings, I felt that it would be following out a more natural process of development to teach them how to construct their own buildings. Mistakes I knew would be made, but these mistakes would teach us valuable lessons for the future.

During the now nineteen years' existence of the Tuskegee school, the plan of having the buildings erected by student labour has been adhered to. In this time forty buildings, counting small and large, have been built, and all except four are almost wholly the product of student labour. As an additional result, hundreds of men are now scattered throughout the South who received their knowledge of mechanics while being taught how to erect these buildings. Skill and knowledge are now handed down from one set of students to another in this way, until at the present time a building of any description or size can be constructed wholly by our instructors and students, from the drawing of the plans to the putting in of the electric fixtures, without going off the grounds for a single workman.

Not a few times, when a new student has been led into the temptation of marring the looks of some building by leadpencil marks or by the cuts of a jackknife, I have heard an old student remind him: "Don't do that. That is our building. I helped put it up."

In the early days of the school I think my most trying experience was in the matter of brickmaking. As soon as we got the farm work reasonably well started, we directed our next efforts toward the industry of making bricks. We needed these for use in connection with the erection of our own buildings; but there was also another reason for establishing this industry. There was no brickyard in the town, and in addition to our own needs there was a demand for bricks in the general market.

I had always sympathized with the "Children of Israel," in their task of "making bricks without straw," but ours was the task of making bricks with no money and no experience.

In the first place, the work was hard and dirty, and it

was difficult to get the students to help. When it came to brickmaking, their distaste for manual labour in connection with book education became especially manifest. It was not a pleasant task for one to stand in the mud-pit for hours, with the mud up to his knees. More than one man became disgusted and left the school.

We tried several locations before we opened up a pit that furnished brick clay. I had always supposed that brickmaking was very simple, but I soon found out by bitter experience that it required special skill and knowledge, particularly in the burning of the bricks. After a good deal of effort we moulded about twenty-five thousand bricks, and put them into a kiln to be burned. This kiln turned out to be a failure, because it was not properly constructed or properly burned. We began at once, however, on a second kiln. This, for some reason, also proved a failure. The failure of this kiln made it still more difficult to get the students to take any part in the work. Several of the teachers, however, who had been trained in the industries at Hampton, volunteered their services, and in some way we succeeded in getting a third kiln ready for burning. The burning of a kiln required about a week. Toward the latter part of the week, when it seemed as if we were going to have a good many thousand bricks in a few hours, in the middle of the night the kiln fell. For the third time we had failed.

The failure of this last kiln left me without a single dollar with which to make another experiment. Most of the teachers advised the abandoning of the effort to make bricks. In the midst of my troubles I thought of a watch which had come into my possession years before. I took this watch to the city of Montgomery, which was not far distant, and placed it in a pawn-shop. I secured cash upon it to the amount of fifteen dollars, with which to renew the brickmaking experiment. I returned to Tuskegee, and, with the help of the fifteen dollars, rallied our rather demoralized and discouraged forces and began a fourth attempt to make bricks. This time, I am glad to say, we were successful. Before I got hold of any money, the time-limit on my watch had expired, and I have never seen it since; but I have never regretted the loss of it.

Brickmaking has now become such an important industry at the school that last season our students manufactured twelve hundred thousand of first-class bricks, of a quality suitable to be sold in any market. Aside from this, scores of young men have mastered the brickmaking trade—both the making of bricks by hand and by machinery—and are now engaged in this industry in many parts of the South.

The making of these bricks taught me an important lesson in regard to the relations of the two races in the South. Many white people who had had no contact with the school, and perhaps no sympathy with it, came to us to buy bricks because they found out that ours were good bricks. They discovered that we were supplying a real want in the community. The making of these bricks caused many of the white residents of the neighbourhood to begin to feel that the education of the Negro was not making him worthless, but that in educating our students we were adding something to the wealth and comfort of the community. As the people of the neighbourhood came to us to buy bricks, we got acquainted with them; they traded with us and we with them. Our business interests became inter-mingled. We had something which they wanted; they had something which we wanted. This, in a large measure, helped to lay the foundation for the pleasant relations that have continued to exist between us and the white people in that section, and which now ex-tend throughout the South.

Wherever one of our brickmakers has gone in the South, we find that he has something to contribute to the well-being of the community into which he has gone; something that has made the community feel that, in a degree, it is indebted to him, and perhaps, to a certain extent, dependent upon him. In this way pleas-ant relations between the races have been stimulated.

My experience is that there is something in human nature which always makes an individual recognize and reward merit, no matter under what colour of skin merit is found. I have found, too, that it is the visible, the tangible, that goes a long ways in softening prejudices. The actual sight of a first-class house that a Negro has built is ten times more potent than pages of discussion about a house that he ought to build, or perhaps could build.

The same principle of industrial education has been carried out in the building of our own wagons, carts, and buggies, from the first. We now own and use on our farm and about the school dozens of these vehicles, and every one of them has been built by the hands of the students. Aside from this, we help supply the local market with these vehicles. The supplying of them to the people in the community has had the same effect as the supplying of bricks, and the man who learns at Tuskegee to build and repair wagons and carts is regarded as a benefactor by both races in the community where he goes. The people with whom he lives and works are going to think twice before they part with such a man.

The individual who can do something that the world wants done will, in the end, make his way regardless of his race. One man may go into a community prepared to supply the people there with an analysis of Greek sentences. The community may not at that time be prepared for, or feel the need of, Greek analysis, but it may feel its need of bricks and houses and wagons. If the man can supply the need for those, then, it will lead eventually to a demand for the first product, and with the demand will come the ability to appreciate it and to profit by it.

About the time that we succeeded in burning our first kiln of bricks we began facing in an emphasized form the objection of the students to being taught to work. By this time it had gotten to be pretty well advertised throughout the state that every student who came to Tuskegee, no matter what his financial ability might be, must learn some industry. Quite a number of letters came from parents protesting against their children engaging in labour while they were in the school. Other parents came to the school to protest in person. Most of the new students brought a written or a verbal request from their parents to the effect that they wanted their children taught nothing but books. The more books, the larger they were, and the longer the titles printed upon them, the better pleased the students and their parents seemed to be.

I gave little heed to these protests, except that I lost no opportunity to go into as many parts of the state as I could, for the purpose of speaking to the parents, and showing them the value of industrial education. Besides, I talked to the students constantly on the subject. Notwithstanding the unpopularity of industrial work, the school continued to increase in numbers to such an extent that by the middle of the second year there was an attendance of about one hundred and fifty, representing almost all parts of the state of Alabama, and including a few from other states.

In the summer of 1882 Miss Davidson and I both went North and engaged in the work of raising funds for the completion of our new building. On my way North I stopped in New York to try to get a letter of recommendation from an officer of a missionary organization who had become somewhat acquainted with me a few years previous. This man not only refused to give me the letter, but advised me most earnestly to go back home at once, and not make an attempt to get money, for he was quite sure that I would never get more than enough to pay my travelling expenses. I thanked him for his advice, and proceeded on my journey.

The first place I went to in the North, was Northampton, Mass., where I spent nearly a half-day in looking for a coloured family with whom I could board, never dreaming that any hotel would admit me. I was greatly surprised when I found that I would have no trouble in being accommodated at a hotel.

We were successful in getting money enough so that on Thanksgiving Day of that year we held our first service in the chapel of Porter Hall, although the building was not completed.

In looking about for some one to preach the Thanksgiving sermon, I found one of the rarest men that it has ever been my privilege to know. This was the Rev. Robert C. Bedford, a white man from Wisconsin, who was then pastor of a little coloured Congregational church in Montgomery, Ala. Before going to Montgomery to look for some one to preach this sermon I had never heard of Mr. Bedford. He had never heard of me. He gladly consented to come to Tuskegee and hold the Thanksgiving service. It was the first service of the kind that the coloured people there had ever observed, and what a deep interest they manifested in it! The sight of the new building made it a day of Thanksgiving for them never to be forgotten.

Mr. Bedford consented to become one of the trustees of the school, and in that capacity, and as a worker for it, he has been connected with it for eighteen years. During this time he has borne the school upon his heart night and day, and is never so happy as when he is performing some service, no matter how humble, for it. He completely obliterates himself in everything, and looks only for permission to serve where service is most disagreeable, and where others would not be attracted. In all my relations with him he has seemed to me to approach as nearly to the spirit of the Master as almost any man I ever met.

A little later there came into the service of the school another man, quite young at the time, and fresh from Hampton, without whose service the school never could have become what it is. This was Mr. Warren Logan, who now for seventeen years has been the treasurer of the Institute, and the acting principal during my absence. He has always shown a degree of unselfishness and an amount of business tact, coupled with a clear judgment, that has kept the school in good condition no matter how long I have been absent from it. During all the financial stress through which the school has passed, his patience and faith in our ultimate success have not left him.

As soon as our first building was near enough to completion so that we could occupy a portion of it—which was near the middle of the second year of the school—we opened a boarding department. Students had begun coming from quite a distance, and in such increasing numbers that we felt more and more that we were merely skimming over the surface, in that we were not getting hold of the students in their home life.

We had nothing but the students and their appetites with which to begin a boarding department. No provision had been made in the new building for a kitchen and dining room; but we discovered that by digging out a large amount of earth from under the building we could make a partially lighted basement room that could be used for a kitchen and dining room. Again I called on the students to volunteer for work, this time to assist in digging out the basement. This they did, and in a few weeks we had a place to cook and eat in, although it was very rough and uncomfortable. Any one seeing the place now would never believe that it was once used for a dining room.

The most serious problem, though, was to get the boarding department started off in running order, with nothing to do with in the way of furniture, and with no money with which to buy anything. The merchants in the town would let us have what food we wanted on credit. In fact, in those earlier years I was constantly embarrassed because people seemed to have more faith in me than I had in myself. It was pretty hard to cook, however, without stoves, and awkward to eat without dishes. At first the cooking was done out-of-doors, in the old-fashioned, primitive style, in pots and skillets placed over a fire. Some of the carpenters' benches that had been used in the construction of the building were utilized for tables. As for dishes, there were too few to make it worth while to spend time in describing them.

No one connected with the boarding department seemed to have any idea that meals must be served at certain fixed and regular hours, and this was a source of great worry. Everything was so out of joint and so inconvenient that I feel safe in saying that for the first two weeks something was wrong at every meal. Either the meat was not done or had been burnt, or the salt had been left out of the bread, or the tea had been forgotten.

Early one morning I was standing near the dining-room door listening to the complaints of the students. The complaints that morning were especially emphatic and numerous, because the whole breakfast had been a failure. One of the girls who had failed to get any breakfast came out and went to the well to draw some water to drink to take the place of the breakfast which she had not been able to get. When she reached the well, she found that the rope was broken and that she could get no water. She turned from the well and said, in the most discouraged tone, not knowing that I was where I could hear her, "We can't even get water to drink at this school." I think no one remark ever came so near discouraging me as that one.

At another time, when Mr. Bedford—whom I have already spoken of as one of our trustees, and a devoted friend of the institution—was visiting the school, he was given a bedroom immediately over the dining room. Early in the morning he was awakened by a rather animated discussion between two boys in the dining room below. The discussion was over the question as to whose turn it was to use the coffee-cup that morning. One boy won the case by proving that for three mornings he had not had an opportunity to use the cup at all.

But gradually, by patience and hard work, we brought order out of chaos, just as will be true of any problem if we stick to it with patience and wisdom and earnest effort.

As I look back now over that part of our struggle, I am glad that we had it. I am glad that we endured all those discomforts and inconveniences. I am glad that our students had to dig out the place for their kitchen and dining room. I am glad that our first boarding-place was in that dismal, ill-lighted, and damp basement. Had we started in a fine, attractive, convenient room, I fear we would have "lost our heads" and become "stuck up." It means a great deal, I think, to start off on a foundation which one has made for one's self.

When our old students return to Tuskegee now, as they often do, and go into our large, beautiful, well-ventilated, and well-lighted dining room, and see tempting, well-cooked food—largely grown by the students themselves—and see tables, neat tablecloths and napkins, and vases of flowers upon the tables, and hear singing birds, and note that each meal is served exactly upon the minute, with no disorder, and with almost no complaint coming from the hundreds that now fill our dining room, they, too, often say to me that they are glad that we started as we did, and built ourselves up year by year, by a slow and natural process of growth.

CHAPTER XI

MAKING THEIR BEDS BEFORE
THEY COULD LIE ON THEM

A LITTLE LATER in the history of the school we had a visit from General J. F. B. Marshall, the Treasurer of the Hampton Institute, who had had faith enough to lend us the first two hundred and fifty dollars with which to make a payment down on the farm. He remained with us a week, and made a careful inspection of everything. He seemed well pleased with our progress, and wrote back interesting and encouraging reports to Hampton. A little later Miss Mary F. Mackie, the teacher who had given me the "sweeping" examination when I entered Hampton, came to see us, and still later General Armstrong himself came.

At the time of the visits of these Hampton friends the number of teachers at Tuskegee had increased considerably, and the most of the new teachers were graduates of the Hampton Institute. We gave our

Hampton friends, especially General Armstrong, a cordial welcome. They were all surprised and pleased at the rapid progress that the school had made within so short a time. The coloured people from miles around came to the school to get a look at General Armstrong, about whom they had heard so much. The General was not only welcomed by the members of my own race, but by the Southern white people as well.

This first visit which General Armstrong made to Tuskegee gave me an opportunity to get an insight into his character such as I had not before had. I refer to his interest in the Southern white people. Before this I had had the thought that General Armstrong, having fought the Southern white man, rather cherished a feeling of bitterness toward the white South, and was interested in helping only the coloured man there. But this visit convinced me that I did not know the greatness and the generosity of the man. I soon learned, by his visits to the Southern white people, and from his conversations with them, that he was as anxious about the prosperity and the happiness of the white race as the black. He cherished no bitterness against the South, and was happy when an opportunity offered for manifesting his sympathy. In all my acquaintance with General Armstrong I never heard him speak, in public or in private, a single bitter word against the white man in the South. From his example in this respect I learned the lesson that great men cultivate love, and that only little men cherish a spirit of hatred. I learned that assistance given to the weak makes the one who gives it strong; and that oppression of the unfortunate makes one weak.

It is now long ago that I learned this lesson from General Armstrong, and resolved that I would permit no man, no matter what his colour might be, to narrow and degrade my soul by making me hate him. With God's help, I believe that I have completely rid myself of any ill feeling toward the Southern white man for any wrong that he may have inflicted upon my race. I am made to feel just as happy now when I am rendering service to Southern white men as when the service is rendered to a member of my own race. I pity from the bottom of my heart any individual who is so unfortunate as to get into the habit of holding race prejudice.

The more I consider the subject, the more strongly I am convinced that the most harmful effect of the practice to which the people in certain sections of the South have felt themselves compelled to resort, in order to get rid of the force of the Negroes' ballot, is not wholly in the wrong done to the Negro, but in the permanent injury to the morals of the white man. The wrong to the Negro is temporary, but to the morals of the white man the injury is permanent. I have noted time and time again that when an individual perjures himself in order to break the force of the black man's ballot, he soon learns to practise dishonesty in other relations of life, not only where the Negro is concerned, but equally so where a white man is concerned. The white man who begins by cheating a Negro usually ends by cheating a white man. The white man who begins to break the law by lynching a Negro soon yields to the temptation to lynch a white man. All this, it seems to me, makes it important that the whole Nation lend a hand in trying to lift the burden of ignorance from the South.

Another thing that is becoming more apparent each year in the development of education in the South is the influence of General Armstrong's idea of education; and this not upon the blacks alone, but upon the whites also. At the present time there is almost no Southern state that is not putting forth efforts in the direction of securing industrial education for its white boys and girls, and in most cases it is easy to trace the history of these efforts back to General Armstrong.

Soon after the opening of our humble boarding department students began coming to us in still larger numbers. For weeks we not only had to contend with the difficulty of providing board, with no money, but also with that of providing sleeping accommodations.

For this purpose we rented a number of cabins near the school. These cabins were in a dilapidated condition, and during the winter months the students who occupied them necessarily suffered from the cold. We charged the students eight dollars a month—all they were able to pay—for their board. This included, besides board, room, fuel, and washing. We also gave the students credit on their board bills for all the work which they did for the school which was of any value to the institution. The cost of tuition, which was fifty dollars a year for each student, we had to secure then, as now, wherever we could.

This small charge in cash gave us no capital with which to start a boarding department. The weather during the second winter of our work was very cold. We were not able to provide enough bed-clothes to keep the students warm. In fact, for some time we were not able to provide, except in a few cases, bedsteads and mattresses of any kind. During the coldest nights I was so troubled about the discomfort of the students that I could not sleep myself. I recall that on several occasions I went in the middle of the night to the shanties occupied by the young men, for the purpose of comforting them. Often I found some of them sitting huddled around a fire, with the one blanket which we had been able to provide wrapped around them, trying in this way to keep warm. During the whole night some of them did not attempt to lie down. One morning, when the night previous had been unusually cold, I asked those of the students in the chapel who thought that they had been frostbitten during the night to raise their hands. Three hands went up. Notwithstanding these experiences, there was almost no complaining on the part of the students. They knew that we were doing the best that we could for them. They were happy in the privilege of being permitted to enjoy any kind of opportunity that would enable them to improve their condition. They were constantly asking what they might do to lighten the burdens of the teachers.

I have heard it stated more than once, both in the North and in the South, that coloured people would not obey and respect each other when one member of the race is placed in a position of authority over others. In regard to this general belief and these statements, I can say that during the nineteen years of my experience at Tuskegee I never, either by word or act, have been treated with disrespect by any student or officer connected with the institution. On the other hand, I am constantly embarrassed by the many acts of thoughtful kindness. The students do not seem to want to see me carry a large book or a satchel or any kind of a burden through the grounds. In such cases more than one always offers to relieve me. I almost never go out of my office when the rain is falling that some student does not come to my side with an umbrella and ask to be allowed to hold it over me.

While writing upon this subject, it is a pleasure for me to add that in all my contact with the white people of the South I have never received a single personal insult. The white people in and near Tuskegee, to an especial degree, seem to count it a privilege to show me all the respect within their power, and often go out of their way to do this.

Not very long ago I was making a journey between Dallas (Texas) and Houston. In some way it became known in advance that I was on the train. At nearly every station at which the train stopped, numbers of white people, including in most cases the officials of the town, came aboard and introduced themselves and thanked me heartily for the work that I was trying to do for the South.

On another occasion, when I was making a trip from Augusta, Georgia, to Atlanta, being rather tired from much travel, I rode in a Pullman sleeper. When I went into the car, I found there two ladies from Boston whom I knew well. These good ladies were perfectly ignorant, it seems, of the customs of the South, and in the goodness of their hearts insisted that I take a seat with them in their section. After some hesitation I consented. I had been there but a few minutes when one of them, without my knowledge, ordered supper to be served to the three of us. This embarrassed me still further. The car was full of Southern white men, most of whom had their eyes on our party. When I found that supper had been ordered, I tried to contrive some excuse that would permit me to leave the section, but the ladies insisted that I must eat with them. I finally settled back in my seat with a sigh, and said to myself, "I am in for it now, sure."

To add further to the embarrassment of the situation, soon after the supper was placed on the table one of the ladies remembered that she had in her satchel a special kind of tea which she wished served, and as she said she felt quite sure the porter did not know how to brew it properly, she insisted upon getting up and preparing and serving it herself. At last the meal was over; and it seemed the longest one that I had ever eaten. When we were through, I decided to get myself out of the embarrassing situation and go into the smoking-room, where most of the men were by that time, to see how the land lay. In the meantime, however, it had become known in some way throughout the car who I was. When I went into the smoking-room I was never more surprised in my life than when each man, nearly every one of them a citizen of Georgia, came up and introduced himself to me and thanked me earnestly for the work that I was trying to do for the whole South. This was not flattery, because each one of these individuals knew that he had nothing to gain by trying to flatter me.

From the first I have sought to impress the students with the idea that Tuskegee is not my institution, or that of the officers, but that it is their institution, and that they have as much interest in it as any of the trustees or instructors. I have further sought to have them feel that I am at the institution as their friend and adviser, and not as their overseer. It has been my aim to have them speak with directness and frankness about anything that concerns the life of the school. Two or three times a year I ask the students to write me a letter criticising or making complaints or suggestions about anything connected with the institution. When this is not done, I have them meet me in the chapel for a heart-to-heart talk about the conduct of the school. There are no meetings with our students that I enjoy more than these, and none are more helpful to me in planning for the future. These meetings, it seems to me, enable me to get at the very heart of all that concerns the school. Few things help an individual more than to place responsibility upon him, and to let him know that you trust him. When I have read of labour troubles between employers and employees, I have often thought that many strikes and similar disturbances might be avoided if the employers would cultivate the habit of getting nearer to their employees, of consulting and advising with them, and letting them feel that the interests of the two are the same. Every individual responds to confidence, and this is not more true of any race than of the Negroes. Let them once understand that you are unselfishly interested in them, and you can lead them to any extent.

It was my aim from the first at Tuskegee to not only have the buildings erected by the students themselves, but to have them make their own furniture as far as was possible. I now marvel at the patience of the students while sleeping upon the floor while waiting for some kind of a bedstead to be constructed, or at their sleeping without any kind of a mattress while waiting for something that looked like a mattress to be made.

In the early days we had very few students who had been used to handling carpenters' tools, and the bedsteads made by the students then were very rough and very weak. Not unfrequently when I went into the students' rooms in the morning I would find at least two bedsteads lying about on the floor. The problem of providing mattresses was a difficult one to solve. We finally mastered this, however, by getting some cheap cloth and sewing pieces of this together so as to make large bags. These bags we filled with the pine straw—or, as it is sometimes called, pine needles—which we secured from the forests near by. I am glad to say that the industry of mattress-making has grown steadily since then, and has been improved to such an extent that at the present time it is an important branch of the work which is taught systematically to a number of our girls, and that the mattresses that now come out of the mattress-shop at Tuskegee are about as good as those bought in the average store. For some time after the opening of the boarding department we had no chairs in the students' bedrooms or in the dining rooms. Instead of chairs we used stools which the students constructed by nailing together three pieces of rough board. As a rule, the furniture in the students' rooms during the early days of the school consisted of a bed, some stools, and sometimes a rough table made by the students. The plan of having the students make the furniture is still followed, but the number of pieces in a room has been increased, and the workmanship has so improved that little fault can be found with the articles now. One thing that I have always insisted upon at Tuskegee is that everywhere there should be absolute cleanliness. Over and over again the students were reminded in those first years—and are reminded now—that people would excuse us for our poverty, for our lack of comforts and conveniences, but that they would not excuse us for dirt.

Another thing that has been insisted upon at the school is the use of the tooth-brush. "The gospel of the tooth-brush," as General Armstrong used to call it, is a part of our creed at Tuskegee. No student is permitted to remain who does not keep and use a tooth-brush. Several times, in recent years, students have come to us who brought with them almost no other article except a tooth-brush. They had heard from the lips of older students about our insisting upon the use of this, and so, to make a good impression, they brought at least a tooth-brush with them. I remember that one morning, not long ago, I went with the lady principal on her usual morning tour of inspection of the girls' rooms. We found one room that contained three girls who had recently arrived at the school. When I asked them if they had tooth-brushes, one of the girls replied, pointing to a brush: "Yes, sir. That is our brush. We bought it together, yesterday." It did not take them long to learn a different lesson.

It has been interesting to note the effect that the use of the tooth-brush has had in bringing about a higher degree of civilization among the students. With few exceptions, I have noticed that, if we can get a student to the point where, when the first or second tooth-brush disappears, he of his own motion buys another, I have not been disappointed in the future of that individual. Absolute cleanliness of the body has been insisted upon from the first. The students have been taught to bathe as regularly as to take their meals. This lesson we began teaching before we had anything in the shape of a bath-house. Most of the students came from plantation districts, and often we had to teach them how to sleep at night; that is, whether between the two sheets—after we got to the point where we could provide them two sheets—or under both of them. Naturally I found it difficult to teach them to sleep between two sheets when we were able to supply but one. The importance of the use of the nightgown received the same attention.

For a long time one of the most difficult tasks was to teach the students that all the buttons were to be kept on their clothes, and that there must be no torn places and no grease-spots. This lesson, I am pleased to be able to say, has been so thoroughly learned and so faithfully handed down from year to year by one set of students to another that often at the present time, when the students march out of chapel in the evening and their dress is inspected, as it is every night, not one button is to be found missing.

CHAPTER XII

RAISING MONEY

WHEN WE opened our boarding department, we provided rooms in the attic of Porter Hall, our first building, for a number of girls. But the number of students, of both sexes, continued to increase. We could find rooms outside the school grounds for many of the young men, but the girls we did not care to expose in this way. Very soon the problem of providing more rooms for the girls, as well as a larger boarding department for all the students, grew serious. As a result, we finally decided to undertake the construction of a still larger building—a building that would contain rooms for the girls and boarding accommodations for all.

After having had a preliminary sketch of the needed building made, we found that it would cost about ten thousand dollars. We had no money whatever with which to begin; still we decided to give the needed building a name. We knew we could name it, even though we were in doubt about our ability to secure the means for its construction. We decided to call the proposed building Alabama Hall, in honour of the state in which we were labouring. Again Miss Davidson began making efforts to enlist the interest and help of the coloured and white people in and near Tuskegee. They responded willingly, in proportion to their means. The students, as in the case of our first building, Porter Hall, began digging out the dirt in order to allow of the laying of the foundations.

When we seemed at the end of our resources, so far as securing money was concerned, something occurred which showed the greatness of General Armstrong—something which proved how far he was above the ordinary individual. When we were in the midst of great anxiety as to where and how we were to get funds for the new building, I received a telegram from General Armstrong asking me if I could spend a month travelling with him through the North, and asking me, if I could do so, to come to Hampton at once. Of course I accepted General Armstrong's invitation, and went to Hampton immediately. On arriving there I found that the General had decided to take a quartette of singers through the North, and hold meetings for a month in important cities, at which meetings he and I were to speak. Imagine my surprise when the General told me, further, that these meetings were to be held, not in the interests of Hampton, but in the interests of Tuskegee, and that the Hampton Institute was to be responsible for all the expenses.

Although he never told me so in so many words, I found out that General Armstrong took this method of introducing me to the people of the North, as well as for the sake of securing some immediate funds to be used in the erection of Alabama Hall. A weak and narrow man would have reasoned that all the money which came to Tuskegee in this way would be just so much taken from the Hampton Institute; but none of these selfish or short-sighted feelings ever entered the breast of General Armstrong. He was too big to be little, too good to be mean. He knew that the people in the North who gave money gave it for the purpose of helping the whole cause of Negro civilization, and not merely for the advancement of any one school. The General knew, too, that the way to strengthen Hampton was to make it a centre of unselfish power in the working out of the whole Southern problem.

In regard to the addresses which I was to make in the North, I recall just one piece of advice which the General gave me. He said: "Give them an idea for every word." I think it would be hard to improve upon this advice; and it might be made to apply to all public speaking. From that time to the present I have always tried to keep his advice in mind.

Meetings were held in New York, Brooklyn, Boston, Philadelphia, and other large cities, and at all of these meetings General Armstrong pleaded, together with myself, for help, not for Hampton, but for Tuskegee. At these meetings an especial effort was made to secure help for the building of Alabama Hall, as well as to introduce the school to the attention of the general public. In both these respects the meetings proved successful.

After that kindly introduction I began going North alone to secure funds. During the last fifteen years I have been compelled to spend a large proportion of my time away from the school, in an effort to secure money to provide for the growing needs of the institution. In my efforts to get funds I have had some experiences that may be of interest to my readers. Time and time again I have been asked, by people who are trying to secure money for philanthropic purposes, what rule or rules I followed to secure the interest and help of people who were able to contribute money to worthy objects. As far as the science of what is called begging can be reduced to rules, I would say that I have had but two rules. First, always to do my whole duty regarding making our work known to individuals and organizations; and, second, not to worry about the results. This second rule has been the hardest for me to live up to. When bills are on the eve of falling due, with not a dollar in hand with which to meet them, it is pretty difficult to learn not to worry, although I think I am learning more and more each year that all worry simply consumes, and to no purpose, just so much physical and mental strength that might otherwise be given to effective work. After considerable experience in coming into contact with wealthy and noted men, I have observed that those who have accomplished the greatest results are those who "keep under the body"; are those who never grow excited or lose self-control, but are always calm, self-possessed, patient, and polite. I think that President William McKinley is the best example of a man of this class that I have ever seen.

In order to be successful in any kind of undertaking, I think the main thing is for one to grow to the point where he completely forgets himself; that is, to lose himself in a great cause. In proportion as one loses himself in this way, in the same degree does he get the highest happiness out of his work.

My experience in getting money for Tuskegee has taught me to have no patience with those people who are always condemning the rich because they are rich, and because they do not give more to objects of charity. In the first place, those who are guilty of such sweeping criticisms do not know how many people would be made poor, and how much suffering would result, if wealthy people were to part all at once with any large proportion of their wealth in a way to disorganize and cripple great business enterprises. Then very few persons have any idea of the large number of applications for help that rich people are constantly being flooded with. I know wealthy people who receive as many as twenty calls a day for help. More than once, when I have gone into the offices of rich men, I have found half a dozen persons waiting to see them, and all come for the same purpose, that of securing money. And all these calls in person, to say nothing of the applications received through the mails. Very few people have any idea of the amount of money given away by persons who never permit their names to be known. I have often heard persons condemned for not giving away money, who, to my own knowledge, were giving away thousands of dollars every year so quietly that the world knew nothing about it.

As an example of this, there are two ladies in New York, whose names rarely appear in print, but who, in a quiet way, have given us the means with which to erect three large and important buildings during the last eight years. Besides the gift of these buildings, they have made other generous donations to the school. And they not only help Tuskegee, but they are constantly seeking opportunities to help other worthy causes.

Although it has been my privilege to be the medium through which a good many hundred thousand dollars have been received for the work at Tuskegee, I have always avoided what the world calls "begging." I often tell people that I have never "begged" any money, and that I am not a "beggar." My experience and observation have convinced me that persistent asking outright for money from the rich does not, as a rule, secure help. I have usually proceeded on the principle that persons who possess sense enough to earn money have sense enough to know how to give it away, and that the mere making known of the facts regarding Tuskegee, and especially the facts regarding the work of the graduates, has been more effective than outright begging. I think that the presentation of facts, on a high, dignified plane, is all the begging that most rich people care for.

While the work of going from door to door and from office to office is hard, disagreeable, and costly in bodily strength, yet it has some compensations. Such work gives one a rare opportunity to study human nature. It also has its compensations in giving one an opportunity to meet some of the best people in the world—to be more correct, I think I should say *the best* people in the world. When one takes a broad survey of the country, he will find that the most useful and influential people in it are those who take the deepest interest in institutions that exist for the purpose of making the world better.

At one time, when I was in Boston, I called at the door of a rather wealthy lady, and was admitted to the vestibule and sent up my card. While I was waiting for an answer, her husband came in, and asked me in the most abrupt manner what I wanted. When I tried to explain the object of my call, he became still more ungentlemanly in his words and manner, and finally grew so excited that I left the house without waiting for a reply from the lady. A few blocks from that house I called to see a gentleman who received me in the most cordial manner. He wrote me his check for a generous sum, and then, before I had had an opportunity to thank him, said: "I am so grateful to you, Mr. Washington, for giving me the opportunity to help a good cause. It is a privilege to have a share in it. We in Boston are constantly indebted to you for doing *our* work." My experience in securing money convinces me that the first type of man is growing more rare all the time, and that the latter type is increasing; that is, that, more and more, rich people are coming to regard men and women who apply to them for help for worthy objects, not as beggars, but as agents for doing their work.

In the city of Boston I have rarely called upon an individual for funds that I have not been thanked for calling, usually before I could get an opportunity to thank the donor for the money. In that city the donors seem to feel, in a large degree, that an honour is being conferred upon them in their being permitted to give. Nowhere else have I met with, in so large a measure, this fine and Christlike spirit as in the city of Boston, although there are many notable instances of it outside that city. I repeat my belief that the world is growing in the direction of giving. I repeat that the main rule by which I have been guided in collecting money is to do my full duty in regard to giving people who have money an opportunity to help.

In the early years of the Tuskegee school I walked the streets or travelled country roads in the North for days and days without receiving a dollar. Often it has happened, when during the week I had been disappointed in not getting a cent from the very individuals from whom I most expected help, and when I was almost broken down and discouraged, that generous help has come from some one who I had had little idea would give at all.

I recall that on one occasion I obtained information that led me to believe that a gentleman who lived about two miles out in the country from Stamford, Conn., might become interested in our efforts at Tuskegee if our conditions and needs were presented to him. On an unusually cold and stormy day

I walked the two miles to see him. After some difficulty I succeeded in securing an interview with him. He listened with some degree of interest to what I had to say, but did not give me anything. I could not help having the feeling that, in a measure, the three hours that I had spent in seeing him had been thrown away. Still, I had followed my usual rule of doing my duty. If I had not seen him, I should have felt unhappy over neglect of duty.

Two years after this visit a letter came to Tuskegee from this man, which read like this: "Enclosed I send you a New York draft for ten thousand dollars, to be used in furtherance of your work. I had placed this sum in my will for your school, but deem it wiser to give it to you while I live. I recall with pleasure your visit to me two years ago."

I can hardly imagine any occurrence which could have given me more genuine satisfaction than the receipt of this draft. It was by far the largest single donation which up to that time the school had ever received. It came at a time when an unusually long period had passed since we had received any money. We were in great distress because of lack of funds, and the nervous strain was tremendous. It is difficult for me to think of any situation that is more trying on the nerves than that of conducting a large institution, with heavy financial obligations to meet, without knowing where the money is to come from to meet these obligations from month to month.

In our case I felt a double responsibility, and this made the anxiety all the more intense. If the institution had been officered by white persons, and had failed, it would have injured the cause of Negro education; but I knew that the failure of our institution, officered by Negroes, would not only mean the loss of a school, but would cause people, in a large degree, to lose faith in the ability of the entire race. The receipt of this draft for ten thousand dollars, under all these circumstances, partially lifted a burden that had been pressing down upon me for days.

From the beginning of our work to the present I have always had the feeling, and lose no opportunity to impress our teachers with the same idea, that the school will always be supported in proportion as the inside of the institution is kept clean and pure and wholesome.

The first time I ever saw the late Collis P. Huntington, the great railroad man, he gave me two dollars for our school. The last time I saw him, which was a few months before he died, he gave me fifty thousand dollars toward our endowment fund. Between these two gifts there were others of generous proportions which came every year from both Mr. and Mrs. Huntington.

Some people may say that it was Tuskegee's good luck that brought to us this gift of fifty thousand dollars. No, it was not luck. It was hard work. Nothing ever comes to one, that is worth having, except as a result of hard work. When Mr. Huntington gave me the first two dollars, I did not blame him for not giving me more, but made up my mind that I was going to convince him by tangible results that we were worthy of larger gifts. For a dozen years I made a strong effort to convince Mr. Huntington of the value of our work. I noted that just in proportion as the usefulness of the school grew, his donations increased. Never did I meet an individual who took a more kindly and sympathetic interest in our school than did Mr. Huntington. He not only gave money to us, but took time in which to advise me, as a father would a son, about the general conduct of the school.

More than once I have found myself in some pretty tight places while collecting money in the North. The following incident I have never related but once before, for the reason that I feared that people would not believe it. One morning I found myself in Providence, Rhode Island, without a cent of money with which to buy breakfast. In crossing the street to see a lady from whom I hoped to get some money, I found a bright new twenty-five-cent piece in the middle of the street-car track. I not only had this twenty-five cents for my breakfast, but within a few minutes I had a donation from the lady on whom I had started to call.

At one of our Commencements I was bold enough to invite the Rev. E. Winchester Donald, D.D., rector of Trinity Church, Boston, to preach the Commencement sermon. As we then had no room large enough to accommodate all who would be present, the place of meeting was under a large, improvised arbour, built partly of brush and partly of rough boards. Soon after Dr. Donald had begun speaking, the rain came down in torrents, and he had to stop, while some one held an umbrella over him.

The boldness of what I had done never dawned upon me until I saw the picture made by the rector of Trinity Church standing before that large audience under an old umbrella, waiting for the rain to cease so that he could go on with his address.

It was not very long before the rain ceased and Dr. Donald finished his sermon; and an excellent sermon it was, too, in spite of the weather. After he had gone to his room, and had gotten the wet threads of his clothes dry, Dr. Donald ventured the remark that a large chapel at Tuskegee would not be out of place. The next day a letter came from two ladies who were then travelling in Italy, saying that they had decided to give us the money for such a chapel as we needed.

A short time ago we received twenty thousand dollars from Mr. Andrew Carnegie, to be used for the purpose of erecting a new library building. Our first library and reading-room were in a corner of a shanty, and the whole thing occupied a space about five by twelve feet. It required ten years of work before I was able to secure Mr. Carnegie's interest and help. The first time I saw him, ten years ago, he seemed to take but little interest in our school, but I was determined to show him that we were worthy of his help. After ten years of hard work I wrote him a letter reading as follows:

DECEMBER 15, 1900.

MR. ANDREW CARNEGIE, 5 W. FIFTY-FIRST ST.,
    NEW YORK.

DEAR SIR: Complying with the request which you made of me when I saw you at your residence a few days ago, I now submit in writing an appeal for a library building for our institution.

We have 1100 students, 86 officers and instructors, together with their families, and about 200 coloured people living near the school, all of whom would make use of the library building.

We have over 12,000 books, periodicals, etc., gifts from our friends, but we have no suitable place for them, and we have no suitable reading-room.

Our graduates go to work in every section of the South,

and whatever knowledge might be obtained in the library would serve to assist in the elevation of the whole Negro race.

Such a building as we need could be erected for about $20,000. All of the work for the building, such as brickmaking, brick-masonry, carpentry, blacksmithing, etc., would be done by the students. The money which you would give would not only supply the building, but the erection of the building would give a large number of students an opportunity to learn the building trades, and the students would use the money paid to them to keep themselves in school. I do not believe that a similar amount of money often could be made go so far in uplifting a whole race.

If you wish further information, I shall be glad to furnish it.

Yours truly,

BOOKER T. WASHINGTON, Principal.

The next mail brought back the following reply: "I will be very glad to pay the bills for the library building as they are incurred, to the extent of twenty thousand dollars, and I am glad of this opportunity to show the interest I have in your noble work."

I have found that strict business methods go a long way in securing the interest of rich people. It has been my constant aim at Tuskegee to carry out, in our financial and other operations, such business methods as would be approved of by any New York banking house.

I have spoken of several large gifts to the school; but by far the greater proportion of the money that has built up the institution has come in the form of small donations from persons of moderate means. It is upon these small gifts, which carry with them the interest of hundreds of donors, that any philanthropic work must depend largely for its support. In my efforts to get money I have often been surprised at the patience and deep interest of the ministers, who are besieged on every hand and at all hours of the day for help. If no other consideration had convinced me of the value of the Christian life, the Christlike work which the Church of all denominations in America has done during the last thirty-five years for the elevation of the black man would have made me a Christian. In a large degree it has been the pennies, the nickels, and the dimes which have come from the Sunday-schools, the Christian Endeavour societies, and the missionary societies, as well as from the church proper, that have helped to elevate the Negro at so rapid a rate.

This speaking of small gifts reminds me to say that very few Tuskegee graduates fail to send us an annual contribution. These contributions range from twenty-five cents up to ten dollars.

Soon after beginning our third year's work we were surprised to receive money from three special sources, and up to the present time we have continued to receive help from them. First, the State Legislature of Alabama increased its annual appropriation from two thousand dollars to three thousand dollars; I might add that still later it increased this sum to four thousand five hundred dollars a year. The effort to secure this increase was led by the Hon. M. F. Foster,[3] the member of the Legislature from Tuskegee. Second, we received one thousand dollars from the John F. Slater Fund. Our work seemed to please the trustees of this fund, as they soon began increasing their annual grant. This has been added to from time to time until at present we receive eleven thousand dollars annually from this Fund. The other help to which I have referred came in the shape of an allowance from the Peabody Fund. This was at first five hundred dollars, but it has since been increased to fifteen hundred dollars.

The effort to secure help from the Slater and Peabody Funds brought me into contact with two rare men—men who have had much to do in shaping the policy for the education of the Negro. I refer to the Hon. J. L. M. Curry, of Washington, who is the general agent for these two funds, and Mr. Morris K. Jesup, of New York. Dr. Curry is a native of the South, an ex-Confederate soldier, yet I do not believe there is any man in the country who is more deeply interested in the highest welfare of the Negro than Dr. Curry, or one who is more free from race prejudice. He enjoys the unique distinction of possessing to an equal degree the confidence of the black man and the Southern white man. I shall never forget the first time I met him. It was in Richmond, Va., where he was then living. I had heard much about him. When I first went into his presence, trembling because of my youth and inexperience, he took me by the hand so cordially, and spoke such encouraging words, and gave me such helpful advice regarding the proper course to pursue, that I came to know him then, as I have known him ever since, as a high example of one who is constantly and unselfishly at work for the betterment of humanity.

Mr. Morris K. Jesup, the treasurer of the Slater Fund, I refer to because I know of no man of wealth and large and complicated business responsibilities who gives not only money but his time and thought to the subject of the proper method of elevating the Negro to the extent that is true of Mr. Jesup. It is very largely through his effort and influence that during the last few years the subject of industrial education has assumed the importance that it has, and been placed on its present footing.

CHAPTER XIII

TWO THOUSAND MILES FOR A
FIVE-MINUTE SPEECH

SOON AFTER the opening of our boarding department, quite a number of students who evidently were worthy, but who were so poor that they did not have any money to pay even the small charges at the school, began applying for admission. This class was composed of both men and women. It was a great trial to refuse admission to these applicants, and in 1884 we established a night-school to accommodate a few of them.

The night-school was organized on a plan similar to the one which I had helped to establish at Hampton. At first it was composed of about a dozen students. They were admitted to the night-school only when they had no money with which to pay any part of their board in the regular day-school. It was further required that they must work for ten hours during the day at some trade or industry, and study academic branches for two hours during the evening. This was the requirement for the first one or two years of their stay. They were to be paid something above the cost of their board, with the understanding that all of their earnings, except a very small part, were to be reserved in the school's treasury, to be used for paying their board in the regular day-school after they had entered that department. The night-school, started in this manner, has grown until there are at present four hundred and fifty-seven students enrolled in it alone.

There could hardly be a more severe test of a student's worth than this branch of the Institute's work. It is largely because it furnishes such a good opportunity to test the backbone of a student that I place such high value upon our night-school. Any one who is willing to work ten hours a day at the brick-yard, or in the laundry, through one or two years, in order that he or she may have the privilege of studying academic branches for two hours in the evening, has enough bottom to warrant being further educated.

After the student has left the night-school he enters the day-school, where he takes academic branches four days in a week, and works at his trade two days. Besides this he usually works at his trade during the three summer months. As a rule, after a student has succeeded in going through the night-school test, he finds a way to finish the regular course in industrial and academic training. No student, no matter how much money he may be able to command, is permitted to go through school without doing manual labour. In fact, the industrial work is now as popular as the academic branches. Some of the most successful men and women who have graduated from the institution obtained their start in the night-school.

While a great deal of stress is laid upon the industrial side of the work at Tuskegee, we do not neglect or overlook in any degree the religious and spiritual side. The school is strictly undenominational, but it is thoroughly Christian, and the spiritual training of the students is not neglected. Our preaching service, prayer-meetings, Sunday-school, Christian Endeavour Society, Young Men's Christian Association, and various missionary organizations, testify to this.

In 1885, Miss Olivia Davidson, to whom I have already referred as being largely responsible for the success of the school during its early history, and I were married. During our married life she continued to divide her time and strength between our home and the work for the school. She not only continued to work in the school at Tuskegee, but also kept up her habit of going North to secure funds. In 1889 she died, after four years of happy married life and eight years of hard and happy work for the school. She literally wore herself out in her never ceasing efforts in behalf of the work that she so dearly loved. During our married life there were born to us two bright, beautiful boys, Baker Taliaferro[4] and Ernest Davidson. The older of these, Baker, has already mastered the brickmaker's trade at Tuskegee.

I have often been asked how I began the practice of public speaking. In answer I would say that I never planned to give any large part of my life to speaking in public. I have always had more of an ambition to *do* things than merely to talk *about* doing them. It seems that when I went North with General Armstrong to speak at the series of public meetings to which I have referred, the President of the National Educational Association, the Hon. Thomas W. Bicknell, was present at one of those meetings and heard me speak. A few days afterward he sent me an invitation to deliver an address at the next meeting of the Educational Association. This meeting was to be held in Madison, Wis. I accepted the invitation. This was, in a sense, the beginning of my public-speaking career.

On the evening that I spoke before the Association there must have been not far from four thousand persons present. Without my knowing it, there were a large number of people present from Alabama, and some from the town of Tuskegee. These white people afterward frankly told me that they went to this meeting expecting to hear the South roundly abused, but were pleasantly surprised to find that there was no word of abuse in my address. On the contrary, the South was given credit for all the praiseworthy things that it had done. A white lady who was teacher in a college in Tuskegee wrote back to the local paper that she was gratified, as well as surprised, to note the credit which I gave the white people of Tuskegee for their help in getting the school started. This address at Madison was the first that I had delivered that in any large measure dealt with the general problem of the races. Those who heard it seemed to be pleased with what I said and with the general position that I took.

When I first came to Tuskegee, I determined that I would make it my home, that I would take as much pride in the right actions of the people of the town as any white man could do, and that I would, at the same time, deplore the wrong-doing of the people as much as any white man. I determined never to say anything in a public address in the North that I would not be willing to say in the South. I early learned that it is a hard matter to convert an individual by abusing him, and that this is more often accomplished by giving credit for all the praiseworthy actions performed than by calling attention alone to all the evil done.

While pursuing this policy I have not failed, at the proper time and in the proper manner, to call attention, in no uncertain terms, to the wrongs which any part of the South has been guilty of. I have found that there is a large element in the South that is quick to respond to straightforward, honest criticism of any wrong policy. As a rule, the place to criticise the South, when criticism is necessary, is in the South—not in Boston. A Boston man who came to Alabama to criticise Boston would not effect so much good, I think, as one who had his word of criticism to say in Boston.

In this address at Madison I took the ground that the policy to be pursued with reference to the races was, by every honourable means, to bring them together and to encourage the cultivation of friendly relations, instead of doing that which would embitter. I further contended that, in relation to his vote, the Negro should more and more consider the interests of the community in which he lived, rather than seek alone to please some one who lived a thousand miles away from him and from his interests.

In this address I said that the whole future of the Negro rested largely upon the question as to whether or not he should make himself, through his skill, intelligence, and character, of such undeniable value to the community in which he lived that the community could not dispense with his presence. I said that any individual who learned to do something better than anybody else—learned to do a common thing in an uncommon manner—had solved his problem, regardless of the colour of his skin, and that in proportion as the Negro learned to produce what other people wanted and must have, in the same proportion would he be respected.

I spoke of an instance where one of our graduates had produced two hundred and sixty-six bushels of sweet potatoes from an acre of ground, in a community where the average production had been only forty-nine bushels to the acre. He had been able to do this by reason of his knowledge of the chemistry of the soil and by his knowledge of improved methods of agriculture. The white farmers in the neighbourhood respected him, and came to him for ideas regarding the raising of sweet potatoes. These white farmers honoured and respected him because he, by his skill and knowledge, had added something to the wealth and the comfort of the community in which he lived. I explained that my theory of education for the Negro would not, for example, confine him for all time to farm life—to the production of the best and the most sweet potatoes—but that, if he succeeded in this line of industry, he could lay the foundations upon which his children and grandchildren could grow to higher and more important things in life.

Such, in brief, were some of the views I advocated in this first address dealing with the broad question of the relations of the two races, and since that time I have not found any reason for changing my views on any important point.

In my early life I used to cherish a feeling of ill will toward any one who spoke in bitter terms against the Negro, or who advocated measures that tended to oppress the black man or take from him opportunities for growth in the most complete manner. Now, whenever I hear any one advocating measures that are meant to curtail the development of another, I pity the individual who would do this. I know that the one who makes this mistake does so because of his own lack of opportunity for the highest kind of growth. I pity him because I know that he is trying to stop the progress of the world, and because I know that in time the development and the ceaseless advance of humanity will make him ashamed of his weak and narrow position. One might as well try to stop the progress of a mighty railroad train by throwing his body across the track, as to try to stop the growth of the world in the direction of giving mankind more intelligence, more culture, more skill, more liberty, and in the direction of extending more sympathy and more brotherly kindness.

The address which I delivered at Madison, before the National Educational Association, gave me a rather wide introduction in the North, and soon after that opportunities began offering themselves for me to address audiences there.

I was anxious, however, that the way might also be opened for me to speak directly to a representative Southern white audience. A partial opportunity of this kind, one that seemed to me might serve as an entering wedge, presented itself in 1893, when the international meeting of Christian Workers was held at Atlanta, Ga. When this invitation came to me, I had engagements in Boston that seemed to make it impossible for me to speak in Atlanta. Still, after looking over my list of dates and places carefully, I found that I could take a train from Boston that would get me into Atlanta about thirty minutes before my address was to be delivered, and that I could remain in that city about sixty minutes before taking another train for Boston. My invitation to speak in Atlanta stipulated that I was to confine my address to five minutes. The question, then, was whether or not I could put enough into a five-minute address to make it worth while for me to make such a trip.

I knew that the audience would be largely composed of the most influential class of white men and women, and that it would be a rare opportunity for me to let them know what we were trying to do at Tuskegee, as well as to speak to them about the relations of the races. So I decided to make the trip. I spoke for five minutes to an audience of two thousand people, composed mostly of Southern and Northern whites. What I said seemed to be received with favour and enthusiasm. The Atlanta papers of the next day commented in friendly terms on my address, and a good deal was said about it in different parts of the country. I felt that I had in some degree accomplished my object—that of getting a hearing from the dominant class of the South.

The demands made upon me for public addresses continued to increase, coming in about equal numbers from my own people and from Northern whites. I gave as much time to these addresses as I could spare from the immediate work at Tuskegee. Most of the addresses in the North were made for the direct purpose of getting funds with which to support the school. Those delivered before the coloured people had for their main object the impressing upon them of the importance of industrial and technical education in addition to academic and religious training.

I now come to that one of the incidents in my life which seems to have excited the greatest amount of interest, and which perhaps went further than anything else in giving me a reputation that in a sense might be called National. I refer to the address which I delivered at the opening of the Atlanta Cotton states and International Exposition, at Atlanta, Ga., September 18, 1895.

So much has been said and written about this incident, and so many questions have been asked me concerning the address, that perhaps I may be excused for taking up the matter with some detail. The five-minute address in Atlanta, which I came from Boston to deliver, was possibly the prime cause for an opportunity being given me to make the second address there. In the spring of 1895 I received a telegram from prominent citizens in Atlanta asking me to accompany a committee from that city to Washington for the purpose of appearing before a committee of Congress in the interest of securing Government help for the Exposition. The committee was composed of about twenty-five of the most prominent and most influential white men of Georgia. All the members of this committee were white men except Bishop Grant,[5] Bishop Gaines,[6] and myself. The Mayor and several other city and state officials spoke before the committee. They were followed by the two coloured bishops. My name was the last on the list of speakers. I had never before appeared before such a committee, nor had I ever delivered any address in the capital of the Nation. I had many misgivings as to what I ought to say, and as to the impression that my address would make. While I cannot recall in detail what I said, I remember that I tried to impress upon the committee, with all the earnestness and plainness of any language that I could command, that if Congress wanted to do something which would assist in ridding the South of the race question and making friends between the two races, it should, in every proper way, encourage the material and intellectual growth of both races. I said that the Atlanta Exposition would present an opportunity for both races to show what advance they had made since freedom, and would at the same time afford encouragement to them to make still greater progress.

I tried to emphasize the fact that while the Negro should not be deprived by unfair means of the franchise, political agitation alone would not save him, and that back of the ballot he must have property, industry, skill, economy, intelligence, and character, and that no race without these elements could permanently succeed. I said that in granting the appropriation Congress could do something that would prove to be of real and lasting value to both races, and that it was the first great opportunity of the kind that had been presented since the close of the Civil War.

I spoke for fifteen or twenty minutes, and was surprised at the close of my address to receive the hearty congratulations of the Georgia committee and of the members of Congress who were present. The Committee was unanimous in making a favourable report, and in a few days the bill passed Congress. With the passing of this bill the success of the Atlanta Exposition was assured.

Soon after this trip to Washington the directors of the Exposition decided that it would be a fitting recognition of the coloured race to erect a large and attractive building which should be devoted wholly to showing the progress of the Negro since freedom. It was further decided to have the building designed and erected wholly by Negro mechanics. This plan was carried out. In design, beauty, and general finish the Negro Building was equal to the others on the grounds.

After it was decided to have a separate Negro exhibit, the question arose as to who should take charge of it. The officials of the Exposition were anxious that I should assume this responsibility, but I declined to do so, on the plea that the work at Tuskegee at that time demanded my time and strength. Largely at my suggestion, Mr. I. Garland Penn, of Lynchburg, Va., was selected to be at the head of the Negro department. I gave him all the aid that I could. The Negro exhibit, as a whole, was large and creditable. The two exhibits in this department which attracted the greatest amount of attention were those from the Hampton Institute and the Tuskegee Institute. The people who seemed to be the most surprised, as well as pleased, at what they saw in the Negro Building were the Southern white people.

As the day for the opening of the Exposition drew near, the Board of Directors began preparing the programme for the opening exercises. In the discussion from day to day of the various features of this programme, the question came up as to the advisability of putting a member of the Negro race on for one of the opening addresses, since the Negroes had been asked to take such a prominent part in the Exposition. It was argued, further, that such recognition would mark the good feeling prevailing between the two races. Of course there were those who were opposed to any such recognition of the rights of the Negro, but the Board of Directors, composed of men who represented the best and most progressive element in the South, had their way, and voted to invite a black man to speak on the opening day. The next thing was to decide upon the person who was thus to represent the Negro race. After the question had been canvassed for several days, the directors voted unanimously to ask me to deliver one of the opening-day addresses, and in a few days after that I received the official invitation.

The receiving of this invitation brought to me a sense of responsibility that it would be hard for any one not placed in my position to appreciate. What were my feelings when this invitation came to me? I remembered that I had been a slave; that my early years had been spent in the lowest depths of poverty and ignorance, and that I had had little opportunity to prepare me for such a responsibility as this. It was only a few years before that time that any white man in the audience might have claimed me as his slave; and it was easily possible that some of my former owners might be present to hear me speak.

I knew, too, that this was the first time in the entire history of the Negro that a member of my race had been asked to speak from the same platform with white Southern men and women on any important National occasion. I was asked now to speak to an audience composed of the wealth and culture of the white South, the representatives of my former masters. I knew, too, that while the greater part of my audience would be composed of Southern people, yet there would be present a large number of Northern whites, as well as a great many men and women of my own race.

I was determined to say nothing that I did not feel from the bottom of my heart to be true and right. When the invitation came to me, there was not one word of intimation as to what I should say or as to what I should omit. In this I felt that the Board of Directors had paid a tribute to me. They knew that by one sentence I could have blasted, in a large degree, the success of the Exposition. I was also painfully conscious of the fact that, while I must be true to my own race in my utterances, I had it in my power to make such an ill-timed address as would result in preventing any similar invitation being extended to a black man again for years to come. I was equally determined to be true to the North, as well as to the best element of the white South, in what I had to say.

The papers, North and South, had taken up the discussion of my coming speech, and as the time for it drew near this discussion became more and more widespread. Not a few of the Southern white papers were unfriendly to the idea of my speaking. From my own race I received many suggestions as to what I ought to say. I prepared myself as best I could for the address, but as the eighteenth of September drew nearer, the heavier my heart became, and the more I feared that my effort would prove a failure and a disappointment.

The invitation had come at a time when I was very busy with my school work, as it was the beginning of our school year. After preparing my address, I went through it, as I usually do with all those utterances which I consider particularly important, with Mrs. Washington, and she approved of what I intended to say. On the sixteenth of September, the day before I was to start for Atlanta, so many of the Tuskegee teachers expressed a desire to hear my address that I consented to read it to them in a body. When I had done so, and had heard their criticisms and comments, I felt somewhat relieved, since they seemed to think well of what I had to say.

On the morning of September 17, together with Mrs. Washington and my three children, I started for Atlanta. I felt a good deal as I suppose a man feels when he is on his way to the gallows. In passing through the town of Tuskegee I met a white farmer who lived some distance out in the country. In a jesting manner this man said: "Washington, you have spoken before the Northern white people, the Negroes in the South, and to us country white people in the South; but in Atlanta, to-morrow, you will have before you the Northern whites, the Southern whites, and the Negroes all together. I am afraid that you have got yourself into a tight place." This farmer diagnosed the situation correctly, but his frank words did not add anything to my comfort.

In the course of the journey from Tuskegee to Atlanta both coloured and white people came to the train to point me out, and discussed with perfect freedom, in my hearing, what was going to take place the next day. We were met by a committee in Atlanta. Almost the first thing that I heard when I got off the train in that city was an expression something like this, from an old coloured man near by: "Dat's de man of my race what's gwine to make a speech at de Exposition to-morrow. I'se sho' gwine to hear him."

Atlanta was literally packed, at the time, with people from all parts of this country, and with representatives of foreign governments, as well as with military and civic organizations. The afternoon papers had forecasts of the next day's proceedings in flaring headlines. All this tended to add to my burden. I did not sleep much that night. The next morning, before day, I went carefully over what I intended to say. I also kneeled down and asked God's blessing upon my effort. Right here, perhaps, I ought to add that I make it a rule never to go before an audience, on any occasion, without asking the blessing of God upon what I want to say.

I always make it a rule to make especial preparation for each separate address. No two audiences are exactly alike. It is my aim to reach and talk to the heart of each individual audience, taking it into my confidence very much as I would a person. When I am speaking to an audience, I care little for how what I am saying is going to sound in the newspapers, or to another audience, or to an individual. At the time, the audience before me absorbs all my sympathy, thought, and energy.

Early in the morning a committee called to escort me to my place in the procession which was to march to the Exposition grounds. In this procession were prominent coloured citizens in carriages, as well as several Negro military organizations. I noted that the Exposition officials seemed to go out of their way to see that all of the coloured people in the procession were properly placed and properly treated. The procession was about three hours in reaching the Exposition grounds, and during all of this time the sun was shining down upon us disagreeably hot. When we reached the grounds, the heat, together with my nervous anxiety, made me feel as if I were about ready to collapse, and to feel that my address was not going to be a success. When I entered the audience-room, I found it packed with humanity from bottom to top, and there were thousands outside who could not get in.

The room was very large, and well suited to public speaking. When I entered the room, there were vigorous cheers from the coloured portion of the audience, and faint cheers from some of the white people. I had been told, while I had been in Atlanta, that while many white people were going to be present to hear me speak, simply out of curiosity, and that others who would be present would be in full sympathy with me, there was a still larger element of the audience which would consist of those who were going to be present for the purpose of hearing me make a fool of myself, or, at least, of hearing me say some foolish thing, so that they could say to the officials who had invited me to speak, "I told you so!"

One of the trustees of the Tuskegee Institute, as well as my personal friend, Mr. William H. Baldwin, Jr. was at the time General Manager of the Southern Railroad, and happened to be in Atlanta on that day. He was so nervous about the kind of reception that I would have, and the effect that my speech would produce, that he could not persuade himself to go into the building, but walked back and forth in the grounds outside until the opening exercises were over.

CHAPTER XIV

THE ATLANTA EXPOSITION ADDRESS

THE ATLANTA Exposition, at which I had been asked to make an address as a representative of the Negro race, as stated in the last chapter, was opened with a short address from Governor Bullock.[7] After other interesting exercises, including an invocation from Bishop Nelson,[8] of Georgia, a dedicatory ode by Albert Howell, Jr., and addresses by the President of the Exposition and Mrs. Joseph Thompson, the President of the Woman's Board, Governor Bullock introduced me with the words, "We have with us to-day a representative of Negro enterprise and Negro civilization."

When I arose to speak, there was considerable cheering, especially from the coloured people. As I remember it now, the thing that was uppermost in my mind was the desire to say something that would cement the friendship of the races and bring about hearty coöperation between them. So far as my outward surroundings were concerned, the only thing that I recall distinctly now is that when I got up, I saw thousands of eyes looking intently into my face. The following is the address which I delivered:—

MR. PRESIDENT AND GENTLEMEN OF THE BOARD OF DIRECTORS AND CITIZENS.

One-third of the population of the South is of the Negro race. No enterprise seeking the material, civil, or moral welfare of this section can disregard this element of our population and reach the highest success. I but convey to you, Mr. President and Directors, the sentiment of the masses of my race when I say that in no way have the value and manhood of the American Negro been more fittingly and generously recognized than by the managers of this magnificent Exposition at every stage of its progress. It is a recognition that will do more to cement the friendship of the two races than any occurrence since the dawn of our freedom.

Not only this, but the opportunity here afforded will awaken among us a new era of industrial progress. Ignorant and inexperienced, it is not strange that in the first years of our new life we began at the top instead of at the bottom; that a seat in Congress or the state legislature was more sought than real estate or industrial skill; that the political convention or stump speaking had more attractions than starting a dairy farm or truck garden.

A ship lost at sea for many days suddenly sighted a friendly vessel. From the mast of the unfortunate vessel was seen a signal, "Water, water; we die of thirst!" The answer from the friendly vessel at once came back, "Cast down your bucket where you are." A second time the signal, "Water, water; send us water!" ran up from the distressed vessel, and was answered, "Cast down your bucket where you are." And a third and fourth signal for water was answered, "Cast down your bucket where you are." The captain of the distressed vessel, at last heeding the injunction, cast down his bucket, and it came up full of fresh, sparkling water from the mouth of the Amazon River. To those of my race who depend on bettering their condition in a foreign land or who underestimate the importance of cultivating friendly relations with the Southern white man, who is their next-door neighbour, I would say: "Cast down your bucket where you are"—cast it down in making friends in every manly way of the people of all races by whom we are surrounded.

Cast it down in agriculture, mechanics, in commerce, in domestic service, and in the professions. And in this connection it is well to bear in mind that whatever other sins the South may be called to bear, when it comes to business, pure and simple, it is in the

South that the Negro is given a man's chance in the commercial world, and in nothing is this Exposition more eloquent than in emphasizing this chance. Our greatest danger is that in the great leap from slavery to freedom we may overlook the fact that the masses of us are to live by the productions of our hands, and fail to keep in mind that we shall prosper in proportion as we learn to dignify and glorify common labour and put brains and skill into the common occupations of life; shall prosper in proportion as we learn to draw the line between the superficial and the substantial, the ornamental gewgaws of life and the useful. No race can prosper till it learns that there is as much dignity in tilling a field as in writing a poem. It is at the bottom of life we must begin, and not at the top. Nor should we permit our grievances to overshadow our opportunities.

To those of the white race who look to the incoming of those of foreign birth and strange tongue and habits for the prosperity of the South, were I permitted I would repeat what I say to my own race, "Cast down your bucket where you are." Cast it down among the eight millions of Negroes whose habits you know, whose fidelity and love you have tested in days when to have proved treacherous meant the ruin of your firesides. Cast down your bucket among these people who have, without strikes and labour wars, tilled your fields, cleared your forests, builded your railroads and cities, and brought forth treasures from the bowels of the earth, and helped make possible this magnificent representation of the progress of the South. Casting down your bucket among my people, helping and encouraging them as you are doing on these grounds, and to education of head, hand, and heart, you will find that they will buy your surplus land, make blossom the waste places in your fields, and run your factories. While doing this, you can be sure in the future, as in the past, that you and your families will be surrounded by the most patient, faithful, law-abiding, and unresentful people that the world has seen. As we have proved our loyalty to you in the past, in nursing your children, watching by the sick-bed of your mothers and fathers, and often following them with tear-dimmed eyes to their graves, so in the future, in our humble way, we shall stand by you with a devotion that no foreigner can approach, ready to lay down our lives, if need be, in defence of yours, interlacing our industrial, commercial, civil, and religious life with yours in a way that shall make the interests of both races one. In all things that are purely social we can be as separate as the fingers, yet one as the hand in all things essential to mutual progress.

There is no defence or security for any of us except in the highest intelligence and development of all. If anywhere there are efforts tending to curtail the fullest growth of the Negro, let these efforts be turned into stimulating, encouraging, and making him the most useful and intelligent citizen. Effort or means so invested will pay a thousand per cent interest. These efforts will be twice blessed—"blessing him that gives and him that takes."

There is no escape through law of man or God from the inevitable:—

> The laws of changeless justice bind
> Oppressor with oppressed;
> And close as sin and suffering joined
> We march to fate abreast.

Nearly sixteen millions of hands will aid you in pulling the load upward, or they will pull against you the load downward. We shall constitute one-third and more of the ignorance and crime of the South, or one-third its intelligence and progress; we shall contribute one-third to the business and industrial prosperity of the South, or we shall prove a veritable body of death, stagnating, depressing, retarding every effort to advance the body politic.

Gentlemen of the Exposition, as we present to you our humble effort at an exhibition of our progress, you must not expect overmuch. Starting thirty years ago with ownership here and there in a few quilts and pumpkins and chickens (gathered from miscellaneous sources), remember the path that has led from these to the inventions and production of agricultural implements, buggies, steam-engines, newspapers, books, statuary, carving, paintings, the management of drugstores and banks, has not been trodden without contact with thorns and thistles. While we take pride in what we exhibit as a result of our independent efforts, we do not for a moment forget that our part in this exhibition would fall far short of your expectations but for the constant help that has come to our educational life, not only from the Southern states, but especially from Northern philanthropists, who have made their gifts a constant stream of blessing and encouragement.

The wisest among my race understand that the agitation of questions of social equality is the extremest folly, and that progress in the enjoyment of all the privileges that will come to us must be the result of severe and constant struggle rather than of artificial forcing. No race that has anything to contribute to the markets of the world is long in any degree ostracized. It is important and right that all privileges of the law be ours, but it is vastly more important that we be prepared for the exercises of these privileges. The opportunity to earn a dollar in a factory just now is worth infinitely more than the opportunity to spend a dollar in an opera-house.

In conclusion, may I repeat that nothing in thirty years has given us more hope and encouragement, and drawn us so near to you of the white race, as this opportunity offered by the Exposition; and here bending, as it were, over the altar that represents the results of the struggles of your race and mine, both starting practically empty-handed three decades ago, I pledge that in your effort to work out the great and intricate problem which God has laid at the doors of the South, you shall have at all times the patient, sympathetic help of my race; only let this be constantly in mind, that, while from representations in these buildings of the product of field, of forest, of mine, of factory, letters, and art, much good will come, yet far above and beyond material benefits will be that higher good, that, let us pray God, will come, in a blotting out of sectional differences and racial animosities and suspicions, in a determination to administer absolute justice, in a willing obedience among all classes to the mandates of law. This, this, coupled with our material prosperity, will bring into our beloved South a new heaven and a new earth.

The first thing that I remember, after I had finished speaking, was that Governor Bullock rushed across the platform and took me by the hand, and that others did the same. I received so many and such hearty congratulations that I found it difficult to get out of the building. I did not appreciate to any degree, however, the impression which my address seemed to have made, until the next morning, when I went into the business part of the city. As soon as I was recognized, I was surprised to find myself pointed out and surrounded by a crowd of men who wished to shake hands with me. This was kept up on every street on to which I went, to an extent which embarrassed me so much that I went back to my boarding-place. The next morning I returned to Tuskegee. At the station in Atlanta, and at almost all of the stations at which the train stopped between that city and Tuskegee, I found a crowd of people anxious to shake hands with me.

The papers in all parts of the United States published the address in full, and for months afterward there were complimentary editorial references to it. Mr. Clark Howell, the editor of the Atlanta *Constitution*, telegraphed to a New York paper, among other words, the following, "I do not exaggerate when I say that Professor Booker T. Washington's address yesterday was one of the most notable speeches, both as to character and as to the warmth of its reception, ever delivered to a Southern audience. The address was a revelation. The whole speech is a platform upon which blacks and whites can stand with full justice to each other."

The Boston *Transcript* said editorially: "The speech

of Booker T. Washington at the Atlanta Exposition, this week, seems to have dwarfed all the other proceedings and the Exposition itself. The sensation that it has caused in the press has never been equalled."

I very soon began receiving all kinds of propositions from lecture bureaus, and editors of magazines and papers, to take the lecture platform, and to write articles. One lecture bureau offered me fifty thousand dollars, or two hundred dollars a night and expenses, if I would place my services at its disposal for a given period. To all these communications I replied that my life-work was at Tuskegee; and that whenever I spoke it must be in the interests of the Tuskegee school and my race, and that I would enter into no arrangements that seemed to place a mere commercial value upon my services.

Some days after its delivery I sent a copy of my address to the President of the United States, the Hon. Grover Cleveland. I received from him the following autograph reply:—

GRAY GABLES, BUZZARD'S BAY, MASS.,
OCTOBER 6, 1895.

BOOKER T. WASHINGTON, ESQ.:

MY DEAR SIR: I thank you for sending me a copy of your address delivered at the Atlanta Exposition.

I thank you with much enthusiasm for making the address. I have read it with intense interest, and I think the Exposition would be fully justified if it did not do more than furnish the opportunity for its delivery. Your words cannot fail to delight and encourage all who wish well for your race; and if our coloured fellow-citizens do not from your utterances gather new hope and form new determinations to gain every valuable advantage offered them by their citizenship, it will be strange indeed.

Yours very truly,

GROVER CLEVELAND.

Later I met Mr. Cleveland, for the first time, when, as President, he visited the Atlanta Exposition. At the request of myself and others he consented to spend an hour in the Negro Building, for the purpose of inspecting the Negro exhibit and of giving the coloured people in attendance an opportunity to shake hands with him. As soon as I met Mr. Cleveland I became impressed with his simplicity, greatness, and rugged honesty. I have met him many times since then, both at public functions and at his private residence in Princeton, and the more I see of him the more I admire him. When he visited the Negro Building in Atlanta he seemed to give himself up wholly, for that hour, to the coloured people. He seemed to be as careful to shake hands with some old coloured "auntie" clad partially in rags, and to take as much pleasure in doing so, as if he were greeting some millionnaire. Many of the coloured people took advantage of the occasion to get him to write his name in a book or on a slip of paper. He was as careful and patient in doing this as if he were putting his signature to some great state document.

Mr. Cleveland has not only shown his friendship for me in many personal ways, but has always consented to do anything I have asked of him for our school. This he has done, whether it was to make a personal donation or to use his influence in securing the donations of others. Judging from my personal acquaintance with Mr. Cleveland, I do not believe that he is conscious of possessing any colour prejudice. He is too great for that. In my contact with people I find that, as a rule, it is only the little, narrow people who live for themselves, who never read good books, who do not travel, who never open up their souls in a way to permit them to come into contact with other souls—with the great outside world. No man whose vision is bounded by colour can come into contact with what is highest and best in the world. In meeting men, in many places, I have found that the happiest people are those who do the most for others; the most miserable are those who do the least. I have also found that few things, if any, are capable of making one so blind and narrow as race prejudice. I often say to our students, in the course of my talks to them on Sunday evenings in the chapel, that the longer I live and the more experience I have of the world, the more I am convinced that, after all, the one thing that is most worth living for—and dying for, if need be—is the opportunity of making some one else more happy and more useful.

The coloured people and the coloured newspapers at first seemed to be greatly pleased with the character of my Atlanta address, as well as with its reception. But after the first burst of enthusiasm began to die away, and the coloured people began reading the speech in cold type, some of them seemed to feel that they had been hypnotized. They seemed to feel that I had been too liberal in my remarks toward the Southern whites, and that I had not spoken out strongly enough for what they termed the "rights" of the race. For a while there was a reaction, so far as a certain element of my own race was concerned, but later these reactionary ones seemed to have been won over to my way of believing and acting.

While speaking of changes in public sentiment, I recall that about ten years after the school at Tuskegee was established, I had an experience that I shall never forget. Dr. Lyman Abbott, then the pastor of Plymouth Church, and also editor of the *Outlook* (then the *Christian Union*), asked me to write a letter for his paper giving my opinion of the exact condition, mental and moral, of the coloured ministers in the South, as based upon my observations. I wrote the letter, giving the exact facts as I conceived them to be. The picture painted was a rather black one—or, since I am black, shall I say "white"? It could not be otherwise with a race but a few years out of slavery, a race which had not had time or opportunity to produce a competent ministry.

What I said soon reached every Negro minister in the country, I think, and the letters of condemnation which I received from them were not few. I think that for a year after the publication of this article every association and every conference or religious body of any kind, of my race, that met, did not fail before adjourning to pass a resolution condemning me, or calling upon me to retract or modify what I had said. Many of these organizations went so far in their resolutions as to advise parents to cease sending their children to Tuskegee. One association even appointed a "missionary" whose duty it was to warn the people against sending their children to Tuskegee. This missionary had a son in the school, and I noticed that, whatever the "missionary" might have said or done with regard to others, he was careful not to take his son away from the institution. Many of the coloured papers, especially those that were the organs of religious bodies, joined in the general chorus of condemnation or demands for retraction.

During the whole time of the excitement, and through all the criticism, I did not utter a word of explanation or retraction. I knew that I was right, and that time and the sober second thought of the people would vindicate me. It was not long before the bishops and other church leaders began to make a careful investigation of the conditions of the ministry, and they found out that I was right. In fact, the oldest and most influential bishop in one branch of the Methodist Church said that my words were far too mild. Very soon public sentiment began making itself felt, in demanding a purifying of the ministry. While this is not yet complete by any means, I think I may say, without egotism, and I have been told by many of our most influential ministers, that my words had much to do with starting a demand for the placing of a higher type of men in the pulpit. I have had the satisfaction of having many who once condemned me thank me heartily for my frank words.

The change of the attitude of the Negro ministry, so far as regards myself, is so complete that at the present time I have no warmer friends among any class than I have among the clergymen. The improvement in the character and life of the Negro ministers is one of the most gratifying evidences of the progress of the race. My experience with them, as well as other events in my life, convince me that the thing to do, when one feels sure that he has said or done the right thing, and is condemned, is to stand still and keep quiet. If he is right, time will show it.

In the midst of the discussion which was going on concerning my Atlanta speech, I received the letter which I give below, from Dr. Gilman, the President of Johns Hopkins University, who had been made chairman of the judges of award in connection with the Atlanta Exposition:—

JOHNS HOPKINS UNIVERSITY, BALTIMORE,
    PRESIDENT'S OFFICE, SEPTEMBER 30, 1895.
    DEAR MR. WASHINGTON: Would it be agreeable to you to be one of the Judges of Award in the Department of Education at Atlanta? If so, I shall be glad to place your name upon the list. A line by telegraph will be welcomed.
                        Yours very truly,
                            D. C. GILMAN.

I think I was even more surprised to receive this invitation than I had been to receive the invitation to speak at the opening of the Exposition. It was to be a part of my duty, as one of the jurors, to pass not only upon the exhibits of the coloured schools, but also upon those of the white schools. I accepted the position, and spent a month in Atlanta in performance of the duties which it entailed. The board of jurors was a large one, consisting in all of sixty members. It was about equally divided between Southern white people and Northern white people. Among them were college presidents, leading scientists and men of letters, and specialists in many subjects. When the group of jurors to which I was assigned met for organization, Mr. Thomas Nelson Page, who was one of the number, moved that I be made secretary of that division, and the motion was unanimously adopted. Nearly half of our division were Southern people. In performing my duties in the inspection of the exhibits of white schools I was in every case treated with respect, and at the close of our labours I parted from my associates with regret.

I am often asked to express myself more freely than I do upon the political condition and the political future of my race. These recollections of my experience in Atlanta give me the opportunity to do so briefly. My own belief is, although I have never before said so in so many words, that the time will come when the Negro in the South will be accorded all the political rights which his ability, character, and material possessions entitle him to. I think, though, that the opportunity to freely exercise such political rights will not come in any large degree through outside or artificial forcing, but will be accorded to the Negro by the Southern white people themselves, and that they will protect him in the exercise of those rights. Just as soon as the South gets over the old feeling that it is being forced by "foreigners," or "aliens," to do something which it does not want to do, I believe that the change in the direction that I have indicated is going to begin. In fact, there are indications that it is already beginning in a slight degree.

Let me illustrate my meaning. Suppose that some months before the opening of the Atlanta Exposition there had been a general demand from the press and public platform outside the South that a Negro be given a place on the opening programme, and that a Negro be placed upon the board of jurors of award. Would any such recognition of the race have taken place? I do not think so. The Atlanta officials went as far as they did because they felt it to be a pleasure, as well as a duty, to reward what they considered merit in the Negro race. Say what we will, there is something in human nature which we cannot blot out, which makes one man, in the end, recognize and reward merit in another, regardless of colour or race.

I believe it is the duty of the Negro—as the greater part of the race is already doing—to deport himself modestly in regard to political claims, depending upon the slow but sure influences that proceed from the possession of property, intelligence, and high character for the full recognition of his political rights. I think that the according of the full exercise of political rights is going to be a matter of natural, slow growth, not an over-night, gourd-vine affair. I do not believe that the Negro should cease voting, for a man cannot learn the exercise of self-government by ceasing to vote, any more than a boy can learn to swim by keeping out of the water, but I do believe that in his voting he should more and more be influenced by those of intelligence and character who are his next-door neighbours.

I know coloured men who, through the encouragement, help, and advice of Southern white people, have accumulated thousands of dollars' worth of property, but who, at the same time, would never think of going to those same persons for advice concerning the casting of their ballots. This, it seems to me, is unwise and unreasonable, and should cease. In saying this I do not mean that the Negro should truckle, or not vote from principle, for the instant he ceases to vote from principle he loses the confidence and respect of the Southern white man even.

I do not believe that any state should make a law that permits an ignorant and poverty-stricken white man to vote, and prevents a black man in the same condition from voting. Such a law is not only unjust, but it will react, as all unjust laws do, in time; for the

effect of such a law is to encourage the Negro to secure education and property, and at the same time it
encourages the white man to remain in ignorance and
poverty. I believe that in time, through the operation
of intelligence and friendly race relations, all cheating
at the ballot-box in the South will cease. It will become apparent that the white man who begins by
cheating a Negro out of his ballot soon learns to cheat
a white man out of his, and that the man who does
this ends his career of dishonesty by the theft of property or by some equally serious crime. In my opinion,
the time will come when the South will encourage all
of its citizens to vote. It will see that it pays better,
from every standpoint, to have healthy, vigorous life
than to have that political stagnation which always results when one-half of the population has no share
and no interest in the Government.

As a rule, I believe in universal, free suffrage, but I
believe that in the South we are confronted with peculiar conditions that justify the protection of the ballot
in many of the states, for a while at least, either by an
educational test, a property test, or by both combined;
but whatever tests are required, they should be made to
apply with equal and exact justice to both races.

CHAPTER XV

THE SECRET OF SUCCESS IN PUBLIC SPEAKING

As to how my address at Atlanta was received by the audience in the Exposition building, I think I prefer to let Mr. James Creelman, the noted war correspondent, tell. Mr. Creelman was present, and telegraphed the following account to the New York *World:*—

ATLANTA, SEPTEMBER 18.

While President Cleveland was waiting at Gray Gables to-day, to send the electric spark that started the machinery of the Atlanta Exposition, a Negro Moses stood before a great audience of white people and delivered an oration that marks a new epoch in the history of the South; and a body of Negro troops marched in a procession with the citizen soldiery of Georgia and Louisiana. The whole city is thrilling to-night with a realization of the extraordinary significance of these two unprecedented events. Nothing has happened since Henry Grady's immortal speech before the New England society in New York that indicates so profoundly the spirit of the New South, except, perhaps the opening of the Exposition itself.

When Professor Booker T. Washington, Principal of an industrial school for coloured people in Tuskegee, Ala. stood on the platform of the Auditorium, with the sun shining over the heads of his auditors into his eyes, and with his whole face lit up with the fire of prophecy, Clark Howell, the successor of Henry Grady, said to me, "That man's speech is the beginning of a moral revolution in America."

It is the first time that a Negro has made a speech in the South on any important occasion before an audience composed of white men and women. It electrified the audience, and the response was as if it had come from the throat of a whirlwind.

Mrs. Thompson had hardly taken her seat when all eyes were turned on a tall tawny Negro sitting in the front row of the platform. It was Professor Booker T. Washington, President of the Tuskegee (Alabama) Normal and Industrial Institute, who must rank from this time forth as the foremost man of his race in America. Gilmore's Band played the "Star-Spangled Banner," and the audience cheered. The tune changed to "Dixie" and the audience roared with shrill "hi-yis." Again the music changed, this time to "Yankee Doodle," and the clamour lessened.

All this time the eyes of the thousands present looked straight at the Negro orator. A strange thing was to happen. A black man was to speak for his people, with none to interrupt him. As Professor Washington strode to the edge of the stage, the low, descending sun shot fiery rays through the windows into his face. A great shout greeted him. He turned his head to avoid the blinding light, and moved about the platform for relief. Then he turned his wonderful countenance to the sun without a blink of the eyelids, and began to talk.

There was a remarkable figure; tall, bony, straight as a Sioux chief, high forehead, straight nose, heavy jaws, and strong, determined mouth, with big white teeth, piercing eyes, and a commanding manner. The sinews stood out on his bronzed neck, and his muscular right arm swung high in the air, with a lead-pencil grasped in the clinched brown fist. His big feet were planted squarely, with the heels together and the toes turned out. His voice rang out clear and true, and he paused impressively as he made each point. Within ten minutes the multitude was in an uproar of enthusiasm—handkerchiefs were waved, canes were flourished, hats were tossed in the air. The fairest women of Georgia stood up and cheered. It was as if the orator had bewitched them.

And when he held his dusky hand high above his head, with the fingers stretched wide apart, and said to the white people of the South on behalf of his race, "In all things that are purely social we can be as separate as the fingers, yet one as the hand in all things essential to mutual progress," the great wave of sound dashed itself against the walls, and the whole audience was on its feet in a delirium of applause, and I thought at that moment of the night when Henry Grady stood among the curling wreaths of tobacco-smoke in Delmonico's banquet-hall and said, "I am a Cavalier among Roundheads."

I have heard the great orators of many countries, but not even Gladstone himself could have pleaded a cause with more consummate power than did this angular Negro, standing in a nimbus of sunshine, surrounded by the men who once fought to keep his race in bondage. The roar might swell ever so high, but the expression of his earnest face never changed.

A ragged, ebony giant, squatted on the floor in one of the aisles, watched the orator with burning eyes and tremulous face until the supreme burst of applause came, and then the tears ran down his face. Most of the Negroes in the audience were crying, perhaps without knowing just why.

At the close of the speech Governor Bullock rushed across the stage and seized the orator's hand. Another shout greeted this demonstration, and for a few minutes the two men stood facing each other, hand in hand.

So far as I could spare the time from the immediate work at Tuskegee, after my Atlanta address, I accepted some of the invitations to speak in public which came to me, especially those that would take me into territory where I thought it would pay to plead the cause of my race, but I always did this with the understanding that I was to be free to talk about my life-work and the needs of my people. I also had it understood that I was not to speak in the capacity of a professional lecturer, or for mere commercial gain.

In my efforts on the public platform I never have been able to understand why people come to hear me speak. This question I never can rid myself of. Time and time again, as I have stood in the street in front of a building and have seen men and women passing in large numbers into the audience-room where I was to speak, I have felt ashamed that I should be the cause of people—as it seemed to me—wasting a valuable hour of time. Some years ago I was to deliver an address before a literary society in Madison, Wis. An hour before the time set for me to speak, a fierce snow-storm began, and continued for several hours. I made up my mind that there would be no audience, and that I should not have to speak, but, as a matter of duty, I went to the church, and found it packed with people. The surprise gave me a shock that I did not recover from during the whole evening.

People often ask me if I feel nervous before speaking, or else they suggest that, since I speak so often, they suppose that I get used to it. In answer to this question I have to say that I always suffer intensely from nervousness before speaking. More than once, just before I was to make an important address, this nervous strain has been so great that I have resolved never again to speak in public. I not only feel nervous before speaking, but after I have finished I usually feel a sense of regret, because it seems to me as if I had left out of my address the main thing and the best thing that I had meant to say.

There is a great compensation, though, for this preliminary nervous suffering, that comes to me after I have been speaking for about ten minutes, and have come to feel that I have really mastered my audience, and that we have gotten into full and complete sympathy with each other. It seems to me that there is rarely such a combination of mental and physical delight in any effort as that which comes to a public speaker when he feels that he has a great audience completely within his control. There is a thread of sympathy and oneness that connects a public speaker with his audience, that is just as strong as though it was something tangible and visible. If in an audience of a thousand people there is one person who is not in sympathy with my views, or is inclined to be doubtful, cold, or critical, I can pick him out. When I have found him I usually go straight at him, and it is a great satisfaction to watch the process of his thawing out. I find that the most effective medicine for such individuals is administered at first in the form of a story, although I never tell an anecdote simply for the sake of telling one. That kind of thing, I think, is empty and hollow, and an audience soon finds it out.

I believe that one always does himself and his audience an injustice when he speaks merely for the sake of speaking. I do not believe that one should speak unless, deep down in his heart, he feels convinced that he has a message to deliver. When one feels, from the bottom of his feet to the top of his head, that he has something to say that is going to help some individual or some cause, then let him say it; and in delivering his message I do not believe that many of the artificial rules of elocution can, under such circumstances, help him very much. Although there are certain things, such as pauses, breathing, and pitch of voice, that are very important, none of these can take the place of *soul* in an address. When I have an address to deliver, I like to forget all about the rules for the proper use of the English language, and all about rhetoric and that sort of thing, and I like to make the audience forget all about these things, too.

Nothing tends to throw me off my balance so quickly, when I am speaking, as to have some one leave the room. To prevent this, I make up my mind, as a rule, that I will try to make my address so interesting, will try to state so many interesting facts one after another, that no one can leave. The average audience, I have come to believe, wants facts rather than generalities or sermonizing. Most people, I think, are able to draw proper conclusions if they are given the facts in an interesting form on which to base them.

As to the kind of audience that I like best to talk to, I would put at the top of the list an organization of strong, wide-awake, business men, such, for example, as is found in Boston, New York, Chicago, and Buffalo. I have found no other audience so quick to see a point, and so responsive. Within the last few years I have had the privilege of speaking before most of the leading organizations of this kind in the large cities of the United States. The best time to get hold of an organization of business men is after a good dinner, although I think that one of the worst instruments of torture that was ever invented is the custom which makes it necessary for a speaker to sit through a fourteen-course dinner, every minute of the time feeling sure that his speech is going to prove a dismal failure and disappointment.

I rarely take part in one of these long dinners that I do not wish that I could put myself back in the little cabin where I was a slave boy, and again go through the experience there—one that I shall never forget—of getting molasses to eat once a week from the "big house." Our usual diet on the plantation was corn bread and pork, but on Sunday morning my mother was permitted to bring down a little molasses from the "big house" for her three children, and when it was received how I did wish that every day was Sunday! I would get my tin plate and hold it up for the sweet morsel, but I would always shut my eyes while the molasses was being poured out into the plate, with the hope that when I opened them I would be surprised to see how much I had got. When I opened my eyes I would tip the plate in one direction and another, so as to make the molasses spread all over it, in the full belief that there would be more of it and that it would last longer if spread out in this way. So strong are my childish impressions of those Sunday morning feasts that it would be pretty hard for any one to convince me that there is not more molasses on a plate when it is spread all over the plate than when it occupies a little corner—if there is a corner in a plate. At any rate, I have never believed in "cornering" syrup. My share of the syrup was usually about two tablespoonfuls, and those two spoonfuls of molasses were much more enjoyable to me than is a fourteen-course dinner after which I am to speak.

Next to a company of business men, I prefer to speak to an audience of Southern people, of either race, together or taken separately. Their enthusiasm and responsiveness are a constant delight. The "amens" and "dat's de truf" that come spontaneously from the coloured individuals are calculated to spur any speaker on to his best efforts. I think that next in order of preference I would place a college audience. It has been my privilege to deliver addresses at many of our leading colleges, including Harvard, Yale, Williams, Amherst, Fisk University, the University of Pennsylvania, Wellesley, the University of Michigan, Trinity College in North Carolina, and many others.

It has been a matter of deep interest to me to note the number of people who have come to shake hands with me after an address, who say that this is the first time they have ever called a Negro "Mister."

When speaking directly in the interests of the Tuskegee Institute, I usually arrange, some time in advance, a series of meetings in important centres. This takes me before churches, Sunday-schools, Christian Endeavour Societies, and men's and women's clubs. When doing this I sometimes speak before as many as four organizations in a single day.

Three years ago, at the suggestion of Mr. Morris K.

Jesup, of New York, and Dr. J. L. M. Curry, the general agent of the fund, the trustees of the John F. Slater Fund voted a sum of money to be used in paying the expenses of Mrs. Washington and myself while holding a series of meetings among the coloured people in the large centres of Negro population, especially in the large cities of the ex-slaveholding states. Each year during the last three years we have devoted some weeks to this work. The plan that we have followed has been for me to speak in the morning to the ministers, teachers, and professional men. In the afternoon Mrs. Washington would speak to the women alone, and in the evening I spoke to a large mass-meeting. In almost every case the meetings have been attended not only by the coloured people in large numbers, but by the white people. In Chattanooga, Tenn., for example, there was present at the mass-meeting an audience of not less than three thousand persons, and I was informed that eight hundred of these were white. I have done no work that I really enjoyed more than this, or that I think has accomplished more good.

These meetings have given Mrs. Washington and myself an opportunity to get first-hand, accurate information as to the real condition of the race, by seeing the people in their homes, their churches, their Sunday-schools, and their places of work, as well as in the prisons and dens of crime. These meetings also gave us an opportunity to see the relations that exist between the races. I never feel so hopeful about the race as I do after being engaged in a series of these meetings. I know that on such occasions there is much that comes to the surface that is superficial and deceptive, but I have had experience enough not to be deceived by mere signs and fleeting enthusiasms. I have taken pains to go to the bottom of things and get facts, in a cold, business-like manner.

I have seen the statement made lately, by one who claims to know what he is talking about, that, taking the whole Negro race into account, ninety per cent of the Negro women are not virtuous. There never was a baser falsehood uttered concerning a race, or a statement made that was less capable of being proved by actual facts.

No one can come into contact with the race for twenty years, as I have done in the heart of the South, without being convinced that the race is constantly making slow but sure progress materially, educationally, and morally. One might take up the life of the worst element in New York City, for example, and prove almost anything he wanted to prove concerning the white man, but all will agree that this is not a fair test.

Early in the year 1897 I received a letter inviting me

to deliver an address at the dedication of the Robert Gould Shaw monument in Boston. I accepted the invitation. It is not necessary for me, I am sure, to explain who Robert Gould Shaw was, and what he did.[9] The monument to his memory stands near the head of Boston Common, facing the State House. It is counted to be the most perfect piece of art of the kind to be found in the country.

The exercises connected with the dedication were held in Music Hall, in Boston, and the great hall was packed from top to bottom with one of the most distinguished audiences that ever assembled in the city. Among those present there were more persons representing the famous old anti-slavery element than it is likely will ever be brought together in the country again. The late Hon. Roger Wolcott, then Governor of Massachusetts, was the presiding officer, and on the platform with him were many other officials and hundreds of distinguished men. A report of the meeting which appeared in the Boston *Transcript* will describe it better than any words of mine could do:—

The core and kernel of yesterday's great noon meeting in honour of the Brotherhood of Man, in Music Hall, was the superb address of the Negro President of Tuskegee. "Booker T. Washington received his Harvard A. M. last June, the first of his race," said Governor Wolcott, "to receive an honorary degree from the oldest university in the land, and this for the wise leadership of his people." When Mr. Washington rose in the flag-filled, enthusiasm-warmed, patriotic, and glowing atmosphere of Music Hall, people felt keenly that here was the civic justification of the old abolition spirit of Massachusetts; in his person the proof of her ancient and indomitable faith; in his strong thought and rich oratory, the crown and glory of the old war days of suffering and strife. The scene was full of historic beauty and deep significance. "Cold" Boston was alive with the fire that is always hot in her heart for righteousness and truth. Rows and rows of people who are seldom seen at any public function, whole families of those who are certain to be out of town on a holiday, crowded the place to overflowing. The city was at her birthright *fête* in the persons of hundreds of her best citizens, men and women whose names and lives stand for the virtues that make for honourable civic pride.

Battle-music had filled the air. Ovation after ovation, applause warm and prolonged, had greeted the officers and friends of Colonel Shaw, the sculptor, St. Gaudens, the memorial Committee, the Governor and his staff, and the Negro soldiers of the Fifty-fourth Massachusetts as they came upon the platform or entered the hall. Colonel Henry Lee, of Governor Andrew's old staff, had made a noble, simple presentation speech for the committee, paying tribute to Mr. John M.

Forbes, in whose stead he served. Governor Wolcott had made his short, memorable speech, saying, "Fort Wagner marked an epoch in the history of a race, and called it into manhood." Mayor Quincy had received the monument for the city of Boston. The story of Colonel Shaw and his black regiment had been told in gallant words, and then, after the singing of

> Mine eyes have seen the glory
> Of the coming of the Lord,

Booker Washington arose. It was, of course, just the moment for him. The multitude, shaken out of its usual symphony-concert calm, quivered with an excitement that was not suppressed. A dozen times it had sprung to its feet to cheer and wave and hurrah, as one person. When this man of culture and voice and power, as well as a dark skin, began, and uttered the names of Stearns and of Andrew, feeling began to mount. You could see tears glisten in the eyes of soldiers and civilians. When the orator turned to the coloured soldiers on the platform, to the colour-bearer of Fort Wagner, who smilingly bore still the flag he had never lowered even when wounded, and said, "To you, to the scarred and scattered remnants of the Fifty-fourth, who, with empty sleeve and wanting leg, have honoured this occasion with your presence, to you, your commander is not dead. Though Boston erected no monument and history recorded no story, in you and in the loyal race which you represent, Robert Gould Shaw would have a monument which time could not wear away," then came the climax of the emotion of the day and the hour. It was Roger Wolcott, as well as the Governor of Massachusetts, the individual representative of the people's sympathy as well as the chief magistrate, who had sprung first to his feet and cried, "Three cheers to Booker T. Washington!"

Among those on the platform was Sergeant William H. Carney, of New Bedford, Mass., the brave coloured officer who was the colour-bearer at Fort Wagner and held the American flag. In spite of the fact that a large part of his regiment was killed, he escaped, and exclaimed, after the battle was over, "The old flag never touched the ground."

This flag Sergeant Carney held in his hands as he sat on the platform, and when I turned to address the survivors of the coloured regiment who were present, and referred to Sergeant Carney, he rose, as if by instinct, and raised the flag. It has been my privilege to witness a good many satisfactory and rather sensational demonstrations in connection with some of my public addresses, but in dramatic effect I have never seen or experienced anything which equalled this. For a number of minutes the audience seemed to entirely lose control of itself.

In the general rejoicing throughout the country

which followed the close of the Spanish-American war, peace celebrations were arranged in several of the large cities. I was asked by President William R. Harper, of the University of Chicago, who was chairman of the committee of invitations for the celebration to be held in the city of Chicago, to deliver one of the addresses at the celebration there. I accepted the invitation, and delivered two addresses there during the Jubilee week. The first of these, and the principal one, was given in the Auditorium, on the evening of Sunday, October 16. This was the largest audience that I have ever addressed, in any part of the country; and besides speaking in the main Auditorium, I also addressed, that same evening, two overflow audiences in other parts of the city.

It was said that there were sixteen thousand persons in the Auditorium, and it seemed to me as if there were as many more on the outside trying to get in. It was impossible for any one to get near the entrance without the aid of a policeman. President William McKinley attended this meeting, as did also the members of his Cabinet, many foreign ministers, and a large number of army and navy officers, many of whom had distinguished themselves in the war which had just closed. The speakers, besides myself, on Sunday evening, were Rabbi Emil G.

Hirsch, Father Thomas P. Hodnett, and Dr. John H. Barrows.

The Chicago *Times-Herald*, in describing the meeting, said of my address:—

He pictured the Negro choosing slavery rather than extinction; recalled Crispus Attucks shedding his blood at the beginning of the American Revolution, that white Americans might be free, while black Americans remained in slavery; rehearsed the conduct of the Negroes with Jackson at New Orleans; drew a vivid and pathetic picture of the Southern slaves protecting and supporting the families of their masters while the latter were fighting to perpetuate black slavery; recounted the bravery of coloured troops at Port Hudson and Forts Wagner and Pillow, and praised the heroism of the black regiments that stormed El Caney and Santiago to give freedom to the enslaved people of Cuba, forgetting, for the time being, the unjust discrimination that law and custom make against them in their own country.

In all of these things, the speaker declared, his race had chosen the better part. And then he made his eloquent appeal to the consciences of the white Americans: "When you have gotten the full story of the heroic conduct of the Negro in the Spanish-American war, have heard it from the lips of Northern soldier and Southern soldier, from ex-abolitionist and ex-masters, then decide within yourselves whether a race that is thus willing to die for its country should not be given the highest opportunity to live for its country."

The part of the speech which seemed to arouse the wildest and most sensational enthusiasm was that in which I thanked the President for his recognition of the Negro in his appointments during the Spanish-American war. The President was sitting in a box at the right of the stage. When I addressed him I turned toward the box, and as I finished the sentence thanking him for his generosity, the whole audience rose and cheered again and again, waving handkerchiefs and hats and canes, until the President arose in the box and bowed his acknowledgments. At that the enthusiasm broke out again, and the demonstration was almost indescribable.

One portion of my address at Chicago seemed to have been misunderstood by the Southern press, and some of the Southern papers took occasion to criticise me rather strongly. These criticisms continued for several weeks, until I finally received a letter from the editor of the *Age-Herald*, published in Birmingham, Ala., asking me if I would say just what I meant by this part of my address. I replied to him in a letter which seemed to satisfy my critics. In this letter I said that I had made it a rule never to say before a Northern audience anything that I would not say before an audience in the South. I said that I did not think it was necessary for me to go into extended explanations; if my seventeen years of work in the heart of the South had not been explanation enough, I did not see how words could explain. I said that I made the same plea that I had made in my address at Atlanta, for the blotting out of race prejudice in "commercial and civil relations." I said that what is termed social recognition was a question which I never discussed, and then I quoted from my Atlanta address what I had said there in regard to that subject.

In meeting crowds of people at public gatherings, there is one type of individual that I dread. I mean the crank. I have become so accustomed to these people now that I can pick them out at a distance when I see them elbowing their way up to me. The average crank has a long beard, poorly cared for, a lean, narrow face, and wears a black coat. The front of his vest and coat are slick with grease, and his trousers bag at the knees.

In Chicago, after I had spoken at a meeting, I met one of these fellows. They usually have some process for curing all of the ills of the world at once. This Chicago specimen had a patent process by which he said Indian corn could be kept through a period of

three or four years, and he felt sure that if the Negro
race in the South would, as a whole, adopt his process,
it would settle the whole race question. It mattered
nothing that I tried to convince him that our present
problem was to teach the Negroes how to produce
enough corn to last them through one year. Another
Chicago crank had a scheme by which he wanted me
to join him in an effort to close up all the National
banks in the country. If that was done, he felt sure it
would put the Negro on his feet.

The number of people who stand ready to consume
one's time, to no purpose, is almost countless. At one
time I spoke before a large audience in Boston in the
evening. The next morning I was awakened by having
a card brought to my room, and with it a message that
some one was anxious to see me. Thinking that it
must be something very important, I dressed hastily
and went down. When I reached the hotel office I
found a blank and innocent-looking individual waiting for me, who coolly remarked: "I heard you talk at
a meeting last night. I rather liked your talk, and so I
came in this morning to hear you talk some more."

I am often asked how it is possible for me to super-
intend the work at Tuskegee and at the same time be
so much away from the school. In partial answer to

this I would say that I think I have learned, in some degree at least, to disregard the old maxim which says, "Do not get others to do that which you can do yourself." My motto, on the other hand, is, "Do not do that which others can do as well."

One of the most encouraging signs in connection with the Tuskegee school is found in the fact that the organization is so thorough that the daily work of the school is not dependent upon the presence of any one individual. The whole executive force, including instructors and clerks, now numbers eighty-six. This force is so organized and sub-divided that the machinery of the school goes on day by day like clockwork. Most of our teachers have been connected with the institution for a number of years, and are as much interested in it as I am. In my absence, Mr. Warren Logan, the treasurer, who has been at the school seventeen years, is the executive. He is efficiently supported by Mrs. Washington, and by my faithful secretary, Mr. Emmett J. Scott, who handles the bulk of my correspondence and keeps me in daily touch with the life of the school, and who also keeps me informed of whatever takes place in the South that concerns the race. I owe more to his tact, wisdom, and hard work than I can describe.

The main executive work of the school, whether I

am at Tuskegee or not, centres in what we call the executive council. This council meets twice a week, and is composed of the nine persons who are at the head of the nine departments of the school. For example: Mrs. B. K. Bruce, the Lady Principal, the widow of the late ex-senator Bruce, is a member of the council, and represents in it all that pertains to the life of the girls at the school. In addition to the executive council there is a financial committee of six, that meets every week and decides upon the expenditures for the week. Once a month, and sometimes oftener, there is a general meeting of all the instructors. Aside from these there are innumerable smaller meetings, such as that of the instructors in the Phelps Hall Bible Training School, or of the instructors in the agricultural department.

In order that I may keep in constant touch with the life of the institution, I have a system of reports so arranged that a record of the school's work reaches me every day in the year, no matter in what part of the country I am. I know by these reports even what students are excused from school, and why they are excused—whether for reasons of ill health or otherwise. Through the medium of these reports I know each day what the income of the school in money is; I know how many gallons of milk and how many pounds of butter come from the dairy; what the bill of fare for the teachers and students is; whether a certain kind of meat was boiled or baked, and whether certain vegetables served in the dining room were bought from a store or procured from our own farm. Human nature I find to be very much the same the world over, and it is sometimes not hard to yield to the temptation to go to a barrel of rice that has come from the store—with the grain all prepared to go into the pot—rather than to take the time and trouble to go to the field and dig and wash one's own sweet potatoes, which might be prepared in a manner to take the place of the rice.

I am often asked how, in the midst of so much work, a large part of which is before the public, I can find time for any rest or recreation, and what kind of recreation or sports I am fond of. This is rather a difficult question to answer. I have a strong feeling that every individual owes it to himself, and to the cause which he is serving, to keep a vigorous, healthy body, with the nerves steady and strong, prepared for great efforts and prepared for disappointments and trying positions. As far as I can, I make it a rule to plan for each day's work—not merely to go through with the same routine of daily duties, but to get rid of the routine work as early in the day as possible, and then to enter upon some new or advance work. I make it a rule to clear my desk every day, before leaving my office, of all correspondence and memoranda, so that on the morrow I can begin a *new* day of work. I make it a rule never to let my work drive me, but to so master it, and keep it in such complete control, and to keep so far ahead of it, that I will be the master instead of the servant. There is a physical and mental and spiritual enjoyment that comes from a consciousness of being the absolute master of one's work, in all its details, that is very satisfactory and inspiring. My experience teaches me that, if one learns to follow this plan, he gets a freshness of body and vigour of mind out of work that goes a long way toward keeping him strong and healthy. I believe that when one can grow to the point where he loves his work, this gives him a kind of strength that is most valuable.

When I begin my work in the morning, I expect to have a successful and pleasant day of it, but at the same time I prepare myself for unpleasant and unexpected hard places. I prepare myself to hear that one of our school buildings is on fire, or has burned, or that some disagreeable accident has occurred, or that some one has abused me in a public address or printed article, for something that I have done or omitted to do, or for something that he had heard that I had said—probably something that I had never thought of saying.

In nineteen years of continuous work I have taken but one vacation. That was two years ago, when some of my friends put the money into my hands and forced Mrs. Washington and myself to spend three months in Europe. I have said that I believe it is the duty of every one to keep his body in good condition. I try to look after the little ills, with the idea that if I take care of the little ills the big ones will not come. When I find myself unable to sleep well, I know that something is wrong. If I find any part of my system the least weak, and not performing its duty, I consult a good physician. The ability to sleep well, at any time and in any place, I find of great advantage. I have so trained myself that I can lie down for a nap of fifteen or twenty minutes, and get up refreshed in body and mind.

I have said that I make it a rule to finish up each day's work before leaving it. There is, perhaps, one exception to this. When I have an unusually difficult question to decide—one that appeals strongly to the emotions—I find it a safe rule to sleep over it for a night, or to wait until I have had an opportunity to talk it over with my wife and friends.

As to my reading; the most time I get for solid reading is when I am on the cars. Newspapers are to me a constant source of delight and recreation. The only trouble is that I read too many of them. Fiction

I care little for. Frequently I have to almost force my-self to read a novel that is on every one's lips. The kind of reading that I have the greatest fondness for is bi-ography. I like to be sure that I am reading about a real man or a real thing. I think I do not go too far when I say that I have read nearly every book and magazine article that has been written about Abraham Lincoln. In literature he is my patron saint.

Out of the twelve months in a year I suppose that, on an average, I spend six months away from Tuskegee. While my being absent from the school so much un-questionably has its disadvantages, yet there are at the same time some compensations. The change of work brings a certain kind of rest. I enjoy a ride of a long dis-tance on the cars, when I am permitted to ride where I can be comfortable. I get rest on the cars, except when the inevitable individual who seems to be on every train approaches me with the now familiar phrase: "Isn't this Booker Washington? I want to introduce myself to you." Absence from the school enables me to lose sight of the unimportant details of the work, and study it in a broader and more comprehensive manner than I could do on the grounds. This absence also brings me into contact with the best work being done in educa-tional lines, and into contact with the best educators in the land.

But, after all this is said, the time when I get the

most solid rest and recreation is when I can be at Tuskegee, and, after our evening meal is over, can sit down, as is our custom, with my wife and Portia and Baker and Davidson, my three children, and read a story, or each take turns in telling a story. To me there is nothing on earth equal to that, although what is nearly equal to it is to go with them for an hour or more, as we like to do on Sunday afternoons, into the woods, where we can live for a while near the heart of nature, where no one can disturb or vex us, surrounded by pure air, the trees, the shrubbery, the flowers, and the sweet fragrance that springs from a hundred plants, enjoying the chirp of the crickets and the songs of the birds. This is solid rest.

My garden, also, what little time I can be at Tuskegee, is another source of rest and enjoyment. Somehow I like, as often as possible, to touch nature, not something that is artificial or an imitation, but the real thing. When I can leave my office in time so that I can spend thirty or forty minutes in spading the ground, in planting seeds, in digging about the plants, I feel that I am coming into contact with something that is giving me strength for the many duties and hard places that await me out in the big world. I pity the man or woman who has never learned to enjoy nature and to get strength and inspiration out of it.

Aside from the large number of fowls and animals

kept by the school, I keep individually a number of pigs and fowls of the best grades, and in raising these I take a great deal of pleasure. I think the pig is my favourite animal. Few things are more satisfactory to me than a high-grade Berkshire or Poland China pig.

Games I care little for. I have never seen a game of football. In cards I do not know one card from another. A game of old-fashioned marbles with my two boys, once in a while, is all I care for in this direction. I suppose I would care for games now if I had had any time in my youth to give to them, but that was not possible.

CHAPTER XVI

EUROPE

IN 1893 I was married to Miss Margaret James Murray, a native of Mississippi, and a graduate of Fisk University, in Nashville, Tenn., who had come to Tuskegee as a teacher several years before, and at the time we were married was filling the position of Lady Principal. Not only is Mrs. Washington completely one with me in the work directly connected with the school, relieving me of many burdens and perplexities, but aside from her work on the school grounds, she carries on a mothers' meeting in the town of Tuskegee, and a plantation work among the women, children, and men who live in a settlement connected with a large plantation about eight miles from Tuskegee. Both the mothers' meeting and the plantation work are carried on, not only with a view to helping those who are directly reached, but also for the purpose of furnishing object-lessons in these two kinds of work that may be followed by our

255

students when they go out into the world for their own life-work.

Aside from these two enterprises, Mrs. Washington is also largely responsible for a woman's club at the school which brings together, twice a month, the women who live on the school grounds and those who live near, for the discussion of some important topic. She is also the President of what is known as the Federation of Southern Coloured Women's Clubs, and is Chairman of the Executive Committee of the National Federation of Coloured Women's Clubs.

Portia, the oldest of my three children, has learned dressmaking. She has unusual ability in instrumental music. Aside from her studies at Tuskegee, she has already begun to teach there.

Baker Taliaferro is my next oldest child. Young as he is, he has already nearly mastered the brickmason's trade. He began working at this trade when he was quite small, dividing his time between this and class work; and he has developed great skill in the trade and a fondness for it. He says that he is going to be an architect and brickmason. One of the most satisfactory letters that I have ever received from any one came to me from Baker last summer. When I left home for the summer, I told him that he must work at his trade half of each day, and that the other half of the day he could spend as he pleased. When I had been away from

home two weeks, I received the following letter from
him:

Tuskegee, Alabama.

My dear Papa: Before you left home you told me to
work at my trade half of each day. I like my work so much
that I want to work at my trade all day. Besides, I want to
earn all the money I can, so that when I go to another
school I shall have money to pay my expenses.

Your son,

Baker.

My youngest child, Ernest Davidson Washington,
says that he is going to be a physician. In addition to
going to school, where he studies books and has manual training, he regularly spends a portion of his time
in the office of our resident physician, and has already
learned to do many of the duties which pertain to a
doctor's office.

The thing in my life which brings me the keenest
regret is that my work in connection with public affairs keeps me for so much of the time away from my
family, where, of all places in the world, I delight to
be. I always envy the individual whose life-work is so
laid that he can spend his evenings at home. I have
sometimes thought that people who have this rare
privilege do not appreciate it as they should. It is such

a rest and relief to get away from crowds of people, and handshaking, and travelling, and get home, even if it be for but a very brief while.

Another thing at Tuskegee out of which I get a great deal of pleasure and satisfaction is in the meeting with our students, and teachers, and their families, in the chapel for devotional exercises every evening at half-past eight, the last thing before retiring for the night. It is an inspiring sight when one stands on the platform there and sees before him eleven or twelve hundred earnest young men and women; and one cannot but feel that it is a privilege to help to guide them to a higher and more useful life.

In the spring of 1899 there came to me what I might describe as almost the greatest surprise of my life. Some good ladies in Boston arranged a public meeting in the interests of Tuskegee, to be held in the Hollis Street Theatre. This meeting was attended by large numbers of the best people of Boston, of both races. Bishop Lawrence[10] presided. In addition to an address made by myself, Mr. Paul Lawrence Dunbar read from his poems, and Dr. W. E. B. Du Bois read an original sketch.

Some of those who attended this meeting noticed that I seemed unusually tired, and some little time after the close of the meeting, one of the ladies who had been interested in it asked me in a casual way if I had ever been to Europe. I replied that I never had. She asked me if I had ever thought of going, and I told her no; that it was something entirely beyond me. This conversation soon passed out of my mind, but a few days afterward I was informed that some friends in Boston, including Mr. Francis J. Garrison, had raised a sum of money sufficient to pay all the expenses of Mrs. Washington and myself during a three or four months' trip to Europe. It was added with emphasis that we *must* go. A year previous to this Mr. Garrison had attempted to get me to promise to go to Europe for a summer's rest, with the understanding that he would be responsible for raising the money among his friends for the expenses of the trip. At that time such a journey seemed so entirely foreign to anything that I should ever be able to undertake that I confess I did not give the matter very serious attention; but later Mr. Garrison joined his efforts to those of the ladies whom I have mentioned, and when their plans were made known to me Mr. Garrison not only had the route mapped out, but had, I believe, selected the steamer upon which we were to sail.

The whole thing was so sudden and so unexpected that I was completely taken off my feet. I had been at work steadily for eighteen years in connection with Tuskegee, and I had never thought of anything else but ending my life in that way. Each day the school seemed to depend upon me more largely for its daily expenses, and I told these Boston friends that, while I thanked them sincerely for their thoughtfulness and generosity, I could not go to Europe, for the reason that the school could not live financially while I was absent. They then informed me that Mr. Henry L. Higginson, and some other good friends who I know do not want their names made public, were then raising a sum of money which would be sufficient to keep the school in operation while I was away. At this point I was compelled to surrender. Every avenue of escape had been closed.

Deep down in my heart the whole thing seemed more like a dream than like reality, and for a long time it was difficult for me to make myself believe that I was actually going to Europe. I had been born and largely reared in the lowest depths of slavery, ignorance, and poverty. In my childhood I had suffered for want of a place to sleep, for lack of food, clothing, and shelter. I had not had the privilege of sitting down to a dining-table until I was quite well grown. Luxuries had always seemed to me to be something meant for white people, not for my race. I had always regarded Europe, and London, and Paris, much as I regard heaven. And now could it be that I was actually going to Europe? Such thoughts as these were constantly with me.

Two other thoughts troubled me a good deal. I

feared that people who heard that Mrs. Washington
and I were going to Europe might not know all the
circumstances, and might get the idea that we had become, as some might say, "stuck up," and were trying
to "show off." I recalled that from my youth I had
heard it said that too often, when people of my race
reached any degree of success, they were inclined to
unduly exalt themselves; to try and ape the wealthy,
and in so doing to lose their heads. The fear that people might think this of us haunted me a good deal.
Then, too, I could not see how my conscience would
permit me to spare the time from my work and be
happy. It seemed mean and selfish in me to be taking
a vacation while others were at work, and while there
was so much that needed to be done. From the time I
could remember, I had always been at work, and I did
not see how I could spend three or four months in doing nothing. The fact was that I did not know how to
take a vacation.

Mrs. Washington had much the same difficulty in
getting away, but she was anxious to go because she
thought that I needed the rest. There were many important National questions bearing upon the life of the
race which were being agitated at that time, and this
made it all the harder for us to decide to go. We finally
gave our Boston friends our promise that we would go,
and then they insisted that the date of our departure be

set as soon as possible. So we decided upon May 10. My good friend Mr. Garrison kindly took charge of all the details necessary for the success of the trip, and he, as well as other friends, gave us a great number of letters of introduction to people in France and England, and made other arrangements for our comfort and convenience abroad. Good-bys were said at Tuskegee, and we were in New York May 9, ready to sail the next day. Our daughter Portia, who was then studying in South Framingham, Mass., came to New York to see us off. Mr. Scott, my secretary, came with me to New York, in order that I might clear up the last bit of business before I left. Other friends also came to New York to see us off. Just before we went on board the steamer another pleasant surprise came to us in the form of a letter from two generous ladies, stating that they had decided to give us the money with which to erect a new building to be used in properly housing all our industries for girls at Tuskegee.

We were to sail on the *Friesland*, of the Red Star Line, and a beautiful vessel she was. We went on board just before noon, the hour of sailing. I had never before been on board a large ocean steamer, and the feeling which took possession of me when I found myself there is rather hard to describe. It was a feeling, I think, of awe mingled with delight. We were agreeably surprised to find that the captain, as well as several of the other officers, not only knew who we were, but was expecting us and gave us a pleasant greeting. There were several passengers whom we knew, including Senator Sewell," of New Jersey, and Edward Marshall, the newspaper correspondent. I had just a little fear that we would not be treated civilly by some of the passengers. This fear was based upon what I had heard other people of my race, who had crossed the ocean, say about unpleasant experiences in crossing the ocean in American vessels. But in our case, from the captain down to the most humble servant, we were treated with the greatest kindness. Nor was this kindness confined to those who were connected with the steamer; it was shown by all the passengers also. There were not a few Southern men and women on board, and they were as cordial as those from other parts of the country.

As soon as the last good-bys were said, and the steamer had cut loose from the wharf, the load of care, anxiety, and responsibility which I had carried for eighteen years began to lift itself from my shoulders at the rate, it seemed to me, of a pound a minute. It was the first time in all those years that I had felt, even in a measure, free from care; and my feeling of relief it is hard to describe on paper. Added to this was the delightful anticipation of being in Europe soon. It all seemed more like a dream than like a reality.

Mr. Garrison had thoughtfully arranged to have us have one of the most comfortable rooms on the ship. The second or third day out I began to sleep, and I think that I slept at the rate of fifteen hours a day during the remainder of the ten days' passage. Then it was that I began to understand how tired I really was. These long sleeps I kept up for a month after we landed on the other side. It was such an unusual feeling to wake up in the morning and realize that I had no engagements; did not have to take a train at a certain hour; did not have an appointment to meet some one, or to make an address, at a certain hour. How different all this was from some of the experiences that I have been through when travelling, when I have sometimes slept in three different beds in a single night!

When Sunday came, the captain invited me to conduct the religious services, but, not being a minister, I declined. The passengers, however, began making requests that I deliver an address to them in the dining-saloon some time during the voyage, and this I consented to do. Senator Sewell presided at this meeting. After ten days of delightful weather, during which I was not seasick for a day, we landed at the interesting old city of Antwerp, in Belgium.

The next day after we landed happened to be one of those numberless holidays which the people of those countries are in the habit of observing. It was a bright, beautiful day. Our room in the hotel faced the main public square, and the sights there—the people coming in from the country with all kinds of beautiful flowers to sell, the women coming in with their dogs drawing large, brightly polished cans filled with milk, the people streaming into the cathedral—filled me with a sense of newness that I had never before experienced.

After spending some time in Antwerp, we were invited to go with a party of a half-dozen persons on a trip through Holland. This party included Edward Marshall and some American artists who had come over on the same steamer with us. We accepted the invitation, and enjoyed the trip greatly. I think it was all the more interesting and instructive because we went for most of the way on one of the slow, old-fashioned canal-boats. This gave us an opportunity of seeing and studying the real life of the people in the country districts. We went in this way as far as Rotterdam, and later went to The Hague, where the Peace Conference was then in session, and where we were kindly received by the American representatives.

The thing that impressed itself most on me in Holland was the thoroughness of the agriculture and the excellence of the Holstein cattle. I never knew, before visiting Holland, how much it was possible for people to get out of a small plot of ground. It seemed to me that absolutely no land was wasted. It was worth a trip to Holland, too, just to get a sight of three or four hundred fine Holstein cows grazing in one of those intensely green fields.

From Holland we went to Belgium, and made a hasty trip through that country, stopping at Brussels, where we visited the battlefield of Waterloo. From Belgium we went direct to Paris, where we found that Mr. Theodore Stanton, the son of Mrs. Elizabeth Cady Stanton, had kindly provided accommodations for us. We had barely got settled in Paris before an invitation came to me from the University Club of Paris to be its guest at a banquet which was soon to be given. The other guests were ex-President Benjamin Harrison and Archbishop Ireland,[12] who were in Paris at the time. The American Ambassador, General Horace Porter, presided at the banquet. My address on this occasion seemed to give satisfaction to those who heard it. General Harrison kindly devoted a large portion of his remarks at dinner to myself and to the influence of the work at Tuskegee on the American race question. After my address at this banquet other invitations came to me, but I declined the most of them, knowing that if I accepted them all, the object of my visit would be defeated. I did, however, consent to deliver an address in the American chapel the following Sunday morning, and at this meeting General Harrison, General Porter, and other distinguished Americans were present.

Later we received a formal call from the American Ambassador, and were invited to attend a reception at his residence. At this reception we met many Americans, among them Justices Fuller[13] and Harlan,[14] of the United States Supreme Court. During our entire stay of a month in Paris, both the American Ambassador and his wife, as well as several other Americans, were very kind to us.

While in Paris we saw a good deal of the now rather famous American Negro painter, Mr. Henry O. Tanner, whom we had formerly known in America. It was very satisfactory to find how well known Mr. Tanner was in the field of art, and to note the high standing which all classes accorded to him. When we told some Americans that we were going to the Luxembourg Palace to see a painting by an American Negro, it was hard to convince them that a Negro had been thus honoured. I do not believe that they were really convinced of the fact until they saw the picture for themselves. My acquaintance with Mr. Tanner reënforced in my mind the truth which I am constantly trying to impress upon our students at Tuskegee—and on our people throughout the country, as far as I can reach them with my voice—that any man, regardless of colour, will be recognized and rewarded just in proportion as he learns to do something well—learns to do it better than some one else—however humble the thing may be. As I have said, I believe that my race will succeed in proportion as it learns to do a common thing in an uncommon manner; learns to do a thing so thoroughly that no one can improve upon what it has done; learns to make its services of indispensable value. This was the spirit that inspired me in my first effort at Hampton, when I was given the opportunity to sweep and dust that schoolroom. In a degree I felt that my whole future life depended upon the thoroughness with which I cleaned that room, and I was determined to do it so well that no one could find any fault with the job. Few people ever stopped, I found, when looking at his pictures, to inquire whether Mr. Tanner was a Negro painter, a French painter, or a German painter. They simply knew that he was able to produce something which the world wanted—a great painting—and the matter of his colour did not enter into their minds. When a Negro girl learns to cook, to wash dishes, to sew, to write a book, or a Negro boy learns to groom horses, or to grow sweet potatoes, or to produce butter, or to build a house, or to be able to practise medicine, as well or better than some one else, they will be rewarded regardless of race or colour. In the long run, the world is going to have the best, and any difference in race, religion, or previous history will not long keep the world from what it wants.

I think that the whole future of my race hinges on the question as to whether or not it can make itself of such indispensable value that the people in the town and the state where we reside will feel that our presence is necessary to the happiness and well-being of the community. No man who continues to add something to the material, intellectual, and moral well-being of the place in which he lives is long left without proper reward. This is a great human law which cannot be permanently nullified.

The love of pleasure and excitement which seems in a large measure to possess the French people impressed itself upon me. I think they are more noted in this respect than is true of the people of my own race. In point of morality and moral earnestness I do not believe that the French are ahead of my own race in America. Severe competition and the great stress of life have led them to learn to do things more thoroughly and to exercise greater economy; but time, I think, will bring my race to the same point. In the matter of truth and high honour I do not believe that the average Frenchman is ahead of the American Negro; while so far as mercy and kindness to dumb animals go, I believe that my race is far ahead. In fact, when I left France, I had more faith in the future of the black man in America than I had ever possessed.

From Paris we went to London, and reached there early in July, just about the height of the London social season. Parliament was in session, and there was a great deal of gaiety. Mr. Garrison and other friends had provided us with a large number of letters of introduction, and they had also sent letters to other persons in different parts of the United Kingdom, apprising these people of our coming. Very soon after reaching London we were flooded with invitations to attend all manner of social functions, and a great many invitations came to me asking that I deliver public addresses. The most of these invitations I declined, for the reason that I wanted to rest. Neither were we able to accept more than a small proportion of the other invitations. The Rev. Dr. Brooke Herford and Mrs. Herford, whom I had known in Boston, consulted with the American Ambassador, the Hon. Joseph Choate, and arranged for me to speak at a public meeting to be held in Essex Hall. Mr. Choate kindly consented to preside. The meeting was largely attended. There were many distinguished persons present, among them several members of Parliament, including Mr. James Bryce, who spoke at the meeting. What the American Ambassador said in introducing me, as well as a synopsis of what I said, was widely published in England and in the American papers at the time. Dr. and Mrs. Herford gave Mrs. Washington and myself a reception, at which we had the privilege of meeting some of the best people in England. Throughout our stay in London Ambassador Choate was most kind and attentive to us. At the Ambassador's reception I met, for the first time, Mark Twain.

We were the guests several times of Mrs. T. Fisher Unwin, the daughter of the English statesman, Richard Cobden. It seemed as if both Mr. and Mrs. Unwin could not do enough for our comfort and happiness. Later, for nearly a week, we were the guests of the daughter of John Bright, now Mrs. Clark, of Street, England. Both Mr. and Mrs. Clark, with their daughter, visited us at Tuskegee the next year. In Birmingham, England, we were the guests for several days of Mr. Joseph Sturge, whose father was a great abolitionist and friend of Whittier and Garrison. It was a great privilege to meet throughout England those who had known and honoured the late William Lloyd Garrison, the Hon. Frederick Douglass, and other abolitionists. The English abolitionists with whom we came in contact never seemed to tire of talking about these two Americans. Before going to England I had had no proper conception of the deep interest displayed by the abolitionists of England in the cause of freedom, nor did I realize the amount of substantial help given by them.

In Bristol, England, both Mrs. Washington and I spoke at the Women's Liberal Club. I was also the principal speaker at the Commencement exercises of the Royal College for the Blind. These exercises were held in the Crystal Palace, and the presiding officer was the late Duke of Westminster, who was said to be, I believe, the richest man in England, if not in the world. The Duke, as well as his wife and their daughter, seemed to be pleased with what I said, and thanked me heartily. Through the kindness of Lady Aberdeen, my wife and I were enabled to go with a party of those who were attending the International Congress of Women, then in session in London, to see Queen Victoria, at Windsor Castle, where, afterward, we were all the guests of her Majesty at tea. In our party was Miss Susan B. Anthony, and I was deeply impressed with the fact that one did not often get an opportunity to see, during the same hour, two women so remarkable in different ways as Susan B. Anthony and Queen Victoria.

In the House of Commons, which we visited several times, we met Sir Henry M. Stanley. I talked with him about Africa and its relation to the American Negro, and after my interview with him I became more convinced than ever that there was no hope of the

American Negro's improving his condition by emigrating to Africa.

On various occasions Mrs. Washington and I were the guests of Englishmen in their country homes, where, I think, one sees the Englishman at his best. In one thing, at least, I feel sure that the English are ahead of Americans, and that is, that they have learned how to get more out of life. The home life of the English seems to me to be about as perfect as anything can be. Everything moves like clockwork. I was impressed, too, with the deference that the servants show to their "masters" and "mistresses,"—terms which I suppose would not be tolerated in America. The English servant expects, as a rule, to be nothing but a servant, and so he perfects himself in the art to a degree that no class of servants in America has yet reached. In our country the servant expects to become, in a few years, a "master" himself. Which system is preferable? I will not venture an answer.

Another thing that impressed itself upon me throughout England was the high regard that all classes have for law and order, and the ease and thoroughness with which everything is done. The Englishmen, I found, took plenty of time for eating, as for everything else. I am not sure if, in the long run, they do not accomplish as much or more than rushing, nervous Americans do.

My visit to England gave me a higher regard for the nobility than I had had. I had no idea that they were so generally loved and respected by the masses, nor had I any correct conception of how much time and money they spent in works of philanthropy, and how much real heart they put into this work. My impression had been that they merely spent money freely and had a "good time."

It was hard for me to get accustomed to speaking to English audiences. The average Englishman is so serious, and is so tremendously in earnest about everything, that when I told a story that would have made an American audience roar with laughter, the Englishmen simply looked me straight in the face without even cracking a smile.

When the Englishman takes you into his heart and friendship, he binds you there as with cords of steel, and I do not believe that there are many other friendships that are so lasting or so satisfactory. Perhaps I can illustrate this point in no better way than by relating the following incident. Mrs. Washington and I were invited to attend a reception given by the Duke and Duchess of Sutherland, at Stafford House—said to be the finest house in London; I may add that I believe the Duchess of Sutherland is said to be the most beautiful woman in England. There must have been at least three hundred persons at this reception. Twice during the evening the Duchess sought us out for a conversation, and she asked me to write her when we got home, and tell her more about the work at Tuskegee. This I did. When Christmas came we were surprised and delighted to receive her photograph with her autograph on it. The correspondence has continued, and we now feel that in the Duchess of Sutherland we have one of our warmest friends.

After three months in Europe we sailed from Southampton in the steamship *St. Louis*. On this steamer there was a fine library that had been presented to the ship by the citizens of St. Louis, Mo. In this library I found a life of Frederick Douglass, which I began reading. I became especially interested in Mr. Douglass's description of the way he was treated on shipboard during his first or second visit to England. In this description he told how he was not permitted to enter the cabin, but had to confine himself to the deck of the ship. A few minutes after I had finished reading this description I was waited on by a committee of ladies and gentlemen with the request that I deliver an address at a concert which was to be given the following evening. And yet there are people who are bold enough to say that race feeling in America is not growing less intense! At this concert the Hon. Benjamin B. Odell, Jr., the present governor of New York, presided. I was never given a more cordial hearing anywhere. A large proportion of the passengers were Southern people. After the concert some of the passengers proposed that a subscription be raised to help the work at Tuskegee, and the money to support several scholarships was the result.

While we were in Paris I was very pleasantly surprised to receive the following invitation from the citizens of West Virginia and of the city near which I had spent my boyhood days:—

CHARLESTON, W. VA., MAY 16, 1899.

PROFESSOR BOOKER T. WASHINGTON, PARIS, FRANCE:

DEAR SIR: Many of the best citizens of West Virginia have united in liberal expressions of admiration and praise of your worth and work, and desire that on your return from Europe you should favour them with your presence and with the inspiration of your words. We most sincerely indorse this move, and on behalf of the citizens of Charleston extend to you our most cordial invitation to have you come to us, that we may honour you who have done so much by your life and work to honour us.

We are,   Very truly yours,

The Common Council of the City of Charleston,

By W. HERMAN SMITH, MAYOR.

This invitation from the City Council of Charleston was accompanied by the following:—

PROFESSOR BOOKER T. WASHINGTON, PARIS, FRANCE:

DEAR SIR: We, the citizens of Charleston and West Virginia, desire to express our pride in you and the splendid career that you have thus far accomplished, and ask that we be permitted to show our pride and interest in a substantial way.

Your recent visit to your old home in our midst awoke within us the keenest regret that we were not permitted to hear you and render some substantial aid to your work, before you left for Europe.

In view of the foregoing, we earnestly invite you to share the hospitality of our city upon your return from Europe, and give us the opportunity to hear you and put ourselves in touch with your work in a way that will be most gratifying to yourself, and that we may receive the inspiration of your words and presence.

An early reply to this invitation, with an indication of the time you may reach our city, will greatly oblige,

Yours very respectfully,

The Charleston *Daily Gazette*, The *Daily Mail-Tribune*; G. W. Atkinson, Governor; E. L. Boggs, Secretary to Governor; Wm. M. O. Dawson, Secretary of State; L. M. La Follette, Auditor; J. R. Trotter, Superintendent of Schools; E. W. Wilson, ex-Governor; W. A. MacCorkle, ex-Governor; John Q. Dickinson, President Kanawha Valley Bank; L. Prichard, President Charleston National Bank;

Geo. S. Couch, President Kanawha National Bank;

Ed. Reid, Cashier Kanawha National Bank;

Geo. S. Laidley, Superintendent City Schools;

L. E. McWhorter, President Board of Education;

Chas. K. Payne, wholesale merchant;

and many others.

This invitation, coming as it did from the City Council, the state officers, and all the substantial citizens of both races of the community where I had spent my boyhood, and from which I had gone a few years before, unknown, in poverty and ignorance, in quest of an education, not only surprised me, but almost unmanned me. I could not understand what I had done to deserve it all.

I accepted the invitation, and at the appointed day was met at the railway station at Charleston by a committee headed by ex-Governor W. A. MacCorkle, and composed of men of both races. The public reception was held in the Opera-House at Charleston. The Governor of the state, the Hon. George W. Atkinson, presided, and an address of welcome was made by ex-Governor MacCorkle. A prominent part in the reception was taken by the coloured citizens. The Opera-House was filled with citizens of both races, and among the white people were many for whom I had worked when a boy. The next day Governor and

Mrs. Atkinson gave me a public reception at the State House, which was attended by all classes.

Not long after this the coloured people in Atlanta, Georgia, gave me a reception at which the Governor of the state presided, and a similar reception was given me in New Orleans, which was presided over by the Mayor of the city. Invitations came from many other places which I was not able to accept.

CHAPTER XVII

LAST WORDS

BEFORE GOING to Europe some events came into my life which were great surprises to me. In fact, my whole life has largely been one of surprises. I believe that any man's life will be filled with constant, unexpected encouragements of this kind if he makes up his mind to do his level best each day of his life—that is, tries to make each day reach as nearly as possible the high-water mark of pure, unselfish, useful living. I pity the man, black or white, who has never experienced the joy and satisfaction that come to one by reason of an effort to assist in making some one else more useful and more happy.

Six months before he died, and nearly a year after he had been stricken with paralysis, General Armstrong expressed a wish to visit Tuskegee again before he passed away. Notwithstanding the fact that he had lost the use of his limbs to such an extent that he was practically helpless, his wish was gratified, and he was brought to Tuskegee. The owners of the Tuskegee Railroad, white men living in the town, offered to run a special train, without cost, out to the main station—Chehaw, five miles away—to meet him. He arrived on the school grounds about nine o'clock in the evening. Some one had suggested that we give the General a "pine-knot torchlight reception." This plan was carried out, and the moment that his carriage entered the school grounds he began passing between two lines of lighted and waving "fat pine" wood knots held by over a thousand students and teachers. The whole thing was so novel and surprising that the General was completely overcome with happiness. He remained a guest in my home for nearly two months, and, although almost wholly without the use of voice or limb, he spent nearly every hour in devising ways and means to help the South. Time and time again he said to me, during this visit, that it was not only the duty of the country to assist in elevating the Negro of the South, but the poor white man as well. At the end of his visit I resolved anew to devote myself more earnestly than ever to the cause which was so near his heart. I said that if a man in his condition was willing to think, work, and act, I should not be wanting in furthering in every possible way the wish of his heart.

The death of General Armstrong, a few weeks later, gave me the privilege of getting acquainted with one of the finest, most unselfish, and most attractive men that I have ever come in contact with. I refer to the Rev. Dr. Hollis B. Frissell, now the Principal of the Hampton Institute, and General Armstrong's successor. Under the clear, strong, and almost perfect leadership of Dr. Frissell, Hampton has had a career of prosperity and usefulness that is all that the General could have wished for. It seems to be the constant effort of Dr. Frissell to hide his own great personality behind that of General Armstrong—to make himself of "no reputation" for the sake of the cause.

More than once I have been asked what was the greatest surprise that ever came to me. I have little hesitation in answering that question. It was the following letter, which came to me one Sunday morning when I was sitting on the veranda of my home at Tuskegee, surrounded by my wife and three children:—

HARVARD UNIVERSITY, CAMBRIDGE, MAY 28, 1896.
PRESIDENT BOOKER T. WASHINGTON,

MY DEAR SIR: Harvard University desires to confer on you at the approaching Commencement an honorary degree; but it is our custom to confer degrees only on gentlemen who are present. Our Commencement occurs this year on June 24, and your presence would be desirable from about noon till about five o'clock in the afternoon. Would it be possible for you to be in Cambridge on that day?

Believe me, with great regard,
                    Very truly yours,
                         CHARLES W. ELIOT.

This was a recognition that had never in the slightest manner entered into my mind, and it was hard for me to realize that I was to be honoured by a degree from the oldest and most renowned university in America. As I sat upon my veranda, with this letter in my hand, tears came into my eyes. My whole former life—my life as a slave on the plantation, my work in the coal-mine, the times when I was without food and clothing, when I made my bed under a sidewalk, my struggles for an education, the trying days I had had at Tuskegee, days when I did not know where to turn for a dollar to continue the work there, the ostracism and sometimes oppression of my race,—all this passed before me and nearly overcame me.

I had never sought or cared for what the world calls fame. I have always looked upon fame as something to be used in accomplishing good. I have often said to my friends that if I can use whatever prominence may have come to me as an instrument with which to do good, I am content to have it. I care for it only as a means to be used for doing good, just as wealth may be used. The more I come into contact with wealthy people, the more I believe that they are growing in the direction of looking upon their money simply as an instrument which God has placed in their hand for doing good with. I never go to the office of Mr. John D. Rockefeller, who more than once has been generous to Tuskegee, without being reminded of this. The close, careful, and minute investigation that he always makes in order to be sure that every dollar that he gives will do the most good—an investigation that is just as searching as if he were investing money in a business enterprise—convinces me that the growth in this direction is most encouraging.

At nine o'clock, on the morning of June 24, I met President Eliot, the Board of Overseers of Harvard University, and the other guests, at the designated place on the university grounds, for the purpose of being escorted to Sanders Theatre, where the Commencement exercises were to be held and degrees conferred. Among others invited to be present for the purpose of receiving a degree at this time were General Nelson A. Miles, Dr. Bell,[15] the inventor of the Bell telephone, Bishop Vincent,[16] and the Rev. Minot J. Savage. We were placed in line immediately behind the President and the Board of Overseers, and directly afterward the Governor of Massachusetts, escorted by the Lancers, arrived and took his place in the line of march by the side of President Eliot. In the line there were also various other officers and professors, clad in cap and gown. In this order we marched to Sanders Theatre, where, after the usual Commencement exercises, came the conferring of the honorary degrees. This, it seems, is always considered the most interesting feature at Harvard. It is not known, until the individuals appear, upon whom the honorary degrees are to be conferred, and those receiving these honours are cheered by the students and others in proportion to their popularity. During the conferring of the degrees excitement and enthusiasm are at the highest pitch.

When my name was called, I rose, and President Eliot, in beautiful and strong English, conferred upon me the degree of Master of Arts. After these exercises were over, those who had received honorary degrees were invited to lunch with the President. After the lunch we were formed in line again, and were escorted by the Marshal of the day, who that year happened to be Bishop William Lawrence, through the grounds, where, at different points, those who had been honoured were called by name and received the Harvard yell. This march ended at Memorial Hall, where the alumni dinner was served. To see over a thousand strong men, representing all that is best in State, Church, business, and education, with the glow and enthusiasm of college loyalty and college pride,— which has, I think, a peculiar Harvard flavour,—is a sight that does not easily fade from memory.

Among the speakers after dinner were President Eliot, Governor Roger Wolcott, General Miles,[17] Dr. Minot J. Savage, the Hon. Henry Cabot Lodge, and myself. When I was called upon, I said, among other things:—

It would in some measure relieve my embarrassment if I could, even in a slight degree, feel myself worthy of the great honour which you do me to-day. Why you have called me from the Black Belt of the South, from among my humble people, to share in the honours of this occasion, is not for me to explain; and yet it may not be inappropriate for me to suggest that it seems to me that one of the most vital questions that touch our American life is how to bring the strong, wealthy, and learned into helpful touch with the poorest, most ignorant, and humblest, and at the same time make one appreciate the vitalizing, strengthening influence of the other. How shall we make the mansions on yon Beacon Street feel and see the need of the spirits in the lowliest cabin in Alabama cotton-fields or Louisiana sugar-bottoms? This problem Harvard University is solving, not by bringing itself down, but by bringing the masses up.

* * * * * * *

If my life in the past has meant anything in the lifting up of my people and the bringing about of better relations between your race and mine, I assure you from this day it will mean doubly more. In the economy of God there is but one standard by which an individual can succeed—there is but one for a race. This country demands that every race shall measure itself by the American standard. By it a race must rise or fall, succeed or fail, and in the last analysis mere sentiment counts for little. During the next half-century and more, my race must continue passing through the severe American crucible. We are to be tested in our patience, our forbearance, our perseverance, our power to endure wrong, to withstand temptations, to economize, to acquire and use skill; in our ability to compete, to succeed in commerce, to disregard the superficial for the real, the appearance for the substance, to be great and yet small, learned and yet simple, high and yet the servant of all.

As this was the first time that a New England university had conferred an honorary degree upon a Negro, it was the occasion of much newspaper comment throughout the country. A correspondent of a New York paper said:—

When the name of Booker T. Washington was called, and he arose to acknowledge and accept, there was such an outburst of applause as greeted no other name except that of the popular soldier patriot, General Miles. The applause was not studied and stiff, sympathetic and condoling; it was enthusiasm and admiration. Every part of the audience from pit to gallery joined in, and a glow covered the cheeks of those around me, proving sincere appreciation of the rising struggle of an ex-slave and the work he has accomplished for his race.

A Boston paper said, editorially:—

In conferring the honorary degree of Master of Arts upon the Principal of Tuskegee Institute, Harvard University has honoured itself as well as the object of this distinction. The work which Professor Booker T. Washington has accomplished for the education, good citizenship, and popular enlightenment in his chosen field of labour in the South entitles him to rank with our national benefactors. The university which can claim him on its list of sons, whether in regular course or *honoris causa*, may be proud.

It has been mentioned that Mr. Washington is the first of his race to receive an honorary degree from a New England university. This, in itself, is a distinction. But the degree was not conferred because Mr. Washington is a coloured man, or because he was born in slavery, but because he has shown, by his work for the elevation of the people of the Black Belt of the South, a genius and a broad humanity which count for greatness in any man, whether his skin be white or black.

Another Boston paper said:—

It is Harvard which, first among New England colleges, confers an honorary degree upon a black man. No one who has followed the history of Tuskegee and its work can fail to admire the courage, persistence, and splendid common sense of Booker T. Washington. Well may Harvard honour the ex-slave, the value of whose services, alike to his race and country, only the future can estimate.

The correspondent of the New York *Times* wrote:—

All the speeches were enthusiastically received, but the coloured man carried off the oratorical honours, and the applause which broke out when he had finished was vociferous and long-continued.

Soon after I began work at Tuskegee I formed a resolution, in the secret of my heart, that I would try to build up a school that would be of so much service to the country that the President of the United States would one day come to see it. This was, I confess, rather a bold resolution, and for a number of years I kept it hidden in my own thoughts, not daring to share it with any one.

In November, 1897, I made the first move in this direction, and that was in securing a visit from a member of President McKinley's Cabinet, the Hon. James

Wilson, Secretary of Agriculture. He came to deliver an address at the formal opening of the Slater-Armstrong Agricultural Building, our first large building to be used for the purpose of giving training to our students in agriculture and kindred branches.

In the fall of 1898 I heard that President McKinley was likely to visit Atlanta, Georgia, for the purpose of taking part in the Peace Jubilee exercises to be held there to commemorate the successful close of the Spanish-American war. At this time I had been hard at work, together with our teachers, for eighteen years, trying to build up a school that we thought would be of service to the Nation, and I determined to make a direct effort to secure a visit from the President and his Cabinet. I went to Washington, and I was not long in the city before I found my way to the White House. When I got there I found the waiting rooms full of people, and my heart began to sink, for I feared there would not be much chance of my seeing the President that day, if at all. But, at any rate, I got an opportunity to see Mr. J. Addison Porter, the secretary to the President, and explained to him my mission. Mr. Porter kindly sent my card directly to the President, and in a few minutes word came from Mr. McKinley that he would see me.

How any man can see so many people of all kinds, with all kinds of errands, and do so much hard work, and still keep himself calm, patient, and fresh for each visitor in the way that President McKinley does, I cannot understand. When I saw the President he kindly thanked me for the work which we were doing at Tuskegee for the interests of the country. I then told him, briefly, the object of my visit. I impressed upon him the fact that a visit from the Chief Executive of the Nation would not only encourage our students and teachers, but would help the entire race. He seemed interested, but did not make a promise to go to Tuskegee, for the reason that his plans about going to Atlanta were not then fully made; but he asked me to call the matter to his attention a few weeks later.

By the middle of the following month the President had definitely decided to attend the Peace Jubilee at Atlanta. I went to Washington again and saw him, with a view of getting him to extend his trip to Tuskegee. On this second visit Mr. Charles W. Hare, a prominent white citizen of Tuskegee, kindly volunteered to accompany me, to reënforce my invitation with one from the white people of Tuskegee and the vicinity.

Just previous to my going to Washington the second time, the country had been excited, and the coloured people greatly depressed, because of several severe race riots which had occurred at different points in the South. As soon as I saw the President, I perceived that his heart was greatly burdened by reason of these race disturbances. Although there were many people waiting to see him, he detained me for some time, discussing the condition and prospects of the race. He remarked several times that he was determined to show his interest and faith in the race, not merely in words, but by acts. When I told him that I thought that at that time scarcely anything would go farther in giving hope and encouragement to the race than the fact that the President of the Nation would be willing to travel one hundred and forty miles out of his way to spend a day at a Negro institution, he seemed deeply impressed.

While I was with the President, a white citizen of Atlanta, a Democrat and an ex-slaveholder, came into the room, and the President asked his opinion as to the wisdom of his going to Tuskegee. Without hesitation the Atlanta man replied that it was the proper thing for him to do. This opinion was reënforced by that friend of the race, Dr. J. L. M. Curry. The President promised that he would visit our school on the 16th of December.

When it became known that the President was going to visit our school, the white citizens of the town of Tuskegee—a mile distant from the school—were as much pleased as were our students and teachers. The white people of the town, including both men and women, began arranging to decorate the town, and to form themselves into committees for the purpose of coöperating with the officers of our school in order that the distinguished visitor might have a fitting reception. I think I never realized before this how much the white people of Tuskegee and vicinity thought of our institution. During the days when we were preparing for the President's reception, dozens of these people came to me and said that, while they did not want to push themselves into prominence, if there was anything they could do to help, or to relieve me personally, I had but to intimate it and they would be only too glad to assist. In fact, the thing that touched me almost as deeply as the visit of the President itself was the deep pride which all classes of citizens in Alabama seemed to take in our work.

The morning of December 16th brought to the little city of Tuskegee such a crowd as it had never seen before. With the President came Mrs. McKinley and all of the Cabinet officers but one; and most of them brought their wives or some members of their families. Several prominent generals came, including General Shafter[18] and General Joseph Wheeler, who were recently returned from the Spanish-American war. There was also a host of newspaper correspondents. The Alabama Legislature was in session at Montgomery at this time. This body passed a resolution to adjourn for the purpose of visiting Tuskegee. Just before the arrival of the President's party the Legislature arrived, headed by the governor and other state officials.

The citizens of Tuskegee had decorated the town from the station to the school in a generous manner. In order to economize in the matter of time, we arranged to have the whole school pass in review before the President. Each student carried a stalk of sugar-cane with some open bolls of cotton fastened to the end of it. Following the students the work of all departments of the school passed in review, displayed on "floats" drawn by horses, mules, and oxen. On these floats we tried to exhibit not only the present work of the school, but to show the contrasts between the old methods of doing things and the new. As an example, we showed the old method of dairying in contrast with the improved methods, the old methods of tilling the soil in contrast with the new, the old methods of cooking and housekeeping in contrast with the new. These floats consumed an hour and a half of time in passing.

In his address in our large, new chapel, which the students had recently completed, the President said, among other things:—

To meet you under such pleasant auspices and to have the opportunity of a personal observation of your work indeed most gratifying. The Tuskegee Normal and Industrial Institute is ideal in its conception, and has already a large and growing reputation in the country, and is not unknown abroad. I congratulate all who are associated in this undertaking for the good work which it is doing in the education of its students to lead lives of honour and usefulness, thus exalting the race for which it was established.

Nowhere, I think, could a more delightful location have been chosen for this unique educational experiment, which has attracted the attention and won the support even of conservative philanthropists in all sections of the country.

To speak of Tuskegee without paying special tribute to Booker T. Washington's genius and perseverance would be impossible. The inception of this noble enterprise was his, and he deserves high credit for it. His was the enthusiasm and enterprise which made its steady progress possible and established in the institution its present high standard of accomplishment. He has won a worthy reputation as one of the great leaders of his race, widely known and much respected at home and abroad as an accomplished educator, a great orator, and a true philanthropist.

The Hon. John D. Long, the Secretary of the Navy, said in part:—

I cannot make a speech to-day. My heart is too full—full of hope, admiration, and pride for my countrymen of both sections and both colours. I am filled with gratitude and admiration for your work, and from this time forward I shall have absolute confidence in your progress and in the solution of the problem in which you are engaged.

The problem, I say, has been solved. A picture has been presented to-day which should be put upon canvas with the pictures of Washington and Lincoln, and transmitted to future time and generations—a picture which the press of the country should spread broadcast over the land, a most dramatic picture, and that picture is this: The President of the United States standing on this platform; on one side the Governor of Alabama, on the other, completing the trinity, a representative of a race only a few years ago in bondage, the coloured President of the Tuskegee Normal and Industrial Institute.

God bless the President under whose majesty such a scene as that is presented to the American people. God bless the state of Alabama, which is showing that it can deal with this problem for itself. God bless the orator, philanthropist, and disciple of the Great Master—who, if he were on earth, would be doing the same work—Booker T. Washington.

Postmaster General Smith closed the address which he made with these words:—

We have witnessed many spectacles within the last few days. We have seen the magnificent grandeur and the magnificent achievements of one of the great metropolitan cities of the South. We have seen heroes of the war pass by in procession. We have seen floral parades. But I am sure my colleagues will agree with me in saying that we have witnessed no spectacle more impressive and more encouraging, more inspiring for our future, than that which we have witnessed here this morning.

Some days after the President returned to Washington I received the letter which follows:—

EXECUTIVE MANSION, WASHINGTON,
DEC. 23, 1899.

DEAR SIR: By this mail I take pleasure in sending you engrossed copies of the souvenir of the visit of the President to your institution. These sheets bear the autographs of the President and the members of the Cabinet who accompanied him on the trip. Let me take this opportunity of congratulating you most heartily and sincerely upon the great success of the exercises provided for and entertainment furnished us under your auspices during our visit to Tuskegee. Every feature of the programme was perfectly executed and was viewed or participated in with the heartiest satisfaction by every visitor present. The unique exhibition which you gave of your pupils engaged in their industrial vocations was not only artistic but thoroughly impressive. The tribute paid by the President and his Cabinet to your work was none too high, and forms a most encouraging augury, I think, for the future prosperity of your institution. I cannot close without assuring you that the modesty shown by yourself in the exercises was most favourably commented upon by all the members of our party.

With best wishes for the continued advance of your most useful and patriotic undertaking, kind personal regards, and the compliments of the season, believe me, always,

Very sincerely yours,

JOHN ADDISON PORTER,
Secretary to the President.
To PRESIDENT BOOKER T. WASHINGTON,
Tuskegee Normal and Industrial Institute,
Tuskegee, Ala.

Twenty years have now passed since I made the first humble effort at Tuskegee, in a broken-down shanty and an old hen-house, without owning a dollar's worth of property, and with but one teacher and thirty students. At the present time the institution owns twenty-three hundred acres of land, over seven hundred of which are under cultivation each year, entirely by student labour. There are now upon the grounds, counting large and small, forty buildings; and all except four of these have been almost wholly erected by the labour of our students. While the students are at work upon the land and in erecting buildings, they are taught, by competent instructors, the latest methods of agriculture and the trades connected with building.

There are in constant operation at the school, in connection with thorough academic and religious training, twenty-eight industrial departments. All of these teach industries at which our men and women can find immediate employment as soon as they leave the institution. The only difficulty now is that the demand for our graduates from both white and black people in the South is so great that we cannot supply more than one-half the persons for whom applications come to us. Neither have we the buildings nor the money for current expenses to enable us to admit to the school more than one-half the young men and women who apply to us for admission.

In our industrial teaching we keep three things in mind: first, that the student shall be so educated that he shall be enabled to meet conditions as they exist *now*, in the part of the South where he lives—in a word, to be able to do the thing which the world wants done; second, that every student who graduates from the school shall have enough skill, coupled with intelligence and moral character, to enable him to make a living for himself and others; third, to send every graduate out feeling and knowing that labour is dignified and beautiful—to make each one love labour instead of trying to escape it. In addition to the agricultural training which we give to young men, and the training given to our girls in all the usual domestic employments, we now train a number of girls in agriculture each year. These girls are taught gardening, fruit-growing, dairying, bee-culture, and poultry-raising.

While the institution is in no sense denominational, we have a department known as the Phelps Hall Bible Training School, in which a number of students are prepared for the ministry and other forms of Christian work, especially work in the country districts. What is equally important, each one of these students works half of each day at some industry, in order to get skill and the love of work, so that when he goes out from the institution he is prepared to set the people with whom he goes to labour a proper example in the matter of industry.

The value of our property is now over $300,000. If we add to this our endowment fund, which at present is $215,000, the value of the total property is now nearly half a million dollars. Aside from the need for more buildings and for money for current expenses, the endowment fund should be increased to at least $500,000. The annual current expenses are now about $80,000. The greater part of this I collect each year by going from door to door and from house to house. All of our property is free from mortgage, and is deeded to an undenominational board of trustees who have the control of the institution.

From thirty students the number has grown to eleven hundred, coming from twenty-seven states and territories, from Africa, Cuba, Porto Rico, Jamaica, and other foreign countries. In our departments there are eighty-six officers and instructors; and if we add the families of our instructors, we have a constant population upon our grounds of not far from fourteen hundred people.

I have often been asked how we keep so large a body of people together, and at the same time keep them out of mischief. There are two answers: that the men and women who come to us for an education are in earnest; and that everybody is kept busy. The following outline of our daily work will testify to this:—

5 A.M., rising bell; 5.50 A.M., warning breakfast bell; 6 A.M., breakfast bell; 6.20 A.M., breakfast over; 6.20 to 6.50 A.M., rooms are cleaned; 6.50, work bell; 7.30, morning study hour; 8.20, morning school bell; 8.25, inspection of young men's toilet in ranks; 8.40, devotional exercises in chapel; 8.55, "five minutes with the daily news;" 9 A.M., class work begins; 12, class work closes; 12.15 P.M., dinner; 1 P.M., work bell; 1.30 P.M., class work begins; 3.30 P.M., class work ends; 5.30 P.M., bell to

"knock off" work; 6 P.M., supper; 7.10 P.M., evening prayers; 7.30 P.M., evening study hours; 8.45 P.M., evening study hour closes; 9.20 P.M., warning retiring bell; 9.30 P.M., retiring bell.

We try to keep constantly in mind the fact that the worth of the school is to be judged by its graduates. Counting those who have finished the full course, together with those who have taken enough training to enable them to do reasonably good work, we can safely say that at least three thousand men and women from Tuskegee are now at work in different parts of the South; men and women who, by their own example or by direct effort, are showing the masses of our race how to improve their material, educational, and moral and religious life. What is equally important, they are exhibiting a degree of common sense and self-control which is causing better relations to exist between the races, and is causing the Southern white man to learn to believe in the value of educating the men and women of my race. Aside from this, there is the influence that is constantly being exerted through the mothers' meeting and the plantation work conducted by Mrs. Washington.

Wherever our graduates go, the changes which soon begin to appear in the buying of land, improving homes, saving money, in education, and in high moral character are remarkable. Whole communities are fast being revolutionized through the instrumentality of these men and women.

Ten years ago I organized at Tuskegee the first Negro Conference. This is an annual gathering which now brings to the school eight or nine hundred representative men and women of the race, who come to spend a day in finding out what the actual industrial, mental, and moral conditions of the people are, and in forming plans for improvement. Out from this central Negro Conference at Tuskegee have grown numerous state and local conferences which are doing the same kind of work. As a result of the influence of these gatherings, one delegate reported at the last annual meeting that ten families in his community had bought and paid for homes. On the day following the annual Negro Conference, there is held the "Workers' Conference." This is composed of officers and teachers who are engaged in educational work in the larger institutions in the South. The Negro Conference furnishes a rare opportunity for these workers to study the real condition of the rank and file of the people.

In the summer of 1900, with the assistance of such prominent coloured men as Mr. T. Thomas Fortune, who has always upheld my hands in every effort, I organized the National Negro Business League, which held its first meeting in Boston, and brought together for the first time a large number of the coloured men who are engaged in various lines of trade or business in different parts of the United states. Thirty states were represented at our first meeting. Out of this national meeting grew state and local business leagues.

In addition to looking after the executive side of the work at Tuskegee, and raising the greater part of the money for the support of the school, I cannot seem to escape the duty of answering at least a part of the calls which come to me unsought to address Southern white audiences and audiences of my own race, as well as frequent gatherings in the North. As to how much of my time is spent in this way, the following clipping from a Buffalo (N.Y.) paper will tell. This has reference to an occasion when I spoke before the National Educational Association in that city.

Booker T. Washington, the foremost educator among the coloured people of the world, was a very busy man from the time he arrived in the city the other night from the West and registered at the Iroquois. He had hardly removed the stains of travel when it was time to partake of supper. Then he held a public levee in the parlours of the Iroquois until eight o'clock. During that time he was greeted by over two hundred eminent teachers and educators from all parts of the United States. Shortly after eight o'clock he was driven in a carriage to Music Hall, and in one hour and a half he made two ringing addresses, to as many as five thousand people, on Negro education. Then Mr. Washington was taken in charge by a delegation of coloured citizens, headed by the Rev. Mr. Watkins, and hustled off to a small informal reception, arranged in honour of the visitor by the people of his race.

Nor can I, in addition to making these addresses, escape the duty of calling the attention of the South and of the country in general, through the medium of the press, to matters that pertain to the interests of both races. This, for example, I have done in regard to the evil habit of lynching. When the Louisiana State Constitutional Convention was in session, I wrote an open letter to that body pleading for justice for the race. In all such efforts I have received warm and hearty support from the Southern newspapers, as well as from those in all other parts of the country.

Despite superficial and temporary signs which might lead one to entertain a contrary opinion, there was never a time when I felt more hopeful for the race than I do at the present. The great human law that in the end recognizes and rewards merit is everlasting and universal. The outside world does not know, neither can it appreciate, the struggle that is constantly going on in the hearts of both the Southern white people and their former slaves to free themselves from

racial prejudice; and while both races are thus struggling they should have the sympathy, the support, and
the forbearance of the rest of the world.

As I write the closing words of this autobiography
I find myself—not by design—in the city of Richmond, Virginia: the city which only a few decades ago
was the capital of the Southern Confederacy, and
where, about twenty-five years ago, because of my
poverty I slept night after night under a sidewalk.

This time I am in Richmond as the guest of the
coloured people of the city; and came at their request to
deliver an address last night to both races in the Academy of Music, the largest and finest audience room in
the city. This was the first time that the coloured people had ever been permitted to use this hall. The day
before I came, the City Council passed a vote to attend
the meeting in a body to hear me speak. The state Legislature, including the House of Delegates and the Senate, also passed a unanimous vote to attend in a body. In
the presence of hundreds of coloured people, many distinguished white citizens, the City Council, the state
Legislature, and state officials, I delivered my message,
which was one of hope and cheer; and from the bottom
of my heart I thanked both races for this welcome back
to the state that gave me birth.

NOTES

1 Actually 1856, according to the best evidence available. Louis R. Harlan, *Booker T. Washington: The Making of a Black Leader,* 1856–1901 (New York, 1972), 3.

2 At Wayland Theological Seminary for the training of black Baptist ministers.

3 Wilbur F. Foster, who in 1880–81 sponsored the bill that established Tuskegee Normal School.

4 Later known as Booker Taliaferro Washington, Jr. (1887–1945). Baker was his nickname.

5 Abraham L. Grant (1847–1911), bishop of the African Methodist Episcopal Church.

6 Wesley John Gaines (1840–1912), bishop of the African Methodist Episcopal Church.

7 Rufus Brown Bullock (1834–1907), Republican governor of Georgia from 1868 to 1871. An Atlanta businessman in 1895, he was a commissioner of the Atlanta Exposition.

8 Cleland Kinloch Nelson (1852–1917), bishop of the Protestant Episcopal Church.

9 Robert Gould Shaw (1837–63) was the white colonel of the black Fifty-fourth Massachusetts Volunteers. He died while leading his troops against the Confederates at Fort Wagner in Charleston harbor.

10 William Lawrence (1850–1941), Protestant Episcopal bishop of Massachusetts.

11 William Joyce Sewell (1835–1901).

12 John Ireland (1838–1918), Roman Catholic archbishop of St. Paul.

13 Melville Weston Fuller (1833–1910), chief justice of the United States Supreme Court (1888–1910).

14 John Marshall Harlan (1833–1911).

15 Alexander Graham Bell (1847–1922).

16 John Heyl Vincent (1832–1920), bishop of the Methodist Episcopal Church.

17 Nelson Appleton Miles (1839–1925), a hero of the Spanish-American War.

18 Major General William Rufus Shafter (1835–1906), commander of United States troops in Cuba in 1898.

INDEX

for *Up from Slavery*